REMODELING THE NATION

Becoming Modern: New Nineteenth-Century Studies
Series Editors

SARAH SHERMAN
Department of English
University of New Hampshire

JANET AIKINS YOUNT
Department of English
University of New Hampshire

ROHAN MCWILLIAM
Anglia Polytechnic University
Cambridge, England

JANET POLASKY
Department of History
University of New Hampshire

This book series maps the complexity of historical change and assesses the formation of ideas, movements, and institutions crucial to our own time by publishing books that examine the emergence of modernity in North America and Europe. Set primarily but not exclusively in the nineteenth century, the series shifts attention from modernity's twentieth-century forms to its earlier moments of uncertain and often disputed construction. Seeking books of interest to scholars on both sides of the Atlantic, it thereby encourages the expansion of nineteenth-century studies and the exploration of more global patterns of development.

For a complete list of books in this series, see www.upne.com and
www.upne.com/series/BMS.html

Duncan Faherty, *Remodeling the Nation: The Architecture of American Identity, 1776–1858*

Jennifer Hall-Witt, *Fashionable Acts: Opera and Elite Culture in London, 1780–1880*

Scott Molloy, *Trolley Wars: Streetcar Workers on the Line*

William C. Dowling, *Oliver Wendell Holmes in Paris: Medicine, Theology, and the Autocrat of the Breakfast Table*

Betsy Klimasmith, *At Home in the City: Urban Domesticity in American Literature and Culture, 1850–1930*

Sarah Luria, *Capital Speculations: Writing and Building Washington, D.C.*

David L. Richards, *Poland Spring: A Tale of the Gilded Age, 1860–1900*

Angela Sorby, *Schoolroom Poets: Childhood, Performance, and the Place of American Poetry, 1865–1917*

REMODELING THE NATION

The Architecture of American Identity, 1776–1858

Duncan Faherty

University of New Hampshire Press
Durham, New Hampshire

Published by University Press of New England
Hanover and London

University of New Hampshire Press

Published by University Press of New England,
One Court Street, Lebanon, NH 03766
www.upne.com

Printed in the United States of America

5 4 3 2 1

A portion of chapter 4 was previously published as "The Borders of Civilization: Susan Fenimore Cooper's View of American Development" in *Susan Fenimore Cooper: New Essays on Rural Hours and Other Works*, edited by Rochelle Johnson and Daniel Patterson. © 2001 by The University of Georgia Press.

LIBRARY OF CONGRESS CATALOGING-IN-PUBLICATION DATA
Faherty, Duncan.
Remodeling the nation : the architecture of American identity, 1776–1858 / Duncan Faherty.
p. cm. — (Becoming modern)
Includes bibliographical references and index.
ISBN-13: 978-1-58465-655-5 (cloth : alk. paper)
ISBN-10: 1-58465-655-7 (cloth : alk. paper)
1. Architecture, Domestic—Social aspects—United States.   2. Architecture and society—United States—History—18th century.   3. Architecture and society—United States—History—19th century.   4. Symbolism in architecture—United States.
5. National characteristics, American. I. Title.
NA7206.F34 2007
728.0973'09033—dc22   2007025157

University Press of New England is a member of the Green Press Initiative. The paper used in this book meets their minimum requirement for recycled paper.

FOR MY FAMILIES

Contents

Acknowledgments

Few, if any, architects accomplish their designs without the assistance of others. Building houses and writing books are collaborative projects, and this book could not have been completed without the support of mentors, teachers, colleagues, and loved ones. Over the course of working on this manuscript I have enjoyed the friendship and intellectual companionship of a number of wonderful people, and my only regret is my inability to adequately convey my deep sense of gratitude. I trust that they will all take comfort in the fact that without them this book would not have been possible.

My deepest intellectual debt is to Bill Kelly. Mentor, teacher, colleague, and friend, in "whom humor and love, like mountain peaks, soar to such a rapt height." Bill generously read countless drafts, often at a moment's notice, and every page of this project has benefited from his pointed criticism, his scholarly expertise, and his unflagging commitment. More than anyone he has helped me distinguish between the productive and the fruitless, and his boundless curiosity and expansive imagination have made this a far better work than otherwise possible.

I am profoundly indebted to Joan Richardson for her guidance, her sensitive reading, and her continual encouragement to "write well." I am extremely grateful to: Marc Dolan for helping me shape and clarify my argument; Louis Masur for encouraging me to find my own critical voice; Peter Manning for making me a more imaginative scholar; and Joe Wittreich for convincing me that this was all possible. It would take pages to properly thank Steve Kruger for his unending support and remarkable guidance. Jim Kincaid was no help whatsoever—which makes me love him all the more. Michael Drexler generously read a portion of my manuscript and challenged me to earn my conclusions, and I want to thank him for always being willing to talk things through. Chris Iannini continually inspired and reassured, and I want to thank him for his steady support. Kim Engber read, listened, and pushed me to think in new ways. David Humphries debated, listened, and always offered sound advice. I want to thank Nancy Comley for her wise counsel and spirited encouragement. Thanks to Carrie Hintz for being an animated interlocutor and valued colleague. Without a doubt I have benefitted from John Weir's keen sense of humor and limitless attention to language. I deeply thank Jamie Skye

Bianco for her generosity of spirit, for constantly challenging me to think through my assumptions, and for consistently modeling her passion for critical inquiry. Justin Rogers-Cooper was a wellspring of support in the final stretch of this project, and I owe him special thanks for a summer's worth of good humor and comradeship. I especially want to thank: Susan Zimmerman for her unwavering faith; Hugh English for his collegial fellowship; Rich McCoy for his helpful advice and welcome reassurance; and Glenn Burger for his hearty and provocative skepticism about early American literature. Special thanks as well to Sari Altschuler, Shirley Carrie, Ann Cohen, Tom Frosch, Brooks Hefner, Wayne Moreland, Tony O'Brien, Sameer Pandya, Rebekah Rutkoff, Amy Tucker, Jesse Schwartz, Bette Weidman, Gordon Whatley, and Devin Zuber for their consistent reinforcement and timely encouragement.

I was extremely fortunate in having David Kazanjian and Thomas Hallock as my readers for University Press of New England. Their searching prompts and pointed questions allowed me to renovate the frame of the project and remodel its chambers accordingly. A heartfelt thanks to them both for their keen critiques and benevolent words of encouragement. I am deeply thankful to my editor Phyllis Deutsch for her practiced care and nonstop advocacy and most importantly for helping make this book a reality.

This project was supported by several grants from the Professional Staff Congress–City University of New York (PSC-CUNY) Research Award Program, funding which made summers of research and writing possible. I would also like to extend my hearty thanks to Barbara Bowen and the other leaders of the PSC for securing release time for junior faculty. This manuscript undoubtably benefitted from the grant of release time they fought so hard for and without question the break from teaching facilitated the final stages of this project. In so many ways the current leadership of the PSC has helped transform what it means to be a junior faculty member at CUNY, and I thank them for all their efforts.

My colleagues at Queens have been discerning readers and unfailing friends, and I want to thank them all for their many acts of kindness and support. Thanks as well to my students, who continue to teach me as much about the myriad meanings of American literature and culture as I do them. My professional life at Queens would have unraveled long ago without the dedication and hard work of Ximena Santilla, Kim Smith, and James Felder—double thanks for all your support. I also thank Andy Beveridge, Clare Carroll, Tamara Evans, Dean Savage, Don Scott, and Frank Warren for making the college as much a home as my own department.

During the course of writing this book, my thinking benefitted a great deal from responses I received from colleagues and participants at a number of conferences. I especially want to thank my colleagues in the Society of Early Americanists, the Charles Brockden Brown Society, the James Fenimore Cooper Society, the Edgar Allan Poe Society, the Society for the Preservation of New England Antiquities, the Modern Language Association, the American Literature Association, and the American Studies Association, and the organizers of several conferences at the McNeil Center for Early American Studies for allowing me to present portions of this project. This project began as a dissertation at the CUNY Graduate Center, and I thank all my colleagues in the Ph.D. Program in English for their intellectual support and the Graduate Center for its generous financial support. A portion of chapter 4 was first published in *Susan Fenimore Cooper: New Essays on* Rural Hours *and Other Works*, edited by Rochelle Johnson and Daniel Patterson (Athens: University of Georgia Press, 2001). I thank the publisher for permission to reprint and the editors for their helpful suggestions and responses.

I owe a special debt of gratitude to Doug Faherty, Lucia Mariani, and Steven Faherty. *Ringraziamenti per il vostri amore, supporto, incoraggiamento e pazienza continuati. Vi amo tutti.* Many years ago, Eddie Hughes taught me to think about the complexities of remodeling and to respect the profound labor involved in renovation. In many ways without those lessons this book would have no foundation. Words cannot really do justice to the thanks I owe Darren Fried, a rare person and outstanding friend whose patience and humor are unfailing. His dedication to his craft has long been an exemplary model (next year, I promise, we will make it to Tampa). Thanks to David Lee for his restless energy, to Melky Carbrera for his unbounded exuberance, to Kermit Ruffians for his barbeque swinging, and to Wycliffe Gordon for cone's coup and the joyride. I owe a special debt of gratitude to Ingrid "Spud" Lemmey for her enduring friendship and unrivaled good cheer. Now that she has finally lost the bet, I thank Ann Kelly for her commitment to reading *Mercedes of Castile*. Karen Lemmey's visual imagination has long been an inspiration, and I owe her thanks for her formidable curiosity and moral support. What I owe Victoria Soffer can not be easily repaid, but I look forward to trying. I profoundly thank her for her sustaining love, enduring patience, and generous optimism.

My final debt is also my greatest. This work is dedicated to my mother, Mary Ann Faherty, who long ago taught me the importance of home and hearth.

And now, "no more: it is morning: it is July in the country: and I am off for the barn."

REMODELING THE NATION

1

"When Buildings Are of Durable Materials"

The American Home and the Structural Legacies of History

The enthusiasm of the audience gathered at the Illinois State House in Springfield had been building all day. The delegates to the 1858 Illinois Republican state convention had convened in solidarity to send a strong message both to their Democratic opponents and to eastern members of their party: they were no longer interested in failing compromises over the issue of slavery. The time for such measures had passed. At eight o'clock the lanky speaker they had been waiting to hear began his address. "If we could know *where* we are, and *whither* we are tending," Abraham Lincoln argued, "we could then better judge *what* to do, and *how* to do it."[1] In the rhetorical opening of his speech, Lincoln asked the audience to ponder the state of the union. Within his speech, Lincoln insisted, as Eric Foner and Olivia Mahoney argue, that "a policy of popular sovereignty" had "replaced the founding fathers' commitment to the 'ultimate extinction' of slavery with a moral indifference that could only result in the institution's expansion throughout the entire country."[2] Years of ineffective legislation that deferred deep-seated problems had left the country in a tailspin, and the nation was losing its chance to redirect its course. As pro-slavery advocates argued for the right of local governments to self-determination, they undermined national cohesion; turning their backs on the legacies framed for them by the Constitution, they eviscerated, Lincoln suggested, the founders' original intent. Echoing the fears of many citizens, Lincoln argued that the country was nearing a critical juncture, a point at which "it will become *all* one thing, or *all* the other" (461).

Lincoln's speech has endured in the cultural imagination of the United States largely because of the evocative metaphor through which it advances his argument.[3] Within the speech he posits that "a house divided against itself cannot stand" (461). Lincoln adopts a biblical phrase (the line appears in three of the New Testament Gospels) to illustrate the horror facing the nation. His choice of language has long been a means of describing, in shorthand, the dire circumstances of the mid–nineteenth century. The historian Richard Sewell seizes on Lincoln's enduring symbol as the main title of his *A House Divided: Sectionalism and Civil War, 1848–1865*, deploying the phrase to retrospectively divide the North and South into separate spheres each imagining that it possessed "a distinct and superior way of life."[4] Imagining the nation as a stable entity endangered by the opposing pulls of abolitionist and pro-slavery factions has prompted us to regard Lincoln's remarks as the most apt metaphor of the late antebellum period.[5] If the two divisions were finally to lose their framing connections, the national house would surely collapse. Yet wreckage was not what Lincoln predicted; he believed that sooner or later, while the house would not "*fall*," it would "cease to be divided" (461). Lincoln was not predicting an architectural apocalypse but rather a shift in how the house was to be governed. Misreading Lincoln's metaphor does not undermine the power of his analysis. His remarks sounded a shrill warning to those who thought that making further concessions was strategically viable. Continual compromise, Lincoln implied, had effectively remodeled the nation surreptitiously. Lincoln understood that localized "popular sovereignty" and "squatter rights" could not decide the political future of new territories; the time for a return to national leadership was at hand.

Domestic imagery had been a standard feature of American political discourse at least as far back as Thomas Jefferson's designation of the Declaration of Independence as a divorce contract between two equal partners. Framers of the Constitution. Architects of Democracy. Founding Fathers. Builders of a Nation. By common understanding, Americans have embraced the house as the most appropriate metaphor for their political and social states. Lincoln's seizure of this metaphor reveals the acuity with which he understood the problems of the moment. The house, the nation, was beset by renovators intent on a radical alteration of its design. That an issue as divisive as slavery provoked Lincoln to speculate about preserving the national house should come as no surprise. "Lincoln's principle, that Congress might intervene to prevent the spread of slavery," Henry Jaffa argues, "meant that it might legislate the domestic institutions of territories and thereby determine the character of future states."[6] Following the implicit reasoning of Jaffa's interpretation, Lincoln's speech effectively argues that Americans needed to redress the connections between domestic institutions and identity formation. The image of the house advances Lincoln's argument so dramatically because it vividly captures the course of national development. In short, Lincoln figures the nation as a house, remodeled and renovated to accommodate the expanding needs of the national collective; national unity is predetermined by the fact that the Republic's citizens are all housed within the same structure.

Casting himself as the conservator of the founders' vision, Lincoln argues that the national house is a historic landmark that needs to be protected from damaging alterations. Lincoln's speech accuses previous legislators of having framed, in seemingly independent compromises, an incipient movement to nationalize and legitimize slavery. Looking back across the length of recent political history, Lincoln underscores how these separated but interconnected acts have worked in concert to remodel national practices. These legislative measures, Lincoln contends, have refashioned the national house to uphold, in perpetuity, the institutions of slavery. The force of Lincoln's argument intends to display how seemingly discordant compromises have renovated national history. The nation will not be ruined by division; rather, Lincoln fears, it will be so dramatically remodeled by pro-slavery forces that it will no longer resemble its original design.

"We can not absolutely *know* that all these exact adoptions are the result of preconcert. But when we see a lot of framed timbers, different portions of which," Lincoln argues, "we know have been gotten out at different times and places by different workmen—Stephen, Franklin, Roger, and James, for instance—and when we see these timbers joined together, and see they exactly make the frame of a house or a mill, all the tenons and mortices exactly fitting, and all the lengths and proportions of the different pieces exactly adapted to their respective places, and not a piece too many or too few—not omitting even scaffolding—or, if a single piece be lacking, we can see the place in the frame exactly fitted and prepared to yet bring such a piece in—in *such* a case, we find it impossible to not *believe* that Stephen and Franklin and Roger and James all understood one another from the beginning, and all worked upon a common *plan* or *draft* drawn up before the first lick was struck" (465–66). Lincoln conflates the distinctive political philosophies of Stephen Douglas, Franklin Pierce, Roger B. Taney, and James Buchanan by figuring them as carpenters working from the same schematic plan. All the apparently different legislative acts blend so seamlessly that it would be naive to imagine, Lincoln implies, that these builders did not envision a single design from the outset.

Lincoln castigates his opponents for upholding that their assorted actions are not all drawn from a single set of blueprints. "Let any one who doubts, carefully contemplate," Lincoln urges, "the *history* of its construction" and "trace the evidences of design" to visualize the "concert of action" from "the beginning" of such affairs as the Nebraska doctrine and the Dred Scott decision (462). Like the uncovered frame of a house, the structure of governmental policy reveals itself if we know how to look. Following some heretofore unseen master plan, the pro-slavery forces have been laboring synergistically, adding timbers to the legislative framework to ensure not only the protection of slavery where it now exists but its proliferation as well. While Lincoln's line "a house divided against itself cannot stand" has become the most famous phrase from this speech, and is perhaps second only to his Gettysburg Address in terms of its lingering currency, the entirety of the speech employs architectural and domestic language as a primary lens for reading the nation. As David Herbert Donald notes, Lincoln had "been thinking about" this speech "for weeks, drafting sentences and paragraphs on stray pieces of paper and the backs of envelopes, storing them in his tall hat." Revising and sharpening his prose, Lincoln had seized on domestic architecture, the metaphor of the nation as a house, to ground his argument. Drafting and redrafting, editing and polishing, Lincoln "fixed" every syllable "in his tenacious memory," so that "he had no need to refer to his manuscript when he delivered it."[7] Lincoln revised in order to focus the weight of his overriding metaphor, laboring to make sure that each part of his speech hammered away at the surety with which pro-slavery politicians had been serially remodeling the nation.

We may design the buildings, Lincoln suggested, but once built, they design us. Lincoln's topographic imagination seized on how the consistent theme of remodeling and rebuilding haunted American cultural development. This figuration of national history as a never-ending process of domestic improvement had been consistently deployed in order to at once defer prior settlement and distinguish the United States from its North American and European antecedents. By translating national history into the rhetoric of the domestic, Lincoln accessed the ways in which post-Revolutionary Americans had habitually imagined the construction of the nation as unfolding in a palimpsestic architectural landscape and not on the famous figure of the tabula rasa. "Indeed," Julia Stern argues, "the entire notion of the 'Founding' of the republic is in fact predicated on its own architectural—spatial, hierarchical, and topographical—formulation."[8] Early Americans wrote obsessively about the palimpsest of America's built landscape, and this perpetual representation of the complexities of settlement and expansion through the frame of the domestic caused them to proffer the architectural figure of the home as the locus for their attempts to understand and interpret both post- and pre-Revolutionary histories. Lincoln sought to rehabilitate the home as a figure crucial to national stability because, as Stern suggests, the construction of the republic was grounded in acts of architectural imagination. From the outset of national foundation, Americans conceptualized their still unsettled state through metaphors of homebuilding. Far from blind to and silent about prior settlement, Americans put their intimate understanding of this history into play by synergistically seeking to both regulate and repress its legacies.

Throughout the late eighteenth and early nineteenth centuries, house building was deployed as a controlling metaphor in novels, short fiction, travelogues, manuals of domestic economy, visual arts, political tracts, speeches, and natural histories. The currency of this image suggests a citizenry attentive to arguments about shaping a national culture, a culture specific to America's geographic uniqueness and attentive to its historical groundings. Americans represented their unfolding histories not simply in terms of exterior imagery—the familiar metaphor of the nation as a middle ground between wilderness and European civilization—but in terms as well of domestic architecture and interior design. Exploring the ways in which this concern with interior spaces and with the construction of houses intersects with broader inquires about the formation of the national temperament yields a deeply textured understanding of antebellum American culture.

In *Remodeling the Nation*, I trace the complex evolution of this recursive figuration of the domestic houses as the wellspring of national identity. Rather than sharply delineating between particular spheres of public and private, differentiating between social activities and discourses, my goal is to display how this continual return to domestic interiors to interpret and remodel national history demonstrates the ways in which early Americans troubled such delineations and enclosures by envisioning them as protean and contested. As Grantland Rice suggests, Jurgen Habermas' figuration of the development of the *res publica* as a space "where the communications of individuals, evacuated of such idiosyncrasies and biases as personality, skills, and social standing, competed with other such communications, and where reason carried the day," emulates the ways in which "proponents of laissez-faire" predicted "a rational and fair society would emerge."[9] While Lincoln held fast to the idea that he could reasonably persuade voters of the justness of his cause, he aptly recognized that Douglas and his supporters countered his arguments by promoting laissez-faire economics, expressed by popular sovereignty, as the determinant for futurity. Even within the discourse of their debates, Lincoln understood the tension in imagining the possibility of evacuating public discourse from idiosyncratic manifestations of ideology.

The intermingling of the public and private spheres, the ambiguous and complex blurring of these spaces to form a multitude of counterpublics instead of a monolithic *res publica*, more accurately underscores what Michael E. Gardiner calls "the heterodox and pluralistic nature of such spheres."[10] As Gardiner maintains, the idea of counterpublics sensitizes "us to the wide variety of normative ideas that regulate interaction in different areas of socio-cultural life."[11] In describing the complexity inherent "even in the blurred usage of the public sphere," Michael Warner argues that "a public is never just a congeries of people, never just the sum of persons who happen to exist."[12] Instead, Warner advances, "it must first of all have some way of organizing itself as a body and of being addressed in discourse."[13] Discourses surrounding national identity, even when they recursively deployed the figure of the house to sound out the multivalent meanings of U.S. histories, were not necessarily inclusive or universalistic. Rather, these discourses oscillated between divergent understandings, vigorously and elaborately debated, of how to manage textually recapitulations of and encounters with prior settlements (of both Native American and European origins) as well as post-Revolutionary histories. Unpacking the composite and equivocal legacies framed by the palimpsest of America's built landscape, post-Revolutionary Americans continually returned, as Lincoln's speech vividly demonstrates, to representations of the nation as house to consider how the design of the nation as domestic space modeled, remodeled, and inflected cultural development. By indexing how architecture fosters social connections, I postulate that houses shape the parameters of cultural development in order to register the interchange between domestic architecture and cultural order. The domestic, as Amy Kaplan reminds us, "has a double meaning that links the space of the familial household to that of the nation," because it differentiates between *native* and foreign concerns.[14] My aim is to foreground this doubleness to chart how Americans sought to plot and replot their cultural inheritances. I extend this strategy across expansive regional and temporal frames to register how representations of the house reflected and encoded emerging American sensibilities.

In the absence of ancient customs or structures, the foundational unit of community construction, the house, became the means by which the nation conceptualized its own history.[15] Conventional wisdom held that the Republic's social structures had grown out of the management of its natural resources, and many Americans came to believe that cultural values were the product of both material culture (the entire shaped human environment) and the landscapes in and upon which that culture was fashioned.[16] An interest in architecture, the human transformation of nature, both as a practical matter and as a register of national practice, was broadly shared during the antebellum period. Prior to the professionalization of architecture in the last quarter of the century, many middle- and upper-class Americans took an active role in the planning of their homes (Thomas Jefferson, George Washington, and Washington Irving are notable examples). Indeed, architecture was generally regarded as one of the fine arts; the Library of Congress—following Jefferson's cataloging scheme—shelved architectural treatises with works of poetry, fiction, and other artistic texts.[17]

As Benedict Anderson theorizes, the process of imagining a community marks a crucial step in national formation, one tied to what Eric Hobsbawm calls "the invention of tradition."[18] For Hobsbawm, the construction of a social imaginary establishes cultural cohesion and behavioral standards and legitimizes institutions and practices. Lincoln built on the invented tradition, the usable past at his disposal, by returning to the domestic. The image of the nation as house had been central to the success of the fledgling political structures formed after the Revolutionary War. Lincoln revalued that specie by resecuring the cultural identity of the nation to the domestic, and more specifically to the house. In the absence of ancient customs or structures, the foundational unit of community construction, the house, became the means by which the nation conceptualized its own history. By as early as the eighteenth century, North America was far from a virgin landscape. Not only had colonial settlers established a rich architectural record, but the "wilderness" of post-Revolutionary North America was itself replete with occupied houses, abandoned homes, and a host of other structures. Some of these residual buildings had discernible origins, while others confounded those who struggled to map their occupational histories. Rather than inscribed on a blank slate, the Republic was actually (and knowingly) built amid a complex series of residual structures. In undertaking the work of nation building, the citizens of the new Republic came to terms with the multiple settlement histories of North America. By decoding the complexity of these architectural flash points, I move in *Remodeling the Nation* to delineate how domestic praxis was continually informed by questions of household design and construction.

By reestablishing the density of the antebellum architectural record of the United States, I refocus attention on the multiple connections between domestic design and cultural production. Not only did houses of consequence exist prior to the nineteenth century, but Americans understood them to be crucial sites of identity formation. From George Washington's Mount Vernon and Thomas Jefferson's Monticello to Washington Irving's Sunnyside and Hawthorne's Old Manse, houses captivated the nation's attention. Semipublic landmarks, these homes were widely seen as defining institutions. Other, less well-known houses ordered and shaped the landscape that surrounded them. Indeed, the design and construction of houses became a locus for debating broadly shared concerns about cultural development. Moreover, by thinking through the variety of counterpublics that undertook the multivalent meanings of the domestic, we can move away from separating a masculine public world from a private feminine space. The house is not a realm removed from a larger public world, but the lens through which Americans of both genders and from a variety of different political and social orientations, a host of counterpublics, sought to examine the state of the Republic.

To trace how images of the house served as a locus for debating broadly shared concerns about cultural development, my focus shifts between various states and regions. Beginning first by examining key sites in Revolutionary Era Virginia, I move to post-Revolutionary Philadelphia and the surrounding Pennsylvania countryside, then to Manhattan and the lower Hudson Valley during the aftermath of the War of 1812, then up the Hudson to Jacksonian Era northwestern New York State, and finally to "renaissance" New England and its preoccupation with the import of the region's architectural history. Moving across and between these different geographical regions, I examine how the house was continually redeployed as an index of American development. Moreover, this shifting geographical focus allows me to demonstrate how different regions played more prominent roles in defining both American domesticity and national identity at various moments in the nation's early history. In focusing on how Washington and Jefferson imagined their house as a national public sites, I seek to lay the foundation for my subsequent considerations of how crucial texts in American literature use the house as a means of questioning how American culture both departed from and participated in European cultural modes. By returning to the house as a window into the complexity of cultural development, writers such as Charles Brockden Brown, Washington Irving, James Fenimore Cooper, and Nathaniel Hawthorne sought to interrogate the legacies of the Revolutionary Era, in effect to sound out the intent of the framers of national design, as well as question the current state of the doubled-edged meaning of domestic practice. The house, much more than any other cultural object, became a means for writers across the first seventy years of American history to scrutinize both the current state of domestic identity as well as consider the future prospects of the nation. Although the house continued to be a crucial means of registering the state of national identity after the Civil War, such coverage lies outside the scope of this project. By focusing on how mid-nineteenth-century texts are in dialog with early post-Revolutionary ones through the frame of the house, I suggest ways in which these earlier periods of U.S. history imagined themselves in dialog not with a list of absences but with the location that a variety of Revolutionary figures argued was the crucial site for determining American identity.

In the remaining sections of chapter 1, "'When Buildings Are of Durable Materials': The American Home and the Structural Legacies of History," I examine how the invocation of domestic imagery to structure republican thought was embodied in George Washington's Mount Vernon and Thomas Jefferson's Monticello. By exploring how Washington and Jefferson sought to bridge the distance between the architectural figurations of nation construction and the actual design of their own houses, I move to demonstrate how they both understood and responded to the idea of imagining republican identity through metaphors of homebuilding. Like many of their contemporaries, George Washington and Thomas Jefferson embodied in their homes the social forms they hoped the emerging nation would adopt. Mount Vernon and Monticello were popularly imagined as among the first "public" institutions in the new Republic, a status that influenced both Washington's and Jefferson's design decisions. Tracing how both Washington and Jefferson understood the ways in which domestic architecture reflected and measured America's connections to European forms, I map how they understood the emergence of the Republic as informed by its connections to these preexisting traditions.

In chapter 2, "'No Longer Assigned Its Ancient Use': Biloquial Architecture and the Problems of Remodeling," I consider the complexity of the idea of the house in post-Revolutionary America by using Philadelphia as a nexus for grounding interpretations of residual architectural structures. Throughout this chapter, I consider the ways in which early American writers utilized domestic imagery to stage broadly shared concerns about personal and social stability. Beginning with an analysis of William Bartram's *Travels Through North & South Carolina, Georgia, East & West Florida*, I argue that representations of indigenous domestic architecture complicated conceptions of Anglo-American settlement and expansion. By looking back toward the tangled banks of North American settlement (even as he ruminates on post-Revolutionary social order), Bartram calls the sustainability of the U.S. experiment into question. By noting these ruins and abandoned homes, Bartram enjoins the Republic to recalibrate its conceptions of North American history to avoid becoming just another failed colonial enterprise. I extend my investigation of this issue by turning to the novels of Charles Brockden Brown. In both *Wieland* and *Edgar Huntly* (1799), Brown displays an intense interest in framing the complexity of pre-Revolutionary America's settlement history architecturally. Brown's novels continually address questions of possession, intention, and design, by privileging houses as sites of identity formation. For Brown, charting the occupational histories of the nation's houses becomes a means to test the nation's political underpinnings. Subsequent to my discussions of Bartram and Brown, I consider the writing of the Corps of Discovery in order to establish how the "wilderness" of post-Revolutionary North America was itself replete with occupied houses and abandoned homes. Collectively, the writings of Bartram, Brown, Meriwether Lewis, and William Clark register an intricate architectural record of decline and fall, complicating cultural perceptions of expansion and construction. Thus, this chapter measures how post-Revolutionary Americans understood nation building and cultural development as acts of reformulation undertaken within an already architecturally dense environment. By concentrating on the ambiguous legacies framed by these residual houses, I address the impact of pre-Revolutionary structures on the Republic's emerging narratives about originality, design, and viability.

In chapter 3, "'Home Bred Virtues and Local Attachments': New York and the Evolution of the American Home," I examine New York's emergence as the cultural and economic center of the Republic. European travelers typically based their accounts of U.S. social life on the domestic practices they encountered in New York homes. I advance a transatlantic contextualization of domesticity, by focusing on the ways in which Washington Irving attempted to preserve and construct a sense of national architectural practice by underscoring the manufactured nature of European cultural production. Both Washington Irving's fiction and his designs at Sunnyside are crucial to unraveling how he advanced his idea of the possibilities attendant to readaptation and remodeling. In his fiction, Irving unveiled the mythic nature of these European domestic "histories," even as he concurrently imported that practice by "historicizing" his own home. In 1832 Irving returned from a seventeen-year absence in Europe and was shocked by the altered landscape of both Manhattan and the Hudson River Valley, changes driven to a considerable extent by the opening of the Erie Canal. His response, exemplified as much by Sunnyside as by his writing, undercut European claims for preeminence, while they simultaneously invented American national histories. I extend my discussion of Irving's thought, and the sea change produced by the emergence of the market revolution, by surveying Thomas Cole's representations of New York's architectural environment. Cole's series *The Course of Empire* (1836), like Irving after his expatriation, demonstrates how Manhattan was transformed by the widespread adoption of Greek Revival architecture, a style intended to embody New York's new imperial status. Moreover, *The Course of Empire* notes the shift in national practices which cotenant such a metamorphosis. Thus, this chapter traces the pivotal position of New York (and its immediate environs) in aesthetic debates over the relationship between domestic design and the future direction of the nation.

Chapter 4, "'The Wants of Posterity': Community Construction and the Composing Order of American Architecture," broadens my discussion of New York's role in the development of national identity. More particularly, I deploy the representation of houses in the work of three generations of the Cooper family to illuminate significant shifts in American attitudes toward nature and community. William Cooper's concerns over American architectural practice reflect a neo-Jeffersonian vision of community construction. Like Jefferson, Cooper believed the nation's capacity to grow was dependent on establishing building practices that rooted settlers in the local. That legacy was a complex one for James Fenimore Cooper, whose fiction recurrently features the relation between domestic design and the processes of identity formation. In such novels as *The Pioneers* (1823), *Home as Found* (1838), and *Wyandotté, or The Hutted*

Knoll (1843), Cooper reads and reinterprets the relationship between household design and community composition. By treating various eras (both real and imagined) of Cooperstown's history, Cooper creates a master narrative for the region. Susan Fenimore Cooper infused her writing with a protoscientific consciousness absent in her ancestors' writing. Her familiarity with the work of such figures as Andrew Jackson Downing, Louis Agassiz, and Charles Lyell provided her with a lens through which she studied and refigured the domestic legacies of her family. The movement from William to Susan Cooper mirrors developments in American domesticity by highlighting how shifts in conceptions of American nature informed household design. Thus, this chapter examines how each of these writers measured the appropriateness of certain types of architectural styles over less sustainable models to describe a paradigmatic American home.

In chapter 5, "'In the Midst of an Uncertain Future': Remodeling the Legacies of American Domesticity," I take up the question of the gendered nature of domestic design. In an extended discussion of the fiction of Edgar Allan Poe, Nathaniel Hawthorne, and Herman Melville, I consider the relation of art and the market as that nexus is reflected in the representation of houses. Traditionally, American cultural criticism has separated a masculine public world from a feminine private one, yet increasingly at midcentury male artists argued that the modernization of the home endangered cultural stability. Rather than casting this response as an emblem of feminization, I describe a more fluid relationship between home and market. By foregrounding the decisive role male "domestic fiction" played in midcentury identity formation, I readdress critical configurations of the domestic to dispel the oversimplification of the separate-spheres argument. In many of his mid-1830s tales, Poe explored the correspondence between identity formation and spatial location. Thus, his stories continually examine the relationship between architecture and social stability. Melville similarly explores the issues of national development and personal identity in a number of his works, but most particularly "Hawthorne and His Mosses" and "I and My Chimney." In such texts as "Sites from a Steeple," "The Old Manse," and *The Scarlet Letter* (1850), Hawthorne analogously examines the consequences of attempting to embody civic order architecturally. Using Poe's and Melville's short fiction to frame my readings of Hawthorne's work, I recount how for all three of these writers the house was a primary vehicle for figuring both the present and the future of national life.

Lincoln's extended domestic metaphor resonated powerfully with his own recent experiences. During the mid-1850s the Lincolns began an extended renovation of their own small cottage in Springfield, because it was no longer suitable for a well-to-do lawyer. Lincoln's contractors, Hannon & Ragsdale, started the renovation project in April 1856. Typically, the availability of land and the low cost of construction materials made it generally more cost-effective to build new dwellings than to redesign old ones. To preserve the smaller structure within a grander production, Lincoln's architects and contractors needed to grasp the intent of the original designers. Properly shoring up a one-story building to sustain the additional weight of a second story was not an easy task, and ensuring that new mortices fit old tenons was arduous work.

By the end of the construction process, Lincoln's "mean little cottage," on Eighth and Jackson streets in Springfield, was transformed "into a handsome two-story Greek Revival house, tastefully painted chocolate brown, with dark green shutters."[19] Although he had been absent during most of the actual remodeling, Lincoln carefully monitored the project. In particular, he came to understand the importance of working with rather than against the designs of the original architects. Existing beams and new timbers had to be carefully worked to fit if the house was to stand; if the second story was divided against the first, or vice versa, the house would collapse. While the facade was to be radically different, the interior portions of the house would retain the original frame within its encapsulating shell.

The "house divided" metaphor became a recurrent theme in Lincoln's senatorial campaign. Douglas made reference to the speech in his opening salvos of the contest, and Lincoln returned to its language in response. Douglas "gave special attention to a speech of mine, delivered here on the 16th of June," Lincoln noted (512). "He says that he carefully read that speech," and "he charges, in substance, that I invite a war of sections" (512). Lincoln insisted that he had not "put anything in that speech as a matter of fact," or made "any inferences which did not appear to me to be true, and fully warrantable" (512). Quoting liberally from his first speech, Lincoln argues in his reply to Douglas only that the nation is at a turning point; nowhere does he propose a permanent separation.

The issue in question was one of constitutional interpretation: for Lincoln, "the framers of our Constitution placed the issue of slavery where the public mind rested in the hope that it was in course of ultimate extinction" (515). The house that the framers had erected did not include slavery as an enduring element. Douglas and his allies, Lincoln maintained, believed that "the men of the present age, by their experience, have become wiser than the framers of the Constitution" (515). These workmen, these reinterpreters of the framers' intent, betrayed the original design of the national home.

Lincoln's original speech, he observed on the occasion of his first debate with Stephen Douglas, sought neither to promote division nor to limit local rights. He did not favor a "dead uniformity of local institutions."[20] Rather he argued that "the great variety of local institutions in the States, springing from differences in the soil, differences in the face of the country, and in climate, are bounds of Union" (17). These variations, he said, "do not make 'a house divided against itself,' but they make a house united" (17). Slavery was "an element of division in the house," because the original framers had not sanctioned its permanence (18). The states were like different rooms within a house; as long as they remained harmonious, the house was stable. Additions designed in opposition to the original architectural sketches, to the Constitution, would bury the prototype beneath an antagonistic facade.

Lincoln's extended commentary on his initial speech was intended to stir cultural memories. In it, he employs the figures of Washington and Jefferson, among others, as house builders, as nation builders, to insist that the founders never envisioned slavery as a foundational feature of the national home. Lincoln's speech is symptomatic of a widely shared conception of the nation as a distinctly American house. His concern about additions joined to an inherited frame is in part an argument about the consequences of slavery for national life. Pro-slavery forces, he says, have been masking the additions of these new frames, making them appear seamless additions to the preexisting structure. Yet they have no intention of preserving the argument of the original construction. His own house in Springfield had gone from a small cottage to a Greek Revival mansion without a loss of structural integrity. The latter aesthetic seamlessly submerged the first: such could be the fate of the national home if Douglas and others were allowed to carry out their designs. The house would not fall; it would be made all one thing, and as such would advance a new social vision. Lincoln tells his audience that they must be willing to dwell in this newly fashioned building. At a certain point, rapidly approaching, in Lincoln's mind, it will be too late to redesign the new facade or break the lease. More than simply employing domestic images to talk about domestic policies, Lincoln grounds his sense of the crisis facing the nation in the language of house building. Douglas bases his attack on that metaphor, and uses the same language Lincoln uses to conduct his defense. Both return, and return again, to the house divided as an essential point that separates their disparate visions. The centrality of that image across the 1858 Illinois senatorial campaign demonstrates the currency of Lincoln's household imagery. Clearly both Douglas and Lincoln thought that the election could be won or lost on how the public interpreted the image of the nation as a house.

II

A little over three weeks after Abraham Lincoln delivered his speech to the Illinois Republican state convention, Susan Fenimore Cooper wrote a letter to her sister in which she "expressed her pleasure at becoming involved in the purchase and restoration of George Washington's home and grave."[21] Five years earlier, Ann Pamela Cunningham had "ignited a nationwide movement of patriotic women" when she began her campaign to restore Washington's dilapidated estate.[22] The Mount Vernon Ladies' Association was committed to preserving Washington's house as a national memorial, and their energy stemmed from a profound faith that Mount Vernon could serve as a structural rebuttal to the "cataclysmic sectional politics" endangering national union.[23] Susan Fenimore Cooper leapt at the chance to contribute to the cause, and shortly after writing her sister she began work on a children's book, *Mount Vernon: A Letter to the Children of America* (1859), aimed at raising funds for the restoration effort. But Cooper's volume is more than just a sentimental appeal for historic preservation, for it is also a carefully crafted volume that eviscerates any mention of Mount Vernon as a plantation powered by slave labor. Cooper presents Mount Vernon as a "quiet country home," with "broad farms" and "rich crops," but offers no sign of who actually harvested those crops.[24] As Patricia West argues, the "success" of the Mount Vernon Ladies' Association "was predicated on the ability of its advocates to gloss over issues that might strike a chord of sectional disharmony."[25] By transforming Mount Vernon into the paradigmatic pastoral ideal, by cleansing it of any associations with slavery and portraying Washington as a the prototypical yeoman farmer, these preservationists reconstructed Washington as a representative man for the entire nation.

Mount Vernon had fallen into utter disrepair by the 1850s, as Washington's descendants had been unable to afford maintaining what had become, particularly since his death in 1799, an international tourist attraction. With an estimated ten thousand annual uninvited visitors, Mount Vernon was one of the most frequently visited "public" spaces in the United States.[26] Yet, for all the public's reverence for Washington, too many visitors treated Mount Vernon as their own private property, so much so, as Elswyth Thane observes, that "the public carried off anything available for souvenirs," even as they "wandered freely and intrusively about the grounds and the home."[27] Visitors alternatively chipped away at Washington's grave and Mount Vernon's exterior in their efforts to secure tokens of their visits. During the late eighteenth century, Mount Vernon was, as W. Barksdale Maynard suggests, "one of the most mentioned colonial buildings, endlessly praised for simplicity and solidity"; but, as Robert J. Allison notes, "fifty years after Washington's death, Mount Vernon was a crumbling ruin."[28]

Unable to sustain the farm or renovate the house, Washington's heirs tried several times to sell the estate to Congress or the state of Virginia, only to have their efforts rebuffed. After being rejected by both the federal and the state government, John Augustine Washington "offered," as Robert F. Dalzell records, the "dilapidated mansion house and a small parcel of land" to "the public."[29] Fearing that the house would fall into the hands of speculators, Ann Pamela Cunningham began her efforts to purchase the house and transform Mount Vernon into a pedagogic primer aimed at rescripting cultural memories of the Revolutionary generation.[30] Cunningham launched a broad public crusade to reestablish Washington as a symbol of national unity, enlisting representatives from every state in the Republic.[31] As Susan Fenimore Cooper's letter demonstrates, Americans from all across the country actively participated in the restoration efforts, readily joining the movement to preserve Mount Vernon as a national memorial aimed at counterbalancing the prevalence of partisanship and sectionalism.[32]

The efforts of the Mount Vernon Ladies' Association to remodel Mount Vernon into a national shrine tapped into the same cultural preoccupation with reading national history through the frame of domestic houses that Lincoln reappropriated in his campaign debates. Both Lincoln and the Mount Vernon Ladies' Association focused attention on the dualistic legacies that Washington and the other framers of the Constitution had bequeathed the nation, the problems inherent in a slaveholding nation having declared its commitment to the self-evident truth of all men's equality. But the restoration efforts at Mount Vernon were not so dramatic a remodeling as might at first be imagined, for they in fact revel a fundamental tension that Washington had taken pains to deal with as he renovated his estate in his own lifetime. The biographer and historian Henry Wiencek observes that "the ultimate contradiction of Mount Vernon" is that Washington "envisioned" a future for the house free from the stain of an enslaved labor force.[33] Washington never lived to see a slaveless Mount Vernon, although his will freed all his slaves, but he took pains in his design of Mount Vernon to mask the presence of slavery on the plantation. Describing the fixation of both Washington and Thomas Jefferson with the construction of their homes, Robert F. Dalzell Jr. argues that "ultimately, it was as tangible expressions—emblems—of personal independence that Monticello and Mount Vernon mattered most to their creators."[34] Moreover, both Washington and Jefferson realized that their houses were imagined, after the Revolutionary War, as public expressions of their visions for American cultural development. This burden weighed on both Washington and Jefferson, and informed the design choices they made about their respective homes.

The remodeling of Mount Vernon as paradigmatic American farmhouse, illustrative of national and not regional mores, undertaken by the Mount Vernon Ladies' Association adumbrates the ways in which Washington himself struggled with having the house serve as an embodiment of his ideal vision for American independence. As "an exemplar of the practical, utilitarian side of the Enlightenment," Jean B. Lee argues, Washington "hoped to make Mount Vernon a model plantation, one that would instruct and inspire the citizenry of the entire nation in habits he deemed essential for the republic."[35] In seeking to fashion Mount Vernon as a model plantation, Washington labored to have his house speak to post-Revolutionary concerns, and it was this narrative that the Mount Vernon Ladies' Association sought to revive. Moreover, the association's remodeling efforts were part and parcel of a larger, widespread "resurgence in the George Washington myth" during the 1850s, as many Americans turned to "the disinterested figure as an appeal to the Union, an attempt to find a figure that could supercede the sectional divisions of the nation."[36] As the nation struggled to keep from fracturing, antebellum Americans turned to Washington, and more particularly to Mount Vernon, to ground their readings of their Revolutionary heritage. Moving to transform Mount Vernon into a structural reification of "associationism," W. Barksdale Maynard writes, "commentators ignored architectural elements that were ornate or delicate, including the arcades linking house and outbuildings, the dining room serliana with rustic cinctures, and Adamesque plasterwork."[37] By fashioning a simplified version of Mount Vernon, antebellum visitors advanced their representations of George Washington as the quintessential republican citizen. In so doing, they underplayed the efforts Washington oversaw to ensure that the house reflected his vision of a republican citizenry in more nuanced ways. Mount Vernon was a monument, like all other eighteenth-century plantation homes, to wealth and slavery, and Washington struggled to find ways of "moderating" the "visual impact" of these realities.[38] The revival of the Washington myth in the 1850s, dilapidated after years of neglect, focused on Mount Vernon because of the ways in which the house had unmistakably established an ambiguous legacy. Mount Vernon could be remodeled because it had always, albeit uneasily, housed contending narratives about national unity, narratives that Washington was keenly aware of when he designed and refigured the house during the length of his residence there. Washington understood that his retirement from public service was going to be a continual public performance, and, without question, his acceptance of that role informed how he orchestrated the design of Mount Vernon.

Figure 1. George Washington's drawing of the west façade of Mount Vernon, 1773. Courtesy of the Mount Vernon Ladies' Association.

In 1754, Washington, at twenty-two, leased Mount Vernon from his sister-in-law, and he later inherited the property at her death. Although picturesquely situated near the banks of the Potomac, it was "a minor, relatively unfertile farm."[39] Unable to reliably grow tobacco in the depleted soil, "starting in 1766," as Joseph J. Ellis writes, Washington planted wheat, becoming "one of the first of the major Virginia planters to make the change."[40] Washington had significant landholdings on the frontier, and so, to a degree, he could imagine Mount Vernon more as an estate, as a house, than as a plantation. Still, Mount Vernon's failure to generate revenue was a difficulty with which Washington continually grappled.[41] He undertook two major revisions of Mount Vernon during his tenure at the house, the first almost immediately after he took possession, the latter begun in the 1770s and lasting throughout the Revolutionary War. Rather than two distinct endeavors, the process of rebuilding and remodeling Mount Vernon "that had begun with the plans he made in 1757 would prove to be a never-ending enterprise" as each "new project would beget another, multiplying both the pleasures and the frustrations of building."[42] Since Mount Vernon never had a binding master plan, these modifications were undertaken as problems arose or new ideas occurred to Washington. Alterations to one aspect of the house or its grounds necessitated readjusting everything else to accommodate the changes within the overall harmony of the design (see fig. 1).

In the first major reconfiguration, Washington raised Mount Vernon's roof one story, thereby doubling its size, and redecorated both its interior and its exterior. Washington also reoriented the house in the landscape, by moving "the main entrance from the water to the land side."[43] But, over-all, little "documentary evidence" exists "to determine in full detail" the extent of the alterations.[44] The surviving records indicate that the original dwelling that Washington redesigned, built by either his father or grandfather, "was little more than a farm house."[45] Architectural historians believe that Washington preserved almost nothing of the initial structure, yet he never seemed to have considered demolishing it and starting afresh.[46] Washington seemed to want to build on a tradition, to argue architecturally that the past could be reworked in the interests of the future. This sense of building for the future is implicit from his earliest modifications of the house. By shifting the public front of the house to its western side with the relocation of the main entranceway, Washington, Robert Dalzell argues, "whether consciously or not," turned "his back on England" and faced west, "where whatever reputation he could claim at that point had been earned."[47] Whatever the motivations, Washington refashioned the small house almost completely, and in so doing turned an inherited relic into a building consistent with his conception of a proper home. The original house, built in the eighteenth century or perhaps surviving from the seventeenth, would be encircled, contained, and preserved within Washington's new, reoriented frame.

This continual reworking bespeaks the centrality of Mount Vernon in Washington's life. Continually experimenting with minor interior features and with the layout of the grounds leading up to the house, Washington had an aesthetic vision he wanted the house to embody. That vision was consistent with Washington's conception of a gentleman farmer in the eighteenth century, and his practices typically mirrored what he took to be those of European country estates.[48] Washington's decision to have the interior walls finished in stucco, for example, was shaped by his belief that it was "the present taste in England," even though he did not know how to prepare stucco, whether or not to paint it, or whether or not his rooms should be "stuccoed below the surbase (chair high) or from thence upwards only?"[49] Even when he did not understand the precepts of European fashion, Washington wanted to follow them.

As was typical of grand eighteenth-century houses, most of Mount Vernon's first floor was devoted to public spaces. Its central passageway was dominated by a staircase that allowed Washington to descend from the private second story to greet his company. The staircase actually comprised three staircases, the first ascending to the height of the first floor, where it terminated in a small landing before joining another short staircase at a right angle, which gave way, again at a right angle, to another short series of stairs. The centered staircase gave visitors the impression of the second-story private areas without offering them any visual access to what they contained. The staircase thus functioned to remind visitors that they were separated from the domestic sphere of the occupants. This figuration of the power relationship between the private and public spaces of the house aligned Mount Vernon's architectural argument with residual practices. The house's interior design, following Washington's intent, maintained a traditional relationship between inhabitants and visitors.

The central passageway, which included the ornate staircase, was one of the most elaborately embellished spaces within the house. Conceiving of the first floor as a semipublic space led Washington to fashion it as the area where Mount Vernon would make "its principal bid for the world's attention and respect."[50] Washington's lavishly completed entrance hall, finished wooden paneling, and other decorative turns indeed solicit attention. The entrance hall was centered in the first floor, with (almost) equal wings on either side. Washington had added the second story to the house in his first rebuilding, offering him the opportunity from very early on to establish a strict division between public and private spaces. By almost doubling the amount of usable space, Washington retrofitted the house as a dwelling place for a large landowner, transforming Mount Vernon from a modest farmhouse into a mansion. Washington wanted to build an impressive dwelling, appropriate for a man of distinction. Upon entering, visitors would be aware that their host, situated in his private second-story realm, was above them, literally and figuratively. The interior of the house signifies not Washington's democratic ethos but his commitment to hierarchy. Washington's embrace of the distinctions between public and private arose from his faithfulness to residual codes of gentility.[51]

Yet establishing privacy at Mount Vernon—given the hordes of endless visitors who descended on the house—was no easy matter. Eventually, the Washingtons were forced to locate a gate at the bottom of their formal staircase to prevent "visitors" from ascending to the second floor.[52] Washington's evocation of the social order implied by his adoption of an English architectural practice—a grand stairway meant to showcase *him* descending—collapsed in the face of the curiosity of a republican citizenry. After his retirement from public service, Washington was still popularly imagined as the public face of the Republic, and Mount Vernon became broadly recognized for its importance as an emblem of his domestic practices and beliefs. The house and the man were imagined as public symbols of the possibilities for national stability in the United States; they both served as metaphors for American identity. Washington was uncomfortable with this celebrity, but he also recognized that it was a burden that he and his house must shoulder. Retiring to Mount Vernon after his terms as the first president of the United States, Washington was inundated with visitors. Instead of finding in Mount Vernon a sanctuary from the pressures of public life, Washington was deluged by the curious. In his correspondence he laments that "so many come here without *proper* introductions."[53] This

situation forced him to spend the majority of his time away from the very
building he had hoped would be a bastion of solitude. In effect, visitors
were more often sheltered at Mount Vernon than was Washington. The
cultural codes of hospitality drove Washington to provide for those who
descended on him, but the practice was nearly unbearable. He had, after
all, returned to Mount Vernon to retire. The distraction of the innumer-
able "strange faces" prevented him from tending to his house, which had
suffered from his prolonged absence in New York and Philadelphia. Writing to his friend and confidant James McHenry, Washington bemoaned
that the more he examined his house, the more he "probed, the deeper" he
found "the wounds" caused by his "absence and neglect of eight years."[54]
The problem that faced Washington was how simultaneously to address
the needs of his *guests* and those of his house. That the American public
now imagined Mount Vernon as a public holding only further complicated
the matter. In effect, Washington wondered if Mount Vernon was
designed to house him or to provide a living room for the nation.[55]
"Indeed," Robert Dalzell argues, "the necessity of putting his private life
on public display had created a paradox that would trouble Washington as
long as he lived."[56]

"Before the War, and even while it existed," Washington wrote to a
friend, "altho' I was eight years from home at one stretch, (except the en
passant visits made to it on My march to and from the Siege of Yorktown)
I made considerable additions to my dwelling house, and alterations in my
Offices, and Gardens; but the dilapidations occasioned by time, and those
neglects which are co-extensive with the absence of Proprietors, have
occupied as much of my time, within the last twelve months in repairing
them, as at any former period in the same space."[57] Washington had finally
returned home, after a period of "five and twenty years, nearly," to be a
"permanent resident at" Mount Vernon, but he did not have the freedom
to restore the house to its optimal condition.[58] After a quarter century in
the direct service of the nation, he was still called on to minister to its citizens, and fulfilling this charge prevented him from having the leisure to
rework Mount Vernon as he saw fit. Washington may have had to curb his
architectural ambitions because of the high cost of construction and the
difficulty of securing skilled carpenters and craftsman, but his correspondence suggests that the biggest impediment he faced in terms of remodeling Mount Vernon was the extraordinary number of visitors who arrived at
his estate wanting a glimpse of his domestic life.

After the Revolution, the cultural perception of equality among all citizens began to test Mount Vernon's design. Americans did not seek an invitation; they just showed up. But there they confronted an interior design
that bespoke not equality but separation. The orchestrated effect on visitors arriving via the inland roads began when they entered Mount Ver-

non's gates, where two undulating pathways led to the house by means of a circular approach. On these paths the house disappeared from direct view, masked behind artfully planted trees and the varied arrangement of foliage across the grounds. Likewise, the groves of trees and the circuitous pathway shielded the slave quarters and storehouse buildings from direct view, in some way masking their presence at Mount Vernon. The slave barracks, which extended as wings from the greenhouse, opened to the rear of the house and had no openings on its front side, so that it was almost impossible to tell from this front view what they contained. These buildings, constructed around 1792–93, replaced a larger and more visible two-story wooden structure that had previously housed the plantation's slaves.[59] The redesign of the slave quarters, in short, as Henry Wiencek observes, allowed Washington to adopt "an architecture that rendered slavery invisible, while at the same time weaving slavery into the fabric of his grand design."[60] Laboring to find some way to erase the visible presence of slavery at Mount Vernon, at least from the inland approach, Washington directed the construction of these barracks so that they appeared not as domestic quarters but as buildings dedicated to some other purpose. Furthermore, the layout of the pathway sought to draw a visitor's attention away from these structures and focus it on the main house. After meandering on his approach, a traveler would finally ascend to the mansion itself, nestled on a high bank of the Potomac so that, behind, one saw only clearings or the river itself. Such a setting made the house appear as a distinctive and solitary element of the environment.

Approaching the house, a visitor would be confronted by a seemingly expensive stone exterior, suggesting both that Mount Vernon was built to last and that its owner had spared no cost. On closer inspection, that illusion vanished. Except for its foundation and chimneys, which are built of brick, Mount Vernon is a wooden dwelling. Following the mandates of eighteenth-century American architectural practice, Washington framed his house with boards, but he devised a strategy to make it appear that he had built his house from stone. The clapboards were divided into a series of rectangular panels, with inclined edges, mimicking the pattern of stone blocks. The walls were then covered with a white paint blended with sand to approximate the rough texture of a masonry facade. Since Washington had preserved the original shell of the first Mount Vernon even as he had expanded, it might have been impossible to shift the character of the house from a wooden framed building to that of a stone structure. Still, by the second half of the eighteenth century many prominent Virginia houses were largely built with masonry, and Washington's invention of the faux stone served to align his house with current construction paradigms. This illusory facade is emblematic, like the obscured slave quarters, of how Mount Vernon tenuously housed a variety of narratives underneath its frame, courting the very ambiguities that the Mount Vernon Ladies' Association played on when they began their restoration efforts.

Situated on the top of a steep bank, the house had a commanding view of passing river traffic. On the eastern front of the house, Washington fashioned a broad piazza to provide a shaded view of the Potomac. On its most publicly exposed side, clear to the view of anyone on the river and not obscured (as the house was on the western front) by foliage, it presented "a generosity of scale, a commanding spaciousness commensurate with the character of the man whose house it was."[61] The open space of the piazza was lined with identical straight-backed wooden chairs, and offered a marked contrast to the darkened wooden panels of the interior. The piazza, "half-rustic, half-sophisticated," made the house "simultaneously simple and grand, a fitting home for the greatest American of his generation, the model republican hero-statesman of the age."[62] Here, on its eastern front, was Mount Vernon's democratic aesthetic. From this piazza, the working portions of the plantation were hidden by the house itself, and it was impossible to see any signs of cultivation or agricultural labor.

Although porches, or piazzas, had appeared in American architecture as early as the mid–eighteenth century, that feature had been limited largely to the Boston and Philadelphia areas.[63] A piazza on a plantation house was an innovation, and, in particular, Mount Vernon's large and unornamented riverfront piazza was an architectural ingenuity. No immediate source for Washington's piazza has been uncovered, no discernible origin for its planning discovered. Washington's correspondence evidences his concern over the design, as he records his search for a flooring material able to withstand continual exposure that he might use for his "long open Gallery." The piazza broke from conventions, violating the "standard proportions" and the reigning "architectural paradigm" in the pursuit of an individualized conception of domestic space.[64] The differences between the eastern river facade and the western inland facade indicate that Mount Vernon had two faces, one suggestive of a democratic design scheme and the other following the rigors of a more conventional eighteenth-century architectural style. Both fronts are tailored to suit the needs of the expectant public, but they do so in conspicuously different ways.

On the river side the innovation of the unique piazza invites commonality, by offering all visitors the natural splendor of the view. On the house's opposite front, Washington advanced a very different aesthetic. Approaching from the interior of the Virginia countryside, visitors were guided along the serpentine walks to a formal entry hallway, which established the wealth and power of their host. Following along this serpentine pathway, they would from various clearings in the foliage see the inner workings of Mount Vernon's planted fields. One entranceway, facing the river, thus marks the house as a modern dwelling, fashioned without precedents, designed for comfort rather than custom. Everyone seated on the porch is on an equal footing and afforded the same advantages; there is no privileged spot, no advantageous location with a better view. Conversely, the house's inland facade is firmly rooted in the available aristocratic traditions, marking off distinction between public and private, between host and guest, between proprietor and visitor. In the middle of these two fronts—at the nexus of these two registers—George Washington resided. Henry Wiencek suggests that "Mount Vernon occupies two landscapes and straddles, as far as that is possible, two realms of time."[65] Facing east from the piazza, one viewed only uncultivated forests, broken on either bank only by the meandering Potomac River. From the western front of the house, one saw highly structured planted fields and attempts to hide the living presence of the slaves who worked the plantation. Washington's position halfway between residual and emerging notions of social order reflected the actual cultural conditions in which he lived. In effect, Mount Vernon's two exteriors suggest the tensions between domestic, and thus social, arrangement and the pursuit of a workable balance in the post-Revolutionary world of the United States. The source of those tensions was largely Washington's reliance on an enslaved labor force, for as Lorena S. Walsh writes, "what Washington could not do was to reconcile his vision of Mount Vernon as a model improved estate with the fundamentally opposed interests of the people he expected to implement his plans."[66] Americans could find in Mount Vernon a dwelling that had managed to make use of the past, even if its owner had entirely reworked its legacy. At the same time, Mount Vernon balanced the uncertainties of that residual practice with the shifting demands of the present and the future. Washington had tried very hard to fabricate this delicate balance at Mount Vernon, and the late antebellum efforts to rescript Washington as an everyman for 1858, as opposed to recalling him as an eighteenth-century Virginia planter, replicated and extended these efforts.

The specific aesthetic or architectural model Washington embodied in Mount Vernon remains difficult to determine. Like the unsettled social landscape of the post-Revolutionary period, the house itself obscures any definitive separation between the public and private realms. A private residence whose chief occupant found solitude only when riding away from it, Mount Vernon lingers as a complicated site. Perhaps because of its ambiguity, it was able to become increasingly important in the middle of the nineteenth century. As the nation drifted toward war, Mount Vernon reemerged as an emblem of stability. The embrace of Mount Vernon as a national shrine erased the ambiguity of Washington's residency. More important, the house still stands as a monument to the difficulties of reconciling the demands of the past and the prospects for the future in the antebellum period. Just as Mount Vernon had a complex cultural role at the close of the eighteenth century, the restoration movement in the mid–nineteenth century played with the historical presentation of domestic life at Washington's home to highlight its more palatable attributes. On the eve of the Civil War, a northern romanticization of Mount Vernon, one voiced most notably by Susan Cooper, sought to downplay its status as a plantation and celebrated it as a prototype for northern yeoman farms. What to make of Mount Vernon and how it related to conceptions of American identity were again a source for debate. Since Washington himself never adequately resolved the tensions over the meaning of his house, that it should still be undefined a half century later is not shocking. The argument embodied in Monticello—another famous American house—by Thomas Jefferson was more forthright.

III

"The genius of architecture," laments Thomas Jefferson in *Notes on the State of Virginia* (1787), "seems to have shed its maledictions over this land," for unfortunately "there are two or three plans, on one of which, according to size, most of the houses in the state are built" (278)."[67] Modeled on prefabricated designs, the majority of Virginia's homes pay little attention, Jefferson observes, to local nuance; directed solely toward the functional, they have no regard for the future. Failing to generate a cultural legacy, Virginians build duplicate houses doomed to collapse or decay. Conceived of as impermanent, these homes fail to tether Virginia's settlers to the space they inhabit, contributing to the migratory patterns of American development. Neglecting the way architecture shapes culture, Americans were replicating, long before the age of mechanical reproduction, endless mistakes. Jefferson, in short, makes eighteenth-century Virginia sound a lot like mid-twentieth-century Levittown.

"The greatest proportion" of Virginia's "private buildings," Jefferson writes, are fashioned of "scantling and boards, plastered with lime" (278). It is, he concludes, "impossible to devise things more ugly, uncomfortable, and happily more perishable" (278). While there are houses of distinction in the state, they are exceptional. An abundance of cheap lumber contributes to a "prejudice" against "houses of brick or stone" as "less wholesome than those of wood" (278).[68] For Jefferson, that superstition had significant consequence. "A country whose buildings are of wood," he argues, "can never increase in its improvements to any considerable degree," for each succeeding generation must devote time and labor to maintain poorly designed buildings (280). "Their duration is highly estimated at 50 years," Jefferson calculates, hence "every half century," the land becomes "a tabula rasa, whereon we have to set out anew, as in the first moment of seating it" (280). Such a practice meant that Virginians, and the nation whose citizens they were meant to represent, were returned cyclically to the position of first contact. Jefferson's concerns were not entirely economic. The absence of an architectural register pointed toward the fragility of the American experiment. In *Notes on the State of Virginia*, as Timothy Sweet convincingly demonstrates, Jefferson sought to ground "America's political virtue on an agrarian base"; in so doing, Jefferson "linked economic intensification (sedentary farming methods and market embeddedness) to national political stability."[69] Sweet rightly maintains that Jefferson's *Notes* oversimplifies the difficulties attendant to moving from transitory subsistence farming to sedentary agricultural practices; similarly, *Notes* reduces the difficulty of manufacturing houses out of brick instead of building with wood.[70] Both of these abridgments serve the same ends, as Jefferson seeks to underscore the necessity of adopting house-building and homesteading practices that root Americans to local landscapes in enduring ways.

Peter S. Onuf argues that Jefferson's *Notes* advances a vision of "republican empire" predicated on looking "westward," away from "the domination of a corrupt British metropolis and the colonial seaports through which it exercised its domination."[71] Tied to this, as Onuf maintains, is the way in which Jefferson contrasts "the internal divisions of a slaveholding oligarchy with an idealized image of a unified republic of patriotic freeholders."[72] In order to ensure the success of these idealized freeholders, Jefferson calls for the adoption of architectural practices that will frame and inculcate appropriate behavior. If Americans continued to establish foundations that were subject to rapid decay, then the nation's social contract would not likely endure. By building permanent houses that tethered landholders to local communities, and shifting to agricultural practices that did not cyclically exhaust the soil (rotating fields away from tobacco and planting wheat in its place), the agrarian republic that *Notes* desperately tries to envision would be both founded and ensured. Jefferson's *Notes* advances, as Rhys Isaac observes, the idea that "farms and estate houses would be the centers of civilization in this new world."[73] The absence of an architectural landscape that fosters a permanent connection to a local community will, Jefferson implies, condemn the Republic to an eternity of new beginnings. *Notes* seeks to counter that possibility by promoting building and agricultural practices that foster rooted stability, going so far as to condemn anything that allows for the continuance of customs or methods that enable change and mobility.[74] "The book marks yet one more attempt," Thomas Hallock observes, "to construct a life over the map, bringing an authorial rage for order over experience that could not be so easily contained."[75]

That Jefferson supported architectural stability might seem at odds with his much quoted response to Shays' Rebellion. In letters to Ezra Stiles, Abigail Adams, James Madison, and, most famously, to William Stephens Smith, Jefferson defended the value of ongoing revolution.[76] "God forbid we should ever be 20 years without such a rebellion," he wrote Smith; "the tree of liberty must be refreshed from time to time with the blood of patriots & tyrants."[77] As Joseph J. Ellis argues, "these were extremely radical statements," which "placed Jefferson far to the left of any responsible political leader of the revolutionary generation."[78] Gordon S. Wood attributes the fact that Jefferson appeared undisturbed by the Shays' Rebellion to his tendency toward "rhetorical exaggeration."[79] Yet Jefferson's tacit approval of even violent civic unrest is not discordant with his insistence that Americans build lasting homes. Jefferson's description of Shays' Rebellion as "an instance of rebellion honorably conducted," speaks to his belief that local affinities—the moral sense of a rooted community—and not a disembodied series of political edicts, would ensure the Republic's well-being (911). Jefferson understood Shays' Rebellion as an uprising of an uninformed people, a vivid reminder that political leaders must stay in constant contact with those whom they serve. If Massachusetts' citizens had remained "quiet under such misconceptions," he argued, that passivity would essentially have marked "the forerunner of death to the public liberty" (911).

For Jefferson, "the remedy" in such situations was "to set [the rebels] right to facts, pardon & pacify them" (911). As Ellis argues, "the Jeffersonian ideal" was "a world in which individual citizens had internalized their social responsibilities so thoroughly that the political architecture Madison was designing was superfluous."[80] America's political framework, in other words, was less important than the actual houses in which Americans would live. As Jan Lewis maintains, "both the Constitution and the process of ratification brought about a politics that was less stable and more popular than its framers anticipated."[81] In houses of consequence, built to last, the citizens of the Republic could incorporate democratic principles, but only if those dwellings were able to link past and present, residents and residences. "When buildings are of durable materials," Jefferson argues, "every new edifice is an actual and permanent acquisition to the state, adding to its value as well as to its ornament" (280). If buildings were consistently imagined as disposable, the practice of domestic architecture, "one of the fine arts," would never flourish, and a distinctly American architectural style, adapted to the nation's ideologies and its environmental circumstances, would never emerge (279). In *Notes*, as Christopher Looby argues, Jefferson seeks to define "smallholding peasants or yeoman farmers" as "central to American political mythology"; crucial to this formulation is the establishment of the proper type of domestic architecture, which would ground the formation of a republican citizenry.[82] Implied within the frame of *Notes* is the idea that homes worth inheriting and inhabiting would promote stability in ways no constitution could effect.

Jefferson's view of home design involves both durability and change, a vision consistent with his hopes for the Republic. Jefferson believed that America needed houses that could withstand alterations: buildings that could be amended by future occupants to better serve their needs. In other words, Jefferson argued that the Republic needed architectural practices that mirrored, in spirit, its political ethos. In describing Jefferson's attitudes toward authorship and ownership of texts, Jay Fliegelman draws a parallel between Monticello and Jefferson's writing and reading practices, which suggest to him how, in Jefferson's design schema, artifacts and individuals "become part of the architectural structure of the room, rather than an intrusive assertion within it."[83] Fliegelman's observation implies the connections that Jefferson believed existed between textual production, domestic architecture, and identity formation. For Jefferson, the Constitution's strengths resided in its flexibility. It could be altered without destroying its original framework. Similarly, the nation needed houses worth preserving even when circumstances necessitated remodeling, because such houses would establish a rooted citizenry committed to the labor of local community construction. In testimony to this belief, Jefferson built and refashioned Monticello. Imagined as a durable structure, Monticello was also a house that was never truly finished.

An almost daily preoccupation for Jefferson, domestic architecture drew his attention during the Revolutionary War, during the length of his public career, and indeed throughout the entirety of his life. Unlike many of his neighbors who built with only the needs of the present generation in mind, Jefferson imagined Monticello as a monument to his life and times. "The future was the screen," Joyce Appleby argues, "upon which Jefferson projected his faith in the unfolding of the human potential under conditions of freedom."[84] Monticello was the screen on which Jefferson projected the future; and while he began planning and designing Monticello in 1769, he did not stop building, tinkering with, and redesigning it until his death in 1826 (see fig. 2). In total, he spent almost fifty-seven years, well over two-thirds of his life, orchestrating the remodeling of his brick mansion. For all the care Jefferson took with his house, his admirers and friends were perplexed by its constantly chaotic condition. Guests found it difficult to believe that Jefferson was comfortable living in a house where inconveniences, such as the lack of securing nails in the second-story floorboards, were endured for lengthy stretches of time. Jefferson never tired of reconceiving Monticello's design. His insistence on micromanaging its construction meant that, as Jack McLaughlin notes, "during his frequent absences construction often came to a halt."[85]

Figure 2. Monticello: first edition (elevation). Architectural drawing by Thomas Jefferson, probably before March 1771. Courtesy of the Massachusetts Historical Society.

Not until he became president did Jefferson relinquish oversight, and only then from absolute necessity.[86]

Jefferson continually warned invited guests that Monticello was unfinished, but few fully grasped what "unfinished" meant. After a tortuous, daylong trip spent slowly navigating muddy roads, Anna Maria Thornton arrived at Monticello on September 18, 1802. "Tho' I had been prepared to see an unfinished house," she wrote in her diary that night, "still I could not help being much struck with the uncommon appearance."[87] When Thornton arrived, Monticello was a barely habitable cavern of raw brick and rough beams, with the new framework incomplete and the original house a patchwork of demolished walls and finished rooms. Jefferson had commenced a major remodeling of Monticello in 1796, and these exterior alterations were not completed until 1809, the final year of his presidency. Unsatisfied with Monticello's original dimensions, Jefferson planned a second version that enveloped the first structure.

Never truly completed, Monticello became something of a palimpsest as Jefferson remodeled its design. The disruption to domestic life caused by this continual tampering was boundless, and the cost of the ceaseless work contributed significantly to his eventual bankruptcy. Such decisions as putting off the enclosure of the framework until the entire house was refitted meant that new timbers were being put into place as other parts of the exposed framework were beginning to rot. These problems were particularly pronounced during the exterior modifications begun in 1796, when temporary roofs and outer walls served as long-standing placeholders. Even as the problematic consequences of Jefferson's architectural decisions became apparent, he remained inflexible. No matter how careful the design drawings, in practice buildings are not as measured and exact as an architect might wish. At Monticello, Jefferson's belief in the power of science to determine a stable measure collided headlong with the realities of early Republican life. His designs and ornamentations exceeded the skills of his hired carpenters and enslaved laborers and craftsmen, yet Jefferson insisted on strict adherence to his drawings.

The first, and perhaps most costly, decision Jefferson made about Monticello was its physical location. His decision to build the house on a mountaintop, considerably removed from all available sources of freshwater, was particularly striking. "It is difficult to think of a contemporary precedent in all of Europe for such an adventuresome, independent decision," William Howard Adams argues, "involving the siting of a new house, where a high hilltop was selected without at least some older, fortified structures dictating the choice."[88] Jefferson did not want to build on someone else's framework, nor was he willing to be bound by notions of economy or convenience in siting Monticello. He wanted an empty canvas on which he could project his vision. Building Monticello on the highest point of his estate allowed Jefferson to suggest, as Rhys Isaac notes, that it "was an archetypal place in profound opposition to another archetypal place, the city that could never, for Jefferson, be on a hill."[89] For Jefferson, it was the house and not diseased cities, as *Notes* makes clear, on which the nation should focus its gaze. The placement of his house atop the highest point on his land also allowed Jefferson to frame an otherwise uncluttered landscape so that the house would appear to be, from certain angles, the only structure on the plantation. By locating the "major service facilities at Monticello below ground," as Robert Dalzell notes, Jefferson reduced the visual impact of slavery at Monticello by effectively submerging it from the visible surface.[90] Jefferson carried this desire to reduce the visual impact of slavery into his interior designs as well, for his much admired dumbwaiter was more than a novel invention; it was also a way of creating a private sphere undisturbed by the overt presence of an enslaved labor force. The placement of Monticello, and the burying of its slave quarters, allowed Jefferson to look out on the landscape and not have his hope for a nation of yeoman farmers disrupted by anything within the foreground of his immediate view.

While Monticello's placement afforded Jefferson picturesque vistas, the choice of location created monumental difficulties. Building a brick house on the top of a mountain, far removed from a water source, caused considerable delay and expense. As he recorded in his *Garden Book*, "a bed of mortar which makes 2000. bricks takes 6 hhds of water"; hence he would either have to order a well dug near the house or require slaves to transport his bricks to the building site.[91] The lack of a well was a problem that would have long-lasting consequences for Jefferson, for even after the house was built, he confronted a continual water shortage until he developed cisterns to collect and store rainwater. The delay in brick making contributed mightily to Jefferson's construction problems, but he held fast to the maxim that a brick house, even in an unusual spot, was the best form for domestic architecture.

Describing the house in an 1809 letter to the architect Benjamin Latrobe, Jefferson wrote: "My essay in Architecture has been so much subordinated to the law of convenience, and affected also by circumstances of change of original design, that it is liable to some unfavorable and just criticisms. But what Nature has done for us is sublime and beautiful and unique."[92] Despite this acknowledgment that his "essay" was bound by circumstance, Monticello remains a testament to Jefferson's resistance to any limit—natural or man-made—that might deflect his vision. His decision to recruit craftsmen in Philadelphia and pay them to relocate to Monticello strikingly exemplifies Jefferson's practice. Building a grand manorial estate during and in the immediate aftermath of the Revolutionary War was financially overwhelming, but Jefferson would settle for no less. Even when delays in materials and shortcomings in the capabilities of available craftsmen demanded adjustments, Jefferson never seriously considered amending his plans. The true costs of construction cannot be figured simply by calculating the enormous direct expenses Jefferson incurred. To them, we must add opportunity costs. Jefferson used a portion of his slaves' time to build Monticello, rather than investing their labor in agricultural work that would have generated capital and income. He refused to sell lumber for profit, reserving his timber for construction. While Jefferson did profit from the surplus nails produced at his Monticello forge, this return did little to offset the economic burden of constant building.[93]

Given the extent of Jefferson's investment, many of his visitors were surprised by what they took to be a fatal design flaw: the lack of a functional connection between the first and second stories of the building. When she asked to be shown to her bedroom, Mrs. Thornton was dismayed that she was expected to "mount a little ladder of a staircase, about two feet wide, and very steep."[94] Her reaction is representative; but, com-

plaints notwithstanding, Jefferson never considered building a grand staircase. Such an addition would have violated both the Palladian architectural
principles that guided his design and his own intentions for Monticello's
entrance hall. A grand staircase would, for Jefferson, be wasted space, and
would destroy the consciously crafted illusion that Monticello was a single-
story dwelling.

Without question, the absence of a central staircase in a Federalist Era
American home was an anomaly. Typically, the main foyer of an eighteenth-
century estate house was dominated by a central staircase, where from its
top a host might greet his guests. Such staircases reified the power relationship between occupant and visitor. A residual architectural form imported
from Europe, the grand staircase created a clearly visible marker of social
distinction. It reminded visitors of the hierarchical separation between
host and guest. Monticello has no such staircase; its second story is
reached instead by two narrow staircases offset in its interior. Architectural
historians have long contended that the absence of a central staircase
reflects Jefferson's opposition to rigid social hierarchies.[95] They contend
that by rejecting an aristocratic form that enforced social distinctions, Jefferson expressed—structurally—his belief that all men were created equal.
Yet this argument fails to consider the disjunction between these "democratic" design principles and Jefferson's pedagogic ambitions. Simply put,
Monticello's vestibule is not an objective correlative of republican ideology
but, rather, a site of instruction.

Like the other Founding Fathers, Jefferson was intimately involved
with the business of framing. Resident in a nation, a landscape, and a house
undergoing continuous transformation, Jefferson realized how intrinsically linked were the fates of all three.[96] Post-Revolutionary Americans
imagined themselves as building from the ground up; Jefferson and his
contemporaries sought a foundation capable of supporting that growth.
Lacking the stability inherent in established structures of belief, Americans
sought emblems to conceptualize the sustaining order they so anxiously
pursued. Among the most prevalent of those metaphors was the house as
grounding for both personal and national identity. Monticello, Jefferson
believed, would both reflect his personal aesthetic and serve as a beacon
for national development.

When the Treaty of Paris ended the Revolutionary War in 1783, the
United States had no home for its rapidly expanding government.
Indeed, Washington began his first term as president in rented rooms in
New York City. In the absence of civic structures, Washington's and Jefferson's homes became surrogate sites of national location, anchors and
emblems of the democratic venture. Washington's struggle to balance
public and private concerns at Mount Vernon played itself out in the
duality of its facades. Even the attempt to carve out a personal space in a

"public" home was a challenge. During one seven-year period, "roughly two-thousand people were entertained at Mount Vernon, many of whom stayed for days on end and visited repeatedly."[97] Similarly, Monticello was continually inundated with visitors; as many as fifty guests were present at any one time. An early biographer of Jefferson cites a family member's complaint: "We had persons from abroad, from all the States of the Union, from every part of the State, men, women, and children. In short, almost every day for at least eight months of the year, brought its contingent of guests."[98] Travelers flocked (weather permitting) to Mount Vernon and Monticello as if they were public holdings, driven by a curiosity to see America's most famous men. Cultural expectations, and the distance of both Monticello and Mount Vernon from urban centers, meant that visitors, invited or unannounced, expected to be fed and lodged by their host.[99]

Both Washington and Jefferson accepted the burden of hospitality, but their respective architectural accommodations to this responsibility sharply underscore their differences.[100] While Washington grudgingly embraced the popular view that cast him as a modern Cincinnatus, Jefferson perceived his relation to the American people in more formal and distant terms. Still, both wanted to maintain some semblance of privacy within their domestic sites. They approached that problem from different premises. Jefferson chose not to focus his visitors' perspective externally, as Washington did with his riverfront piazza, but instead situated them within his house. Although he had selected Monticello's mountaintop location because of the views it provided, Jefferson did not erect a shaded porch where his visitors could linger; instead he brought them into the vestibule, where he provided a different kind of view.

Monticello's entrance hall was completed sometime between 1812 and 1816, and from that point on it became the only public room that all Jefferson's visitors were assured of seeing.[101] Jefferson meticulously supervised the completion of the foyer's interior design, commissioning the portraitist Gilbert Stuart to mix a "true grass green" color for its floor.[102] As Monticello curator Susan R. Stein has argued, "several distinctive architectural features heightened the dramatic impression that characterized the Entrance hall."[103] The only double-storied room within Monticello, its vaulted ceiling conveyed a "sensation of grandeur."[104] Yet even as the hall's dimensions suggested a sense of loftiness, the multitude of objects on display rooted the viewer's attention.

Crossing the threshold of the main doors of Monticello, Jefferson's visitors entered a foyer crowded with carefully arranged Native American artifacts, natural history specimens, mechanical inventions, paintings, sculptures, maps, and curios from the Lewis and Clark expedition. Above them, at the end of the room, a narrow balcony connected the wings of the house; paneled doors located on either side of the room and under the balcony restricted access to Monticello's private spaces. Jefferson's most lavishly furnished room, the foyer, contained, in addition to its displays, three tables (two marble topped, one mahogany), a mirror, a globe, and twenty-eight expensively finished Windsor chairs.[105] The first room visitors saw, the foyer, Jefferson understood, would serve as an introduction to his home and to his domestic vision. The foyer was by no means a "democratic" space; its primary purpose was to distinguish the public from the private. Jefferson created a boundary by omission between the public and the private by not building a central staircase. As Jan Lewis writes, Jefferson "enjoyed the public, but he wanted it to be on his terms," and his design of Monticello's interior reflects that desire for control spatially.[106] In the entrance hall, the balcony at the far end of the room and the doors on the surrounding walls immediately notified visitors that they were excluded from most of the house. The public visitors to Monticello, like the slaves hidden behind Jefferson's dumbwaiter or buried in quarters below the house itself, remained shielded from the privacy of Jefferson's interior life.[107] The entryway room was and is a strange foyer, for it does not provide entrance into anything beyond itself. Jefferson's furnishings extend this rhetoric of exclusion to suggest that he designed this public space with pedagogic intent.

Given the dimensions of the room and its densely decorated wall space, the twenty-eight Windsor chairs would seem to have been organized in a series of rows. Far from encouraging contact between visitors, such an arrangement would have focused attention on the objects on display. As Susan Stewart argues, the "task of filling in the immediate environment with things" is "a matter of ornamentation and presentation in which the interior is both a model and a projection of self-fashioning."[108] In undertaking that project in his foyer, Jefferson sought to guide the interaction between his guests and his displays by modeling the layout of the room on that of a classroom or gallery. Where Washington called his visitors' attention to the shady view from Mount Vernon's portico, Jefferson had less interest in creature comfort. Indeed, the crowded foyer of Monticello must have been distinctly uncomfortable. Both Washington and Jefferson were influenced by the tradition of plantation architecture, but while Washington embraced the notion of Mount Vernon as the big house, a center for communal gathering and interaction, Jefferson's floor plan rejects that conception at every turn. Washington's use of a central staircase enforced the structural separation between public and private, between occupants and visitors. Rather than creating a communal gathering space in Monticello's lone public room, Jefferson built a museum, offering visitors the chance for individual observation and contemplation. Jefferson worked to bring his visitors' attention inside, to contemplate not nature's vistas but the domesticated nature that he displayed inside his own creation, a giant cabinet of curiosities.

The items on display in Jefferson's foyer further document his distinctive conception of public and private domestic spheres. As Stewart observes, the filling in of interior space is an exercise in self-representation. Yet Jefferson's ambition in the room was not simply to represent himself but to demonstrate how the interior of a house could be an enduring monument to cultural identity. As he had argued in *Notes on the State of Virginia*, durable homes had broad consequences. Such houses were a boon to larger social and political networks, for they acted as anchors and examples for future builders. They would serve to ground community development and foster the development of a lasting local moral sense. Even as chaos reigned in other portions of Jefferson's house, the intent of the foyer remained the same: it was a space of constancy amid the flood tide of alteration. Jefferson conceived of the room as a repository where education was the primary goal. "The only means to assure a population capable of making informed choices was to edify it," according to Susan R. Stein, "and Jefferson seized every opportunity to advance his cause."[109] In selecting the objects for display in his foyer, Jefferson struggled to craft an argument about the social conditions of the Republic. Understanding the implications of both selection and arrangement, Jefferson sought artifacts evocative of American particularity. Two artifacts, in particular, underscore with striking clarity Jefferson's cultural and social beliefs: the great seven-day clock placed above the house's main doors, and the display of mastodon bones excavated for Jefferson by William Clark.

Monticello's seven-day clock exemplifies the possibility of control in a fragmented world. Much remarked on by Jefferson's contemporaries, the clock has dual faces, one serving the interior of the entrance hall and the other, located on the front exterior wall, providing an accurate reading of the time to those on the plantation's grounds. The interior face marks the hours and minutes on the clock's larger dial and the seconds on an inset smaller dial. It is equipped with cannonball weights, which, based on their relative height against the wall, display the day of the week. Jefferson began planning the clock as early as 1792, years before the foyer was fully completed, so its fatal design flaw should come as no surprise: the length of the descent of the clock weights is greater than the room's height. Jefferson's solution, as he recorded in a letter to his contractor, was for the weights to "descend naked till they get to the floor where they may enter a square hole and go [on?] to the cellar floor."[110] As a result, Jefferson needed to be in the basement to see whether it was Saturday or Sunday.

Jefferson was not dissuaded in his attempt to display time by the physical constraints of his foyer, but his decision to bore holes through the floorboards is less pragmatic than it might first appear. The clock serves a symbolic purpose as well as an actual one. Within the foyer, guests were called on to witness that even in the face of adversity Jefferson was unwilling to compromise principle. Accordingly he did not abandon his technological innovation because it did not fit; instead, he modified the environment. Like Jefferson's insistence that crops be planted on scientifically determined dates, regardless of actual conditions, his great clock belies his commitment to reason. He resists compromise; challenged, he continues to imagine a functional foundation expressive of his beliefs.

The many mastodon bones Jefferson collected and displayed in juxtaposition with Native American artifacts and detailed maps of the explored regions of North and South America also speak to Jefferson's curatorial ambitions. European accounts of American nature, following the Count de Buffon, Georges-Louis Leclerc, described the new nation in terms of degeneration. Monticello's mastodon bones, along with its mounted pairs of American moose and elk antlers and the partial skull of an American bison, provided fossil evidence to materially refute these European prejudices. Further, these objects drew attention to the uniqueness of American nature, indicating that the New World was the locus of new species and an independent natural history. Jefferson's exhibits underscored the predominant role nature was playing in the formation of American identity, and his foyer charged visitors to appreciate how American natural history was transforming received aesthetic values.[111]

Scholars of the early Republic have long read *Notes on the State of Virginia* as a sustained defense of America's unique environment and its distinctive social practices.[112] In *Notes*, Jefferson offers evidence of America's complexity to justify its independence. As that text seeks to map the contours of national experience, so too does Monticello's foyer. Although Mrs. Thornton and others may have been horrified by Monticello's narrow staircases, Jefferson adamantly refused to reconsider his design. By rejecting the traditional architectural arrangement of an entrance hall, he transformed the role of his foyer for his visitors. Rather than using his entranceway as a traditional public space to accommodate visitors, Jefferson chose to locate his guests in his museum-like parlor, where they would experience beliefs that their host held dear.

Designing his foyer as a pedagogic exercise—a primer for national identity—was consistent, of course, with the tenor of Jefferson's public career. While he continually tinkered with other portions of the house, the foyer remained unaltered, perhaps because in its design and decoration Jefferson had found the best expression of his vision of the emerging Republic. In its display cases and wall mountings, Jefferson inscribed his vision of national identity and positioned himself as teacher and guide. His arrangement of artifacts situated the United States within the context of Western history and tradition; but more importantly, Monticello's foyer reminded its visitors that despite America's organic ties to European culture, its citizens occupied a new physical space. That new environment required the formulation of distinct architectural designs, modeled perhaps on existing prototypes, but able to represent the emerging cultural forms of the United States. Even as Jefferson understood that the new Republic had to align building practices with environmental circumstances, he realized that the citizenry of the emerging nation would be framed by the houses they occupied. This concern fueled both Washington's and Jefferson's interest in domestic architecture, even as it attuned other writers and artists to the importance of the home in shaping cultural development in the Republic. Between the articulation of national development offered by these framers of national origins and Lincoln's return to their privileging of the domestic as the site of national identity construction, Americans returned again and again to the house to sound out the meanings of their inherited histories and to explore the future they were intended to inhabit. Across the length of *Remodeling the Nation*, I move to explore how this continual return to the domestic informed and inflected unfolding conceptions of national identity as generations of Americans sought to build on the foundations constructed by Washington and Jefferson, which established the house as the wellspring of national development.

2

"No Longer Assigned Its Ancient Use"

Biloquial Architecture and the Problems of Remodeling

"In fact, according to my ideas," Henry Laurens observed in 1766, "no coloring can do justice to the forlorn state of poor Billy Bartram."[1] Instead of returning to Philadelphia after accompanying his father, John Bartram, on a botanical expedition to South Carolina, Georgia, and the Floridas in 1765, William Bartram—against the strong objections of his father—had attempted to establish a rice and indigo plantation on the banks of the St. Johns River. The venture was an outright disaster, almost over before it really had begun. "Only a handful of months since John had returned home," historian Thomas P. Slaughter writes, "there wasn't much of William left."[2] By the time Henry Laurens arrived to check on the progress of his friend's son in August of 1766, William had almost entirely wasted away. Instead of finding fields cleared and cultivation well advanced, Laurens discovered that "the house, or rather hovel, that he lives in, is extremely confined, and not proof against the weather."[3] The area would "without doubt, produce good rice, when properly" prepared and planted, but Laurens had no faith that the fever-addled William possessed the capacity for such arduous work.[4] Without question, in Laurens' opinion, William Bartram had failed in his attempt to build a house in the Florida wilderness.

Six months prior to Laurens' visit, John Bartram had—at considerable expense—shipped supplies, provisions, and slaves from South Carolina to provide William with the materials necessary for his settlement. In return for this substantial aid, John Bartram extracted a promise from his son not to quit when things became difficult. John understood that homesteading was arduous work, and he feared that William had romanticized the realities of house and farm building. By demanding that his son vow to stay the course, John hoped to bind William to seeing his project through to fruition. Laurens was well aware of John's edict, yet he still tried to persuade his friend to release William from his oath. "Possibly, sir, your son, though a worthy, ingenious man," Laurens cautiously wrote John, "may not have resolution, or not that sort of resolution, that is necessary to encounter the difficulties incident to, and unavoidable in his present state of life."[5] Unless he was permitted to leave, Laurens concluded, William would perish under the strain of a failing venture.

With his father's blessing, William Bartram abandoned his embryonic plantation and returned to Philadelphia in November 1766. Over the next few years, Bartram struggled to establish himself by alternatively working as a farmhand, a commissioned illustrator, and finally as a merchant. Yet bad luck seemed to follow poor Billy Bartram, and in 1770 he fled Philadelphia to escape persistent creditors. Bartram resurfaced in North Carolina, where he unsuccessfully tried to collect on outstanding debts. Eventually his family settled his overdue obligations, clearing the way for William to return north. But instead of retreating home, William notified his family that he intended to venture again to the Floridas on a botanical expedition to draw, observe, and collect samples. John Bartram's reply suggests that he understood his son, on some level, to be hinting that he intended to resettle in the Southeast. "We are surprised at thy wild notion of going to Augustine," John wrote his son in July 1772; "indeed I don't intend to have any more of my estate spent there or to ye southward upon any pretense whatever."[6]

Without any forthcoming family aid, William solicited the English naturalist John Fothergill for sponsorship. Backed by Fothergill's purse, Bartram traveled southward on his second expedition in 1773. At every turn, Bartram's account of his journey, *Travels Through North & South Carolina, Georgia, East & West Florida* (1791), records the difficulty of establishing and maintaining new settlements. Far from being a pristine wilderness, the interior of the Southeast, at least in Bartram's text, serves as an architectural graveyard. Simply put, observations of failed ventures continually haunt Bartram's *Travels.* These decaying structures and abandoned towns reveal the consequences of poorly executed planning, as Bartram carefully indexes the waves of settlers, all of whom—Native American, British, French, Spanish—miscarried in attempting to create lasting settlements.[7]

For all Bartram's attention to the abandoned houses and ruined settlements that littered the southeastern frontier of the North American landscape, his *Travels* avoids any explicit acknowledgment of his own failed plantation project. Indeed as he "passes near the old plantation he ran," as Thomas Hallock succinctly describes, "nothing is said."[8] Typically, those critics who have noted Bartram's omission of his abandoned plantation house have conjoined it to his supposed neglect of the cultural context of his botanical expedition, figuring both as symptomatic of what Myra Jehlen characterizes as Bartram's "general disregard for the political life around him."[9] While Bartram's expedition took him across the southern front of the Revolutionary War during the mid-1770s, *Travels* remains noticeably silent about the conflict. Comparing *Travels* with Jefferson's *Notes on the State of Virginia* and J. Hector St. John de Crèvecoeur's *Letters from an American Farmer*, Douglas Anderson contends that Bartram "seems to be writing about a different continent altogether" because of his lack of attention to the political backdrop against which his journey takes place.[10] Reading Bartram in a similar vein, Kris Fresonke has more recently dismissed him as "botanically devotional" and "politically abstracted."[11] While Bartram never overtly mentions the American Revolution directly, this silence does not mean that *Travels* is ahistorical or that it merely depicts a deconceptualized vision of unspoiled nature. Such readings neglect how Bartram registers political contexts by reading the ruined landscape of the Southeast, creating in *Travels* a lexicon of failed ventures aimed at informing and shaping post-Revolutionary expansion and settlement. Bartram's tacit silence about the failures of "American" settlement projects is also indicative of the political dimensions of his text, as he labors to assign all failed ventures to pre-Revolutionary social orders. The ruins haunt the landscape, but they do not condemn post-Revolutionary U.S. settlement projects; rather, they stand as warnings about the difficulties attendant to domesticating this wilderness.

Bartram does not envision *Travels* as a recounting of the Revolution but rather as a natural history intent, as Christopher Iannini observes, on claiming "the Floridas as a superabundant resource for the new republic."[12] In his indispensable reading of *Travels*, Iannini maintains that Bartram's taxonomic attempt to annex the Floridas becomes "troubled by the author's intimate awareness of the region as a contested borderland between the plantation empires of the Carolinas and the Spanish West Indies."[13] Bartram registers the tensions between the new Republic's laying claim to the Southeast and the region's complex settlement histories (and the connections that these settlements share with the specter of Caribbean colonization), primarily through his attention to failed settlement ventures. By continually dwelling on the import of these abandoned homes, Bartram calls into question, by implication, the viability of post-Revolutionary colonization. In so doing, Bartram's *Travels* adumbrates a broadly shared post-Revolutionary concern with the presence of ruined homes in the "unclaimed" frontiers of the emergent Republic.

In questioning the parameters by which we might consider the United States as a postcolonial nation, Michael Warner argues that "national culture began with a moment of sweeping amnesia about colonialism"; extending this argument, Warner rather definitively posits that "Americans learned to think of themselves as living in an immemorial nation, rather than in a colonial interaction of cultures."[14] Yet Bartram's focus on

the ruined settlements (undertaken by a range of colonizing and indigenous cultures) that he "discovers" in the midst of the southeastern frontiers of the new nation complicate Warner's claims. In essence, Bartram's
examination of the relics of previous settlements demonstrates his concerns with the challenges facing the United States as it sought to construct
a national identity. This demonstrates the political dimensions of Bartram's taxonomic imagination. The idea that "a society needs to represent
itself to itself in order to certify its existence and its legitimacy," for
Christopher Looby, exemplifies the "American republic in the immediate
post-revolutionary period."[15] By sounding out the implications of these
previous failures, Bartram navigates between the anteceding layers of
inscription present in the "wilderness" to establish how they inform the
capacity of the United States to constitute its own legitimacy.

Bartram's catalog of flora and fauna simultaneously records a roster of
failed attempts at domestication, an inventory that registers the hazardous
nature of settlement in the uncolonized spaces of the Southeast. "Implicit"
in the "taxonomic" writings of many early American writers, as Christopher Looby describes, was the idea that within "the knowledge of the
names and qualities of the beings in nature was not only the basis of
the American's control over his environment, but also might be, in some
sense, the foundation of the collective life of the new nation of which he
was a member."[16] *Travels* seems to presume the truth of the flip side of
Looby's argument as well, that the indecipherable nature of these numerous ruins compromised the stability of the emerging nation. If all these
other settlement attempts resulted in failure, what does that mean, *Travels*
wonders again and again, for the new nation struggling to construct itself?
The political implications of Bartram's *Travels* reside in his taxonomic col-
lections of failed settlement patterns, the collective weight of which testifies
to the uncertainties facing the possibilities for national expansion and social
stability. The multivalent colonial history of North America did not evapo-
rate after the break from British rule; rather, as Jennifer Rae Greeson argues,
"at best, early nationalists could aver that the demise of their coloniality
was imminent."[17] The minute details of the Revolution do not inform Bartram's post-Revolutionary reconstruction of a pre-Revolutionary venture;
rather, he seeks in *Travels* to detail how the history of settlement failure
might affect the foundation of a new national culture.

As the nation struggled, in the midst of continued cultural uncertainty,
to define its own political and geographic boundaries, Bartram's imagination seems to have been haunted by scenes of Nature reasserting control
over human productions, by sites of vegetation pulling down fences and
reclaiming formerly cultivated fields. Moving across the southern borders
of British North America during the Revolutionary War, Bartram witnessed Revolutionary turmoil even if he sublimated that context in the

reconstruction of his experiences in *Travels*. As Edward J. Cashin details in *William Bartram and the American Revolution on the Southern Frontier*, Bartram was far from ignorant of the political turmoil in which he operated during his 1770s botanical expedition. Bartram transcribed his field notes into *Travels* after the Revolution and did so in Philadelphia not far from where the delegates of the Constitutional Convention were forging a new political identity for the nation. Indeed many influential delegates, including Washington, George Mason, Alexander Hamilton, and James Madison, visited Bartram's gardens as they labored on the Constitution.[18] Drafting *Travels* near the center of national debates about the construction of a new political architecture for the emerging United States influenced Bartram to think more about how his text could speak to the future of the nation as opposed to recapitulate its past. In his important reading of Bartram's expedition and its aftermath, historian Edward J. Cashin concludes that Bartram figured *Travels* as "the best tool he had" to contribute to the "building [of] the 'magnificent structure'" that the framers of the Constitution were laboring over just a few miles away in downtown Philadelphia.[19]

While Bartram suffuses the political contexts for his travels within his narrative, he does discover, as Douglas Anderson writes, "that the American Revolution is taking place on a continent accustomed to revolution, to the succession of one form of civilization and the disappearance of another."[20] The dense record of failed ventures that *Travels* catalogs evinces how Bartram's vision of American development (and his configuration of North American natural history) was deeply informed by his observations of failed colonial ventures. In this sense *Travels* serves as a settlement primer, aimed at displaying the root causes for the failure of previous colonization attempts. Bartram's account offers an extended commentary on nonnative incursion and retreat. His text complicates the record of the American frontier by exposing the fallacy that the land was ever a tabula rasa by portraying both lost Native American architectural production as well the presence of ruined European buildings. Bartram's narrative itemizes relics not only of Native American and British provenance but of French and Spanish origin as well. The wild terrain he traverses is not destitute of human presence; on the contrary, at every turn it demonstrates the difficulty of maintaining new settlements. Collectively, these architectural ruins testify to the variegated cultural circumstances of the eighteenth-century American frontier.

As Bartram records the native flora and fauna of the uncharted territories, he simultaneously adumbrates the litany of failed attempts at domesticating the nature he observes. Moreover, *Travels* registers how this terrain is replete with nonwhite inhabitants whose refusal to be removed, relocated, or rendered stationary impacts the viability of the Republic's claims on the area. Bartram's intentional blindness about the failures of Anglo-American settlement (including his own aborted attempt at founding a plantation) are, arguably, a strategic attempt to counterbalance the complexities raised by the presence of other unsuccessful ventures and the uncertainties embodied in the continued presence of the nonwhite residents of the region.[21] Glossing over his own failure, Bartram creates the sense that the majority of these ruined homes bear little direct connection to the citizens of the new nation; instead of focusing on relics of a contemporary nature, he moves to displace these ruined homes well into the pre-Revolutionary past. Bartram describes these aborted ventures by "means of the same rhetoric," Pamela Regis argues, that he "uses to describe plants or the soil of a given area."[22] In employing the same language to describe both the manufactured and the naturally indigenous features of the environment, Bartram rescripts the complexity of pre-Revolutionary history to clear the ground for post-Revolutionary development. By merging the totality of pre-U.S. history into one manageable narrative, Bartram figures the interior of the Southeast as, in Regis' words, a place "waiting for history to happen and for individuals to live their lives there."[23] In consigning previous settlement attempts to the dustbin of history, Bartram implies that they provide object lessons for his contemporaries—providing them with an opportunity to read these ruins and not replicate the mistakes of previous builders.

Bartram's first expedition to Florida in 1765 occurred during a relatively stable political period; indeed, his father's journey was funded by the British monarchy. But Bartram's second field trip, the solo one recounted in the 1791 *Travels*, occurred during the tumultuous 1770s. Traveling during a time of increasing transatlantic tension made Bartram sensitive to the relation between stable authority and viable settlement. As the thirteen colonies contemplated a political break from Great Britain, Bartram witnessed the failures of colonization. He knew firsthand the difficulties of homesteading, but observing the abandonment of projects undertaken with significantly greater resources must have been disturbing.

Coming upon the deserted homes of planters, passing through the walls of ruined forts—emblems of the failure of European powers to establish themselves in the North American forests—Bartram occupied a unique position during the Revolutionary War. Moreover, he wrote *Travels* a decade after the war's conclusion in the midst of substantial political uncertainty and activity. Crafting his text at this later moment, Bartram aimed his observations at a postcolonial nation. Although he never explicitly addresses this context, his meditations on the causes of Native American wars, and the rhetoric he uses to justify them, indicate his concerns over the political course that the United States has chosen. In his reading of the ongoing warfare of the Creeks and Chactaws, Bartram draws an analogy, as he often does throughout his text, between the Native American tribes he encounters and the citizens of the emerging nation: "Thus we see that war or the exercise of arms originates from the same motives, and operates in the spirits of the wild red men of America, as it formerly did in the renowned Greeks and Romans, or modern civilized nations, and not from a ferocious, capricious desire of shedding human blood as carnivorous savages" (248). Rather, he continues, "their martial prowess and objects of desire and ambition proceed from greater principles and more magnanimous intentions, even that of" forming "one universal confederacy or common wealth" (248). The desire to achieve autonomy fueled both Native American and Revolutionary American military strategies. By eliding the cultural differences between the Creeks and the rebelling English colonies, Bartram allows for the possibility of contiguous historical narratives, and deepens the resonance of the ruins he describes.

Early in *Travels*, Bartram describes returning to an ancient "magnificent Indian mount" near the shores of Lake George, which he first observed in 1765. During his initial visit, the area "possessed an almost inexpressible air of grandeur": Bartram marveled at how the mount was framed by a broad highway, an "oblong artificial lake," and a solemn orange grove bordered by a sea of "palms and laurel magnolias" (64). But in the seven years separating his two excursions, the landscape underwent considerable change. What once appeared to him as wilderness (despite the evidence of Native American labor) now strikes him as irreparably altered. The architectural remains of Native American culture have not changed, and they are not the cause of his altered perception. They do not function as obstacles or impediments or warnings to would-be colonizers, but as scenes evoking wonder and awe. Bartram reads this artificial lake and clearing as impermanent and unconnected with European settlement. His description of this site as appearing wild and strange in 1765 echoes his culture's dominant perception of Native American building practices. By displacing these Native American structures into antiquity, Bartram makes them picturesque relics. In associating them with an untamed wilderness, he displaces the history of Native American possession. Safely classified as antiques, these structures represent a cultural order consigned to the realm of curiosity.

Artists of the late eighteenth and early nineteenth centuries often employed the trope of ancient ruins to meditate on the relation of their era to its historical precursors.[24] For Bartram, Native American ruins play no similar role; they are not precursors to his own civilization. It is not those ruins but more recent buildings, now as dilapidated as the Native American relics, that disrupt the harmony of the picturesque scene and frightfully demonstrate the difficulty of mastering new terrain. In the short interval between his two visits, European settlers built here, farmed, lived, and passed on. It is no longer the uncultivated wild he first explored in the 1760s; European settlement has marked the area as changed, in a way in which Native American building could not. What once seemed beautiful and sublime is now blemished. A glowing landscape, which "flattered and entertained" the imagination in 1765, appears "like a desart to a great extent" in 1773 (65). Where the Native American ruins created sensations of admiration, the failed settlement of "an English gentleman" enkindle only dismay. What was briefly a sizable plantation is now in total decay. Sadly, Bartram records how the "venerable [Native American] grove" has been demolished and "planted with indigo, corn, and cotton," only to be "deserted" (65). For Bartram, the ruins of an Anglo-American settlement do not evoke sensations of "grandeur"; rather they are the cause of mournful reflection. The more recent instance of architectural inscription is harrowing. The romantic beauty of the Native American terraforming has been disturbingly overwritten by a commercial experiment. Only decaying fences and rearranged vegetation survive to attest to the settlement attempt undertaken by the English land agent—a dilapidated vision that traumatizes Bartram; for not only did the English planter violate the "natural" beauty of the area, he also left nothing but ungenerative waste in his wake. The scene radically conveys just how rapidly such an endeavor can be pursued and vacated, and this recognition unsettles Bartram.

Even more disturbing than the wreckage of a failed plantation, Bartram notes how entire towns have been left to decompose. In rapid succession, Bartram moves across two areas of failed domestication to create the sensation that what constitutes the wild is an unending series of abandoned colonization projects. Stopping at Frederica, Georgia, Bartram observes the "vestiges of plantations" and a dilapidated fort on an "island [which] had formerly been cleared and planted by the English" (40). Now "overgrown with forests," the island's only evidence of English colonization are the ruined walls and crumbling bricks (40). Leaving Frederica, Bartram sails to the site of another relic of European origin, "fort Picolata," which to his "disappointment" he finds "dismantled and deserted" (52). "The fortress," he writes, "is very ancient, and was built by the Spaniards" (52). Clearly intended as a foothold for a more enduring settlement, it too has now been deserted. The two forts, the English and the Spanish, either decaying or already ruined, testify to the myriad attempts already undertaken to colonize the southern wetlands of North America and document the complex settlement record of this "wilderness."[25]

About thirteen miles from Augusta, Georgia, Bartram discovers another instance of multilayered settlement. Notably, he reads these ruins in a different way, one that looks to create a sustainable past for American development. Bartram begins his treatment of the Silver Bluff area by reading the earliest attempts to domesticate the area, recording both aborted Native American and Spanish attempts at settlement. Equating the remains of "ancient" Spanish miners with the conical mounds of the vanished Native Americans, Bartram deposits these layers of architectural inscription safely into the past (261). Both groups have retreated into the mists of time even as nature has reasserted itself to reclaim their labor. Since both groups failed to establish any permanent presence, Bartram suggests that they were unqualified to bring a lasting order to the area.

Importantly, the area does not become wild again, because another order has arrived to continue the work of domestication. The area is now "the property and seat of G. Golphin [sic], esquire, a gentleman of very distinguished talents and great liberality" (198). George Galphin was "an American patriot during the Revolution," the historian Thomas Slaughter notes, and "was instrumental in persuading Lower Creeks not to fight against the Americans" during the Revolutionary War.[26] Galphin "possessed the most extensive trade, connections and influence," Bartram records, "amongst the South and South-West Indian tribes" of any non-native settler (198–99). By preventing the British from securing an alliance with the Lower Creeks and forcing the Americans to engage on yet another front, Galphin played a crucial role in the success of the Revolutionary cause. As a result of his hard work and his connections, in *Travels* Bartram suggests that Galphin flourished where others had failed, successfully building a "pleasant villa" on the outlines of the other ruins (198).

Bartram's celebration of Galphin's capabilities—particularly since *Travels* is written after the Revolutionary War—fosters an endorsement of Galphin's politics. Concluding his account of the Silver Bluff area, Bartram suggests that "perhaps Mr. Golphin's [sic] buildings and improvements will prove to be the foundation of monuments of infinitely greater celebrity and permanency than either of the preceding establishments" (199). Bartram hopes that this republican citizen will prosper where previous settlers failed. Still, even as Bartram imagines this third venture to be a durable foundation for future growth, the equivocation of "perhaps" introduces his prophetic vision of the future. The overwhelming evidence he finds in the desolation of these uninhabited regions testifies to the adversity that settlements face; seemingly, the odds are against Galphin. Perhaps, since Galphin builds with an eye toward planting his roots in the region, and because he trades and communicates with neighboring Native American tribes, *Travels* leads readers to hope that he might thrive. By having a more expansive imagination—not simply figuring the wilderness as just a means of making a profit—Galphin becomes the closest thing to a model settler in Bartram's text.

As Bartram assuredly knew by the time he wrote *Travels*, Galphin did not survive the Revolution. As the British army marched through Georgia in 1780, Galphin's slaves fled his plantation and sought refuge among the

British forces. In May of 1780, with the Revolutionary cause looking doomed on the southern front, Galphin surrendered himself to British forces in Charleston. Just seven months later, in December 1780, Galphin died, as historian Edward J. Cashin notes, believing that the Americans had lost the war. In the end, Galphin "had lost a fortune in the American effort."[27] Framed as a model settler within the confines of Bartram's *Travels* in 1791, Galphin had actually died a ruined planter over eleven years earlier. But *Travels* does not eulogize Galphin; rather Bartram portrays him as founding a different, perhaps sustainable, model for settlement and development. Far from crafting an apolitical tract, Bartram rearranges historical fact in *Travels* to posit and endorse a different set of possibilities for national expansion. Instead of recording Galphin's settlement as yet one more set of ruins in the wilderness, Bartram willfully erases how the Revolution ruined Galphin. Or, to put it another way, Bartram allows his readers to dwell with the Galphin of the 1770s rather than providing an accurate account of how Galphin had fared by 1791. Such a narrative presentation leaves readers of *Travels* with some prospect for hope, rather than with the knowledge that Galphin's house became just another failed layer of inscription on landscape. By suppressing the actual legacies of Revolutionary history, *Travels* allows readers to remain optimistic about the possibilities for post-Revolutionary homesteading.

Bartram argues that the future settlements to be manufactured in this *wilderness*, whether as reasoned as his portrait of Galphin's or not, will be fashioned upon the foundations already laid by a preceding group. In essence, the project of house and nation building in the United States is a process of rebuilding. Across the length of his southern excursion, Bartram can travel nowhere without encountering a record of previous occupation. Collectively these architectural ruins testify to the complex cultural circumstances of the eighteenth-century frontier. The wilderness of the Americas was not a tabula rasa. Rather, it was littered with the remains of unsuccessful attempts to domesticate the landscape.

Bartram's own plantation was a variation on this theme of failure. Funded entirely by his father and guided by John Bartram's dictates, William Bartram was completely isolated and dependent on slave labor as he undertook the domestication of the St. Johns River estate. The threat of racial violence—be it at the hands of disgruntled Native Americans or by rebellious slaves—reoccurs throughout *Travels*, ever present as an underlying fear that undermines these settlements. Bartram's stylized portrait of Galphin's more systematic approach stands as an alternative model to these scattered, vulnerable settlement ventures. Working in conjunction with the vital interests of U.S. authority, and having made peaceful treaties with the surrounding Native Americas, Galphin seemingly builds for the future with the reasonable expectation of protection from distant authority. Bartram's silence concerning Galphin's actual history stems from the same impulse that causes him to erase his own failure: in both cases Bartram hopes to clear the landscape of ruins that call into question the future of post-Revolutionary America. By attempting to sever any ties between the structural wreckage he observes in the wilderness and U.S. settlement efforts, Bartram labors to differentiate between pre-Revolutionary history and the future prospects of the United States. Long removed from his own settlement attempt, and living in his deceased father's house, William Bartram refigured the ruined houses cluttering the North American wilderness to construct a usable past for the United States. Still, the narrative that Bartram projects remains complicated by the histories he suppresses. Even as he tries to displace all the decimated houses that captivate his attention in *Travels* into a distant past, other abandoned homes remain to haunt the optimistic narrative he seeks to contribute to the construction of a new nation.

II

John Bartram built his house on the banks of the Schuylkill River with "hewn stone split out of ye rock with my own hands."[28] Bartram envisioned his house and his grounds as emblems of his understanding of North American nature, and he struggled to arrange his productions so that they harmonized, as Thomas Slaughter suggests, the variegated "ways—aesthetic, scientific, religious—in which he saw the world."[29] When Bartram remodeled his estate in 1770, his designs indicate that he made accommodations to each of these various facets of his personality. By raising the roof and extending the frame of the house, Bartram nearly doubled its size, an alteration that finally provided his family enough room to suit their needs. In a bid to reconceptualize the public facade of the house, Bartram ordered the construction of a recessed porch on the riverfront side of the house, aesthetically marked by the three supporting Ionic masonry columns (see fig. 3). A lingering dispute with his fellow Quakers (a quarrel that resulted in Bartram forgoing his lifetime habit of attending meetings) led Bartram to chisel his religious beliefs into a stone, which he transformed into a second-story windowsill. The inscription declared, "It is God Alone Almyty Lord the Holy One by Me Adord 1770 John Bartram." The placement of this carving was the capstone of Bartram's remodeling project.

When William Bartram returned to Philadelphia after his natural history expedition to the Floridas in 1777, he moved back in with his parents. William lived in his father's house—a physical testimony to John's industry, aesthetic sensibilities, as well as his particular religious convictions—

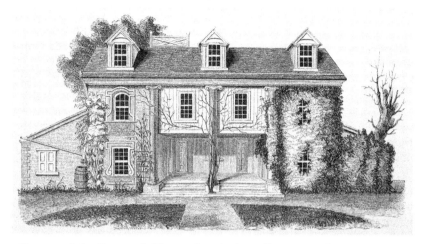

Figure 3. John Bartram's House, frontispiece illustration, from *Memorials of John Bartram and Humphrey Marshall.* Collection of The New-York Historical Society (negative number 79717d).

for the remaining forty-six years of his life. It was in the study directly underneath John's inscription, the historian Thomas Slaughter notes, that William produced *Travels*.[30] If William, as he wrote *Travels*, ever considered the import of his father's religious sentiments or the fact that his father had succeeded (when he himself had failed) at constructing a house with his "own hands," he left no record to that effect. But like many of the other pre-Revolutionary houses that informed *Travels*, John Bartram's house ghosts William Bartram's narrative. Given William's preoccupation with the import of how residual structures would affect the future course of the emerging nation, his location within his father's house during the production of *Travels* likely influenced his conception of the links between architecture and cultural order.

The weighted legacy of inhabiting a house designed by another's hand lies at the center of Charles Brockden Brown's first novel, *Wieland; or, The Transformation: An American Tale* (1798). Set at another farmhouse on the banks of the Schuylkill River, at its core *Wieland* maps the intersections of domestic violence and the burdens of settlement histories.[31] While it might seem forced to draw parallels between Bartram's *Travels* and Brown's *Wieland*, arguably the two texts have more in common than is typically imagined.[32] The elder Wieland fashions his farmhouse and his strange temple—marked by its "twelve Tuscan columns," a design aesthetic reflective of the same classical impulses as John Bartram's Ionic columns—in response to his experiences in the North American wilderness.[33] As Alan Axelrod writes, "the extremity" of Wieland's "wilderness experience" prompts an "architectural reaction" in him, manifesting itself as an attempt to order the "limitless American wilds" by constructing a classically styled house and temple.[34] Whereas William Bartram retreated from the wild to dwell on the meanings of ruined houses that unsettled his taxonomic imagination, Theodore Wieland Sr. reemerges from the wild and deploys domestic architecture as a buffer against the chaos he has witnessed there.

Like Bartram's *Travels*, Brown's *Wieland* focuses on mapping the meanings that residual houses embody for those who stand to inherit them; yet, rather than domesticating these relics, Brown charts the ways in which these houses engender instability and violence. Houses contained the resonances of the past, and Brown's preoccupation with the meanings of domestic spaces suggests that he saw architectural sites as a wellspring for considering the interdependence of the past and the future. Built structures in the "unsettled" portions of the United States were visual reminders of the nation's links to its pre-Revolutionary pasts. Comprehending this, Brown continually focuses on the consequences of architectural design for character formation, and he questions the viability of an emerging cultural order that fails to acknowledge its ties to earlier forms. Throughout *Wieland*, Brown (like Bartram in *Travels*) examines how a pre-existing house shapes the behavior of individuals who end up inhabiting someone else's designs. In so doing, Brown uses houses to signify the multivalent meanings of possession.

"Brown's early letters and fictions," Robert Lawson-Peebles argues, "demonstrate the spatial nature of his imagination."[35] Lawson-Peebles' observation mirrors many of the first critical assessments of Brown's oeuvre. William Dunlap, Brown's earliest biographer, prefigures Lawson-Peebles' reading by highlighting Brown's obsessive focus on the effects of the built environment on the actions and lives of his characters.[36] Dunlap connects the recurrence of this theme in Brown's fiction to a personal interest in architecture, noting for instance that throughout his life Brown "would for hours be absorbed in architectural studies," continually "measuring proportions with his compasses, and drawing plans."[37] In a review of Dunlap's biography, Gulian C. Verplanck figures Brown's concern with architecture as his defining strength as a novelist. Brown, Verplanck argues, "is peculiarly successful in describing a deserted house, silent and dark in the day-time, while a faint ray streams through the crevices of the closed doors and shutters, discovering in a peculiar twilight that it had been once occupied, and that every thing remained undisturbed since its sudden desertion."[38] Verplanck's review foregrounds Brown's pointed ability to describe how the residential history of a house lingers long after particular tenants have abandoned it, evincing the depth of Brown's absorption with houses as registers of the ways in which the past continues to inform the present. In underscoring how Brown's novels contain many minutely detailed portraits of houses, Verplanck unpacks how the precision of Brown's architectural descriptions allows him to create a foundation for episodes that otherwise would seem fantastic. Despite their wildly improbable plotlines, Brown's novels achieve a sense of realism by focusing attention so clearly on the design and construction of buildings. Simply put, as Lawson-Peebles, Dunlap, and Verplanck all recognize, Brown constitutes his novels with a particular attention to how domestic design frames and shapes behavior. By returning to architectural scenes at decisive moments, Brown continually places possession, intention, and design at the forefront of his narratives.

At the beginning of *Wieland*, the narrator describes that Theodore Wieland Sr. migrated to Pennsylvania to proselytize among the Native residents of America's wilderness. He attempted to carry out that zealous mission until "a nearer survey of savage manners once more shook his resolution" (10). No longer interested in converting Native Americans, the elder Wieland remained in America as a gentleman farmer. "The cheapness of land, and the service of African slaves" around Philadelphia, "gave him who was poor in Europe all the advantages of wealth" in America (10). After establishing his farm, the elder Wieland reembarked on his mission, only to fail again; he returned from this second venture in the wilderness "with a constitution somewhat decayed" (11). One night, upon entering the temple he had designed for his solitary worship, the elder Wieland encountered a strange light that burned his clothes and scarred him with wounds from which he never recovered. No explanation is ever proffered for this occurrence, and his children are left to wonder how to interpret and occupy the strange temple and house bequeathed to them.

After the orphaned Theodore Wieland Jr. and his sister Clara, the narrator of *Wieland*, come of age, they return to their father's house and take possession of his estate and temple. Almost immediately after they reinhabit these spaces, they attempt to repurpose a building that their father designed as "the temple of his Deity" and transform the space into a building with a different meaning (12). After Clara concludes her summary of her father's biography, she turns her attention to describing the present circumstances of her family. Early on she naively declares that "the temple" is "no longer assigned to its ancient use" (23). Clara's brief observation encapsulates the ways in which this new generation of Wielands (the first North American branch of the family) presume that they can simply undo the legacies of the past by superficially remodeling a residual architectural production. By purchasing a bust of Cicero, acquiring a harpsichord, and adding some rudimentary furniture, Theodore and Clara suppose that they can transform their father's monument to his monomaniacal religious convictions into a center for communal exchange and "social affections" (24). This delusory shift encapsulates larger cultural shifts unfolding in the emerging Republic, as many Americans at that time promoted the idea of a collective unity based not on the sui generis meanings of settlements but on the promise of filial relations.

In their belief that they can remodel their father's temple without acknowledging that its history has any hold on them, Clara and Theodore are misguided. Arguably, the "transformation" noted in Brown's alternative title for the novel refers to the abortive efforts that Theodore and Clara undertake to simply disown the past. The temple's original intent compromises their ability to alter the structure, incarnating Brown's recurrent concern with how the demands of the past come to bear on the present through the persistence of architectural productions. Theodore and Clara choose to convert "the temple of his Deity" into a summer salon, and by failing to account for the building's original intent, they bring about their own ruin (12). Theodore Wieland Sr.'s house and temple physically testify to the encounter of the Old and New Worlds, and his children attempt to inherit the structures of that exchange but disavow the totality of its histories. Theodore and Clara seek to overwrite the meanings assigned to residual structures, and as such they replicate the ways in which many post-Revolutionary Americans promoted the idea that, even in the midst of the actual chaos and uncertainty around them, they inhabited a nation unfettered by the past.[39] Like the deserted homes and forts that Bartram encounters, Wieland Sr.'s house and temple prove the reality of the elaborate palimpsest of America's built landscape. These residual structures unsettle any hope that the remodeling of the past will prove to be either sustainable or uncomplicated. In *Wieland*, Brown crafts a text—from a post-Revolutionary position—grounded in pre-Revolutionary history. By locating the novel in the colonial period, Brown implies that the Revolution did not destabilize a balanced social order but was just one more convulsion in America's unsettled course. The evidence of these continual revolutions was embodied in the complexities of the architectural remnants strewn about the landscape.

Unpacking the complexity of the much remarked incestuous thread in *Wieland*, Julia A. Stern argues that "in a republic whose first political task is to define itself against the Old World through decidedly manichean means, incest disrupts and deconstructs the taxonomical efforts that further enable citizens to 'dis-cover' their selfhood differentially."[40] Theodore and Clara seek to redefine their father's temple via the same manichean impulse that Stern traces in post-Revolutionary politics; by extension the incestuous relationship they inhabit with their father's architectural designs disrupts their ability to define themselves. The temple grounds Brown's argument that the past cannot be so easily abandoned, serving as the locus for his continual reaffirmation throughout the novel of the idea that the younger Wielands tenant their father's history as fully as they inhabit his structural productions. Echoing Stern's reading of the novel, Christopher Looby advocates reading the undercurrents of incest in the novel in light of how Brown presents properly aligned domestic order as a measure of political stability; incestuous behavior, Looby argues, is fundamentally "anti-social."[41] Occupying their father's temple and pretending that it signifies something else, Theodore and Clara enact an anti-social relationship with the past, one predicated on the idea that they can simply choose to ignore the intent offered up by previous social and structural orders. By virtue of his presentation of Theodore and Clara's attempt to forge an original, unfettered relationship with their environment, Brown points to the ways in which the Wielands' history intimates the position of the United States in the post-Revolutionary period.

Leisured and isolated, Theodore and Clara try to ignore how the burdens of history impact their lives. "In short, the house of Wieland is haunted by its past," Elizabeth Jane Wall Hinds argues, "and in this third generation of self-destruction, that inheritance comes close to annihilating the family for good."[42] Theodore and Clara connect most concretely with the past through the buildings that their patriarchal "Founding Father" designed in response to his encounter with the unsettled wilderness of Pennsylvania. Theodore and Clara inherit the history of that attempted conversion and colonization, and in their naivete they figure that they can simply refurbish that legacy so as to domesticate its meanings. As Brown makes clear, the break from complex historical narratives is not so easily performed. Theodore and Clara cannot simply figure their inheritance as a tabula rasa freed from the exchanges that have preceded them. The self-sufficiency that they play at, in the insular community they create, becomes dangerously compromised because of their myopic refusal to fully question the import of residual foundations. "In Brown's 'American Tale,'" Peter Kafer argues, "one generation's traits get passed down, transmogrified, to the next generation, which suffers accordingly."[43] Theodore and Clara ignore the totality of their heritage, and, as Kafer advances, they endure the distress of having to fully come to terms with the legacies that they inhabit. Typically, readers displace the threat to the superficially Edenic order that Theodore and Clara attempt to construct onto the alien figure of Carwin, the mysterious stranger who for inexplicable reasons decides to torment the Wielands and their circle by projecting his voice. But more is at stake in *Wieland* than the issue of whether or not Carwin's insurgency drives Theodore to violence. Carwin's machinations can explain only Theodore Jr.'s transformation; they do nothing to resolve the mystery of Theodore Sr. or define the legacies that he leaves for his chil-

dren. At best, Carwin bears responsibility for only one of the transforma-
tions that the novel charts; since many of these alterations predate him,
Carwin cannot answer for them all.[44]

Early in the novel, Theodore Wieland and his brother-in-law Pleyel
debate the possibility of adopting "the picture of a single family" as "a
model from which to sketch the condition of a nation" (30). While
Theodore embraces the idea that the picture of a single family can represent a national historical narrative, Pleyel dismisses the idea as "absurd"
(30). Almost as soon as they raise the question, Theodore and Pleyel abandon their discussion because of an interruption. The disagreement
"incites, as it were, an undecidable question," Christopher Looby notes,
"in the reader about the representative status of the Wielands *vis—vis*
American society."[45] Looby continues by noting how Brown quickly
diverts attention from the debate, circling away from the issues raised by
Theodore and Pleyel and turning the narrative toward other concerns.
Still, the question framed by Theodore and Pleyel resonates across the rest
of the novel like a pregnant pause, for, as Edward Sill Fussell observes, "it
is just this exaggeration and absurdity upon which *Wieland* is constructed
and from which it derives its wild yet public power."[46]

The public power of Brown's novel resides in how his portrait of a single family reflects and encodes the history of the emerging nation. In her
influential reading of *Wieland*, Jane Tompkins argues that "the third generation of Wielands embody America's passage from Puritan narrowness
to large-minded enlightenment views not only in their character and education, but in the setting and activities Brown assigns them."[47] Positioned
as the inheritors of the mantle of pre-Revolutionary settlement histories,
Theodore and Clara and the buildings that they inherit incarnate the tangled banks of American history. "Brown's America," as Bill Christophersen
suggests, "was—to borrow an image from *Wieland*—a temple on a cliff."[48]
Struggling to find its equilibrium, the emerging Republic tottered amid
rampant paranoia and instability in the years leading up to the publication
of *Wieland*; Brown's novel maps the chaos of the period by presenting, in
the words of Shirley Samuels, "national concerns" as "domestic dilemmas,
since in order to preserve the nation it was conceived as necessary to preserve the family as a carefully constituted supporting unit."[49] Framing the
precariousness of early republican life, Brown's portrait of the Wieland
estate at Mettingen sketches the conditions of post-Revolutionary America by sounding out the multivalent meanings of its biloquial architectural
landscape.

"By coining the term 'biloquialism,'" as David Kazanjian argues, Brown
avoids the "antirational" connotations attached to ventriloquism; moreover, Brown's neologism allows him to define Carwin's talent as a "merely
doubled voice, a single copy alongside a single original, no matter how

many forms that 'copy' might take."[50] The doubling of a single copy alongside a single original marks more than Carwin's practice, for it defines both Theodore Wieland Jr.'s relationship to his father as well as the two distinct natures of the temple. This biloquial doubling mirrors the manicheism recursively swirling across the novel: Carwin presents himself as both a "native" of Pennsylvania and as an alien intruder from Europe; Clara figures her house as both "sweet and tranquil asylum" and as a too easily penetrated space (199 and 193). The idea of a copy alongside an original speaks to the state of early republican history as well. Theodore and Clara constitute their independence on the basis of muting the voices of the past; in effect they deny the multilayered discourses surrounding them. Carwin's copies fool them because they are continually deaf to the resonance of any other narrative except the one they choose to hear. In his extended soliloquy at the end of the novel, Carwin confesses to an affinity for the temple, admitting to Clara that "many a night have I passed under its roof, revolving no pleasing meditations" (199). While Carwin never explains what about the temple continually draws him toward it, his attachment to "the position and ornaments of *the temple*" stands as one of the oddest details of his confession (199). Carwin's fear at being discovered in the temple drives him to deploy his biloquialism for the first time in *Wieland*, and it is the hearing of this unbodied voice from the temple that begins Theodore's descent into madness.

In addition to his affinity for the temple, Carwin admits being similarly attached to Clara's house.[51] During one of his uninvited visits, Carwin tries to hide himself by projecting his voice into Clara's closet and hinting at her eventual rape and murder. Rationally, Clara understands that it would be impossible for anyone to secure himself in her closet without her knowledge, yet the idea that her house has been violated by strangers paralyzes her. The scene exhibits how Clara, in particular, becomes confused by the instability of her environment. Hearing voices threatening her virtue and safety, Clara proclaims with horror that her house, "which had hitherto been an inviolate asylum, [is] now beset with danger" (60). Caught off guard by this domestic intrusion, Clara exposes a mistaken belief in the sanctity of home. She had thought herself immune to danger because of an unfounded sense of the invulnerability of her residence. Immediately after hearing strange noises around her private chamber, she vividly describes her house's physical design:

My habitation was a wooden edifice, consisting of two stories. In each story were two rooms, separated by an entry, or middle passage, with which they communicated by opposite doors. The passage, on the lower story, had doors at the two ends, and a stair-case. Windows answered to the doors on the upper story. Annexed to this, on the eastern side, were wings, divided in like manner, into an upper and lower room; one of them comprized a kitchen, and chamber above it for the servant, and communicated, on both stories, with the parlor adjoining it below, and the chamber adjoining it above. The opposite wing is of smaller dimensions, the rooms not being above eight feet square. The lower of these was used as a depository of household implements, the upper was a closet in which I deposited my books and papers. They had but one inlet and that was from the room adjoining. There was no window in the lower one, and in the upper, a small aperture which communicated light and air, but would scarcely admit the body. The door which led into this, was close to my bed-head, and was always locked, but when I myself was within. The avenues below were accustomed to be closed and bolted at nights. (56–57)

Brown's minute description of Clara's house suggests that no one could unknowingly secrete himself within her closet. When she comes to believe that Carwin has entered her chamber, rationality offers her no productive way to navigate her future course. Brown's microscopic attention to the material composition of Clara's house creates a deep-seated critique of reason as a guiding social principle. In its design the house exemplifies vernacular structures of the period, separating the kitchen and servants' quarters from the main living spaces. This architectural arrangement separates the public from the private, increasing Clara's ultimately ungrounded sense of security. Despite her expectations, the privacy of her chambers is easily profaned. Brown uses Clara's house to expose the proximity of danger; even within a space designed to secure her from the intrusion of the outside world, she is beset by external dangers.

This invasion of the private by the dangerous currents of the public sphere marks the core of Brown's message in *Wieland.* Failing to account for the demands of the unstable American scene, the Wielands guilelessly think that they occupy a solid foundation without ever coming to terms with the realities of the spaces or environments that they inhabit. Only after Pleyel has rejected her, convinced by Carwin's duplicity of her lack of chastity, does Clara realize that the danger that confronts her cannot be warded off with "doors and bars" (110). The disruptions of the Wielands' domestic space—Carwin admits his ability to being able "to lock and unlock" doors "without the aid of a key"—hinge on the failure of the Wielands to question deeply the spaces they inhabit (206). For Brown, it is precisely this misplaced faith in the unexamined sanctity of the home as a sustainable foundation that allows the Wielands to be continually duped. This is the same cultural problem that Bartram sought to address by indexing abandoned homes; for Bartram understood, like Brown after him, that unless post-Revolutionary Americans came to terms with the import of pre-Revolutionary structures they would be deluding themselves about the ease of settlement and expansion. For both Bartram and Brown, structures emblematic of one set of cultural values cannot easily be remade to serve another purpose, and, moreover, no space can be safely occupied without addressing its history. The Wielands mistakenly believe that the sites they occupy embody the rationality they project onto the world, and that this immunizes them against the convulsions recorded in the totality of their environment's history.

Theodore and Clara believe that by changing the utility of a building, they can shift its significance. They imagine that they can readily convert the temple into an outdoor drawing room, or an outlying farmer's cottage into a secure stronghold. This misguided theory does not take into account the social instability of pre-Revolutionary America. Their own familial history ought to have taught them that pre-Revolutionary America was a haven for dissenters, fundamentalists, and those seeking to mask previous identities and connections. Simply willing that history away would not make its legacies disappear. Looking back into America's history to test the soundness of its foundations, Brown discovers a culture adrift because it lacks a sustaining political or social order. After he completed *Wieland*, Brown sent a copy to Vice President Thomas Jefferson.[52] Perhaps, like Bartram before him, Brown delivered the book to Jefferson because he thought that his novel would contribute to the discursive construction of the "magnificent structure" being manufactured by the emerging nation.[53] Whatever Brown's intentions were, the novel clearly asks its readers to consider the import of residual structures for the unfolding of the present.

III

In his brief preface to *Edgar Huntly; or, Memoirs of a Sleep-Walker* (1800), Charles Brockden Brown announces his intention "to exhibit a series of adventures, growing out of the condition of our country."[54] Surveying the terrain of literary production, Brown calls for American writers to divorce themselves from derivative European models. Instead, they should root their productions in "the sources of amusement" that "are peculiar to ourselves" (3). By focusing on their own history and environment, American writers would no longer have to import alien themes for their subject matter. Brown frames his argument quite simply: the rich wellspring of "the incidents of Indian hostility, and the perils of the western wilderness" offer "far more suitable" sources "for a native of America" to explore than any foreign "Gothic castles and chimeras" (3). The concluding turn of the preface declares that these suitable subjects constitute "the ingredients of this tale," as Brown announces *Edgar Huntly*'s primary concerns as the complexities of frontier settlement (3). On the surface, Brown's preface

appears straightforward rather than deceptive; yet within the introductory
frame lingers the uncertainty generated by the elusive term "a native of
America." While the preface confidently deploys the phrase, the text of
Edgar Huntly recursively destabilizes any surety of definition, continually
rendering any denotation of the term as, at best, contingent. The use of
this phrase at the threshold of a novel concerned with the interactions of
squatters, settlers, aliens, immigrants, Native Americans, troublesome
land claims, and orphaned Euro-Americans suggests that Brown's definition of the "perils of the western wilderness" has as much to do with questions of national identity and domestication as it does with wild animals
and darkened forests.

Brown's preface subtlety conjures a unitary, cohesive subjectivity for
both "Americans" and "American" history, even as his novel points to the
fraught hybridity of a national identity conjured by the rhetorically facile
"ourselves." Just as he questioned cultural stability in *Wieland* by exploring
the ramifications of remodeling previous sites to establish new meanings,
Brown returns in *Edgar Huntly* to the relationship between the legacies of
history and the cultural narratives on which the emerging Republic was
seeking to ground itself. As Caroll Smith-Rosenberg declares in her compelling reading of *Edgar Huntly*, post-Revolutionary Euro-Americans
"quite self-consciously fused two subject positions: the victorious postcolonial and the colonizer, heir to Britain's imperial venture in North
America. Facing east, Euro-Americans positioned themselves as Sons of
Liberty; facing west, they were the progenitors of a vast new empire."[55]
The Janus-faced nature of post-Revolutionary American identity resides at
the center of *Edgar Huntly*, as the novel calculates how the "incidents" of
western settlement and expansion reflect the legacies of the emerging
Republic's connections to the Atlantic frontier. "The determination not
only to break with European prehistories but to wipe out the very notion
of the 'sins of the past' that informed the American Enlightenment," as
Luke Gibbons writes, did not manifest itself as a denial of history, but
rather as a continual questioning of "its relevance for the present."[56] In
Edgar Huntly, Brown deconstructs the optimistic figuration of a cohesive
American subjectivity (which his preface taps into) by mapping how North
America's complex settlement histories destabilize cultural cohesion.

Tracing this unsteadiness on a frontier located just on the outskirts of
the nation's capital allows Brown to highlight how the complexities of the
past cannot be easily disinherited. The terrain of *Edgar Huntly* surveys the
same ground haunted by the infamous Walking Treaty, wherein Anglo-
American settlers cheated the Delaware out of a large sweep of land by
doctoring maps and falsifying documents. The Delaware agreed in 1737 to
abide by the tenets of a 1686 treaty, which allowed Pennsylvania to claim
an area of land that could be walked in a day and a half. In preparation for

this *walking* purchase, the chief justice of Pennsylvania, James Logan, ordered brush and undergrowth cleared along the expanse in question, effectively creating a highway deep into Delaware territory. Logan commissioned several "walkers" to run into the wilderness for thirty-six hours, resulting in their covering almost three times as much ground as they normally would have been able to traverse.[57] Logan's highly orchestrated landgrab outraged the Delaware, but they were nevertheless forcibly removed from the area. It is in this disputed landscape that Edgar Huntly walks; "so when Edgar travels north and west into Norwalk," Peter Kafer writes, "he is traveling into a place where the past hangs heavy, where its energies, its angers, its terrors, from 'about thirty years ago' still haunt."[58] Located just outside Philadelphia, with all its attendant associations with the birth of the Republic, and in the midst of this ominous colonizing history, Edgar Huntly walks the razor's edge separating the nation's disparate histories as he seeks to secure his own future.

By so carefully positioning Huntly in between these two contending registers, Brown ties Huntly's personal quest to larger concerns. "Brown treats his characters," Stephen Shapiro writes, "as mutable bearers of social forces rather than as vessels of emotional interiority."[59] Following the line of Shapiro's argument, Brown deploys Huntly as the carrier of the tensions inherent in the nation's eastward- and westward-facing histories. In a typically Brownian moment, Huntly figures his own interiority to highlight the ways in which his experiences embody more than just a personal history. "Most men are haunted by some species of terror or antipathy," Huntly suggests, "which they are, for the most part, able to trace to some incident which befel [*sic*] them in their early years" (173). Huntly reduces his biography into a parable to produce an object lesson: the habits of mind that shape adult behavior can generally be traced to some crucial primal scene. The specific events to which Huntly alludes to as haunting his development stem from an incident of hostility between Euro-American settlers and the Native Americans they sought to dispossess. As such, Huntly admits that the cause of his current actions emanates from the consequences of colonizing violence, turning his parable into an illustration of national concerns.

"During the last war," Huntly relates, "notwithstanding the progress of population, and the multiplied perils of such an expedition, a band of" Native Americans "penetrated into Norwalk, and lingered long enough to pillage and murder some of the neighboring inhabitants" (172–73). During this particular outbreak of frontier incursion and retreat, Huntly endured the loss of home and family as his paternal home was "pillaged" and "burnt to the ground," while his "parents and an infant child were murdered in their beds" (173). Brown strategically utilizes Huntly's losses to consider the multivalent meanings of the domestication of the frontier.

Orphaned by the ongoing conflict between settlers and the dispossessed Native Americans, Huntly stands as the bearer of a salient thread of America's colonial history. Toward the conclusion of his narrative, Huntly acknowledges that "my uncle's barn yard and orchard" sit atop land that was formerly a Delaware "village," which was deserted "in consequence of the perpetual encroachments of the English colonists" (207). That village, abandoned, burned, and buried underneath Euro-American homesteads, complicates Huntly's re-creation of his disenfranchisement. By uncovering these variegated foundations, Brown addresses the murkiness of nation formation by acknowledging the intricacy of all territorial claims.

At the same time, Huntly's destitute position, given his loss of paternal protection and guidance, means that he finds himself responsible for his own self-fashioning. Without the security of a prospective inheritance, Huntly finds himself precariously dependent on the mercy of others for sustenance and support. Frontier violence has driven Huntly to inhabit a structure he can never inherit, forcing him to undertake an unsupported and unguided search for autonomy. Brown foregrounds how the dissolution of patriarchal authority shapes Huntly's maturation in order to position him as a representative of the state of the emerging Republic more generally. Huntly, like the nation he stands in for, struggles amid uncertainties after the break from colonial rule, inhabiting a landscape replete with all kinds of legacies of frontier violence.[60] The evocative prehistory that Brown crafts for Edgar Huntly roots the novel, set sometime in the mid-1780s, in America's colonial and Revolutionary histories. Huntly's narrative deconstructs the progressive theory of American settlement by representing the fragility of Anglo-American development. By registering the mercurial foundations upon which previous generations of settlers erected their claims to the land, Brown suggests how unsteady the project of nation building actually was.[61]

Mirroring the tactic he used in *Arthur Mervyn* of having his protagonist typify the perilous fate of young men in the nascent United States, Brown creates Huntly to explore the ways in which post-Revolutionary Americans struggled with their fractured inheritances. Huntly's parentless condition mirrors that of several minor characters, notably Clithero, Waldegrave, and Weymouth. Considering the sad trajectory of their histories, Huntly laments the repetitious "mournful tale" of young men in America (154). All too often, Huntly complains, American men "wander from their rustic homes in search of fortune" (154). "Prone to enterprize," young Americans "are scattered over every sea and every land in pursuit of that wealth which will not screen them from disease and infirmity, which is missed much oftener than found, and which, when gained, by no means compensates them for the hardships and vicissitudes endured in the pursuit" (154). In Brown's formulation, this misguided economy threatens cultural growth by

promoting risk without the promise of return. Outside the safety of a settled community, disconnected American men dwell in a state of constant
flux. Removed from "their rustic homes," they risk dissolution. Huntly's
observation posits that well-regulated homes serve as the primary source of
social stability and as antidote to post-Revolutionary chaos. Simultaneously, the novel displays the difficulty facing young American men seeking
houses of their own and exhibits how their efforts compete with the lingering aftereffects of the violence of colonization. In his efforts to return to
republican civilization, Huntly must navigate between ruins and the legacies manifest in abandoned structures and multiple layers of architectural
inscription. Self-fashioned as a representative figure, Huntly traces his own
motivations to the loss of his paternal home, even as he fails to consider the
import of the fact that his own uncle's farmstead stands atop a dispossessed
Delaware village. Like Theodore and Clara Wieland, Huntly inherits a
weighted architectural landscape that continues to confound his attempts
at reductive mapping and interpretation.

In reading Huntly's reactions to his experiences in the wilderness of
Norwalk, which continually "defy his reason and deceive him with false
openings," Paul Downes argues that this "landscape haunts not simply
because of its archaic decay but also because of its revolutionary reorgani-
zation."[62] Littered with residual decaying structures and tenuously overwritten by post-Revolutionary structures of thought and feeling, the terrain that Huntly moves across continually resists his efforts at mastery;
even as Huntly proclaims that "no one was more acquainted with this
wilderness than I," he also quickly confesses that "my knowledge was
extremely imperfect" (97). Within the novel Brown probes the boundaries
of Huntly's imperfect awareness by having him move both east and west
across the area's settlement histories, and as such the text registers the
palimpsest that is the American wilderness.

Focusing on Huntly's efforts to securely locate himself allows Brown to
consider the paucity of this generation's inheritance. Continually, Huntly
dreams about ensuring his future, not via his own industry, but by procuring some windfall that will allow him a life of landed gentility.[63] "In short,"
Elizabeth Hinds writes, "what Edgar has erroneously believed to be his
various inheritances prove time and again to be a chimera of security."[64]
While their settler forefathers had the protection of a paternalistic Crown,
members of Huntly's generation come to maturity without such protection. Sydney J. Krause figures this transition as a "pattern of generational
decline—the falling off in integrity from fathers to sons—that virtually
permeates the novel."[65] Brown places Huntly in the wilderness to make
him reenact, in geographic reverse, the role of a pioneer. Huntly's attempt
to return to civilization, after awakening (he imagines) as a prisoner of a
hostile band of Delaware, dominates the central sections of the novel.

Huntly marks his return from wilderness to civilization architecturally, measuring his proximity to safety by the improvements of a transformed landscape. The sight of "the footsteps of cattle," and a "much beaten" path, all evidencing "human residence," revive his "drooping spirits" (205). He approaches a clapboard house rapturously, celebrating its "window of four panes" and "chimney of brick, well burnt," as signaling his location once more "among beings like myself" (205). Huntly arrives at this small cottage of a farmer after a protracted struggle with a band of Delaware at a more isolated house. Here he discovers that he has not been lost at all, but rather was in familiar territory all along. Reorientated, Huntly recalls the particular history of the hut where he engaged his Delaware pursuers, and in so doing he focuses on the ways in which residual structures house, yet fail to contain, the hybridity of national identity.

In his pathbreaking account of late-eighteenth-century ideologies of farming that circulated in the emerging Republic, Timothy Sweet notes that in Huntly's *eastern* movement from wilderness back to civilization he ventures across "three farmsteads in turn," each of which signifies a different stage of "frontier settlement."[66] These three houses—a bedraggled hut described as "suited to the poverty and desolation which surrounded it," a "small and low" farmhouse, and finally a larger farmhouse, which Huntly declares a "model of cleanliness and comfort"—exhibit the differences between the various settlement strata, in effect creating a reverse map of the unfolding of the domestication of the wilderness (183, 205, and 226). By marking Huntly's journey from wilderness to civilization architecturally, Brown accentuates how houses register environmental and cultural histories. The ramshackle hut tenants a variety of marginalized and possibly destabilizing figures, and Brown implies that necessity of reading the entirety of a house's occupational history in order to interpret its import for the community whose margins it haunts. The hut becomes the container for all the figures that imperil the projection of a cohesive national identity. Like the ruined houses littering Bartram's view of the Southeast and akin to the unreadable legacy of the Wieland temple, the hut in *Edgar Huntly* troubles the surety of national narratives and grounds Brown's interrogation of the prospects for future cultural stability.

Bill Christophersen concludes his reading of *Edgar Huntly* with the observation that "Brown's America" was the "home of the enslaved and the enlightened, the savage and the elect, the shyster and the hayseed, the rebel and the republican, the Federalist and the Republican."[67] Almost all of these variegated tenants are housed, at one point or another, in *Edgar Huntly*'s decisive hut, underscoring its importance in registering the "the condition of our country." For all the novel's narrative spiraling, the divergent plot strands contained in *Edgar Huntly* are all fused in the occupational history of Old Deb's hut. Many critics have underscored the connec-

tions between *Edgar Huntly* and the Alien and Sedition Acts, but few have
noted how this frontier hut quite specifically houses both the seditious and
the alien figures of the novel.[68] Brown presents the hut as containing a
variety of figures marginalized because of his culture's xenophobia; as such,
Brown figures this hut as a wellspring for advancing his concerns about the
multifaceted nature of American identity.

After Huntly awakens in the cave and battles the Delaware who he mistakenly thinks have kidnapped him, he moves to find his way back to the
safety of more settled regions. During his conflict with the Delaware,
Huntly rescues a farmer's daughter who has in fact been abducted, and as
they flee the Delaware they stumble across an isolated hut where Huntly
decides they should take refuge before pressing on. This borderland cottage is now inhabited by a Delaware woman named Old Deb, who refused
to follow her fellow Delaware when they willingly (in Huntly's narrative)
removed themselves from the area. "She declared her resolution," Huntly
recalls, "to remain behind, and maintain possession of the land which her
countrymen should impiously abandon" (207). Yet Old Deb's hut has a
complex history, one that reveals the layers of inscription on the American
landscape. Although the Delaware had a claim to the territory, the house
was not built by Deb's people; rather, the structure was fabricated by a
more recent immigrant. The question of the rightful possession of the
land becomes the dominant theme of the novel. By unpacking the history
of the hut's ownership, Brown foregrounds the significance of the past for
a nation struggling to shape an identity. Rather than echoing the retalia-
tion central to Huntly's own personal narrative, Brown transforms Deb's
hut into a testing ground for divergent territorial claims. By housing a
variety of claims in one domestic site, Brown considers the ways in which
architecture informs cultural development.

The precision of Brown's description of Old Deb's hut stands in stark
contrast to the rest of the text, which is otherwise, as Jared Gardner writes,
"notably devoid of vividly defined landmarks."[69] As exacting as his description of Clara Wieland's chambers, Brown's account of the hut reads like a
set of blueprints designed to allow the reader to easily replicate the structure in question:

> It consisted of a few unhewn logs laid upon each other, to the height of eight
> or ten feet, including a quadrangular space of similar dimensions, and cov-
> ered by thatch. There was no window, light being sufficiently admitted into
> the crevices between the logs. These had formerly been loosely plastered
> with clay, but air and rain had crumbled and washed the greater part of this
> rude cement away. Somewhat like a chimney, built of half-burnt bricks, was
> perceived at one corner. The door was fastened by a leathern thong, tied to
> a peg. (183)

When Huntly's knocks and calls remain unanswered, he enters the hut to warm himself and the "half frozen" "unhappy girl" he has recently liberated from captivity (183). Brown continues his dioramic representation when Huntly crosses the threshold of the hut, graphically capturing the furnishings and objects strewn around the interior, exemplified by his snapshot of "a cedar bucket" filled with "a little water, full of droppings from the roof, drowned insects and sand" (184). The "stale rye-loaf" and some dying "embers" indicate that the hut was recently abandoned, and Huntly feels no reservations over helping himself to the food or having invaded anyone's privacy. For Huntly the hut evidences civilization, and he feels confident in his "power to appease any indignation" the owner "might feel at the liberties" Huntly has "taken" (184). Huntly's narrative reconstruction of the cottage marks it as typical of the coarse shanties built by those first settling a wilderness, and based on this evidence Huntly immediately links—culturally and ethnically—its occupant to his "native" community of post-Revolutionary Americans.[70] For Huntly, houses, unquestionably, suggest a participation in the same cultural order that he has left behind, as he conjectures that whoever occupies the hut would "readily afford us all the information and succour that we needed" (184). Huntly's equation of houses with post-Revolutionary American society belies his inability to actually read the dense settlement of the landscape he professes to have an intimate knowledge of. The cottage's actual history manifests its role as shelter for contending claims, further complicating the simplistic narrative of the wilderness as a blank slate awaiting only the "arrival" of an expanding nation. All the problems charted in the novel branch out of the question of possession, and only by mapping the history of a house, Brown insinuates, can the complexity of a site's supposed connections to a particular social order be properly determined. Located just "three miles" from much more expensively finished houses, this hut also marks the thinness of the line separating civilization from frontier, the tenuousness of the line separating the nation's eastward- and westward-facing histories from one another (286).

The rude cottage was first "erected by a Scottish emigrant, who not being rich enough to purchase land, and entertaining a passion for solitude and independence, cleared a field in the unappropriated wilderness, and subsisted on its produce" (210). Ominously, Huntly records that "after some time he disappeared," and his absence leads Huntly's community to assume that he "was murdered by Indians" (210). "Shortly" after his disappearance, Deb "took possession of his hut, his implements of tillage, and his corn-field" (210). Deb's repossession of the land, presumably grounded in her ancestral claims to the entire domain of Norwalk, remains unchallenged by the American community on whose margins the Scottish emigrant sought to establish his "independence." Conversely, at the first sign of danger to a more substantial house, a posse immediately seeks vengeance and restitution.[71] That a murder could have remained uninvestigated appears strange given Huntly's description of his "neighbourhood" (14). Huntly notes that "each farmer" is "surrounded by his sons and kinsmen," and that his community's scheme is a "patriarchal one" (14). But for all its seeming cohesiveness, the community does not care about anyone residing outside its bounds. Since the solitary Scottish farmer was not organically bound to the community, his demise does not overtly trouble them. Far from a safe place, Huntly occupies a decidedly xenophobic patriarchal world. More troubling is Huntly's failure to notice that his *secure* community actually lacks any authoritative figures; instead it abounds with the legacies of absent fathers and dispossessed sons.

By taking up residence—albeit temporarily—in Old Deb's cottage, Huntly occupies the position of an early marginalized settler. Disconnected from his society's codifying structures of thought and feeling, he becomes unhinged. In the forest he changes into a wild man. Suggestively, it is his occupation and his defense of the cottage that mark his passage into the role of primal frontier warrior. Huntly's early forays into the wilderness demonstrate unfamiliarity with the physical necessities of colonization, as he consistently ventures out unprepared for the task at hand. Unsuited for the gravity of his situation, Huntly confesses that "to be a distant and second-hand spectator of events was widely different from witnessing them myself and partaking of their consequences" (91). Just another lamented son of America, Huntly finds himself adrift without direction. At the novel's conclusion, Clithero—another dispossessed and alien son—takes refuge in Deb's now once more abandoned hut, adding another inhabitant to the site. Venturing to visit Clithero, Huntly finds the hut "by no means in so ruinous a state as when I last visited it" (286). Sustaining himself by working as a day laborer on a nearby farm, Clithero seems, in Huntly's eyes, at last destined to reclaim this marginalized site from the uncertainties that have tenanted it. Yet, as quickly as Brown posits such an idea he pulls the rug out from underneath Huntly's hopes, reaffirming the hut as a location for all the unsettled figures within the narrative. After Huntly informs Clithero of his innocence concerning Ms. Lorimer, who did not die as Clithero had imagined, he expects Clithero to happily become a fixed member of the Norwalk community. Huntly acts to "out-root" guilt but ends up unhinging Clithero (288). As Elizabeth Jane Wall Hinds argues, "houses and other properties in *Edgar Huntly* literally and symbolically reiterate the social orders they host."[72] Deb's hut paradigmatically represents the tenor of Hinds' observation: functioning as home to all the marginalized and dispossessed figures within the novel, it effectively houses no social orders but rather remains as a foundation for all the figures who cannot find a place for themselves within the patriarchal and xenophobic communities of post-Revolutionary Pennsylvania. Although continually abandoned, the hut is never unoccupied. Given how readily someone always seems to take possession of the cottage, Brown adumbrates just how many aberrant figures cannot find a place for themselves in Huntly's community.

By framing the novel's landscape architecturally, Brown offers a multivalent reading of republican society. The house of Huntly's uncle was fashioned by the same impulse that destroyed the home of Huntly's father: both structures are by-products of one group seeking to eradicate the presence of another by overwriting, or tearing down, its homes. Huntly fails to connect one situation with another and thus never comprehends that his foes' motivations are the same as his own. The territorial claims made by Old Deb (in the sense that she dwells in a house built by another), by the Scotch immigrant, and by Huntly's family exist on top of claims made by previous settlers. These disparate justifications combine as the novel confronts the issue of who actually has the authority to domesticate the land. By making houses the stage upon which all sovereignty claims play out, Brown renders all arguments about possession equally valid and groundless.

Without the binding power of a central authority, the early Republic was a world at risk. Huntly's battle at the isolated frontier hut presents the historically labyrinthine process of occupancy and removal that the novel indexes. Development and expansion appear to be governed by little more than whim and chance. Unless something changes, the unfolding of that process will remain chaotic. Discordant individuals are not driven out of the society but are harbored on its borders, a constant sign of the fragility of the cultural order in *domesticated* regions. As the history of the hut indicates, no authority exists to help those not already part of the community. Analogously, this social order does not recognize any new additions to its ranks. The Scottish emigrant arrives in the Pennsylvania frontier to establish his independence, but instead of finding a welcoming community such as the one Andrew the Hebridean encountered in *Letters from an American Farmer*, he awkwardly becomes shunted off to the margins, and his murder becomes little more than local legend. In the landscape of *Edgar Huntly*, Brown depicts a stagnant community, too self-absorbed to expand beyond its limited confines.

Huntly's regression into brutality demarcates the insularity of the community. Only by becoming what he abhors, what he imagines the Delaware to be like, can he survive. If such is the fate of all houseless sons, then the Republic's future will be as precarious as its past. The struggle over the frontier cottage registers the complexities of America's settlement histories. Instead of constituting a measured and reasonable expansion, future acts of settlement will fall victim to circumstances as violent as those

that preceded them. New houses will be as vulnerable to seizure and multiple "owners," and the new nation will have failed to secure its future. Just
as disturbing as abandoned houses, the Scottish farmer's hut exhibits the
ways in which claims to the land can be easily undone if they are not
rooted in social connection. This emigrant farmer who ventured to Pennsylvania to secure his independence failed to find a place for himself under
the umbrella of the term "native of America." Across the length of his
walking, Huntly, born in Pennsylvania, discovers the dense record of previous native settlement, which further troubles the guarantee of the book's
preface's of a cohesive national identity.

Huntly's taxonomy of occupancy reflects the same discoveries that Bartram unearths in his own catalog of palimpsestic houses, even as his experiences in the wilderness prefigure those Meriwether Lewis, another
walker, who would leave Philadelphia just a few years after the publication
of *Edgar Huntly* to map his way across the wilderness of North America. In
1805, on the continent's westernmost frontier, Lewis would oversee the
construction of a series of huts that sought to mark off the Corps of Discovery's independence from those around them. Moreover, like the house
built by Brown's Scottish emigrant, these structures—and the cultural narratives they reflected and encoded—further served to unsettle any mythic
conception of the wilderness as a blank slate free from evidence of previous
settlement.

IV

"In the evening" of 10 December 1805, Sergeant Patrick Gass reported,
"we laid the foundation of our huts."[73] The task of building a winter camp
would occupy the Corps of Discovery, under the command of Captains
Meriwether Lewis and William Clark, for the next nineteen days. Frontier
construction was arduous under optimal conditions; at Fort Clatsop the
difficulties proved extreme. "During [the last] month," Gass wrote, "we
have had three fair days; and there is no prospect of a change" (10:182).
Similarly, Clark complained "the winds" were so "violent" that trees were
"falling in every direction," as "whorl winds, with gusts of rain Hail &
Thunder" struck and crashed around them (6:128). As the seasonal rains of
the Pacific Northwest continued without abatement, sleeping in thread-
bare leather tents—so "rotten that the Smallest things tares [them] into
holes"—had become unbearable (6:127). In order to gain some semblance
of shelter, Clark wrote, "we Covered our Selves as well as we could with
Elk Skins, & Set up the greater part of the night, all wet" (6:126). The men
relentlessly complained of fevers, aches, bruises, and rashes, underscoring
the need for proper housing.[74] But circumstances made construction slow

going, for even as the men were "all well employ'd in cutting logs and raising winter cabins," fashioning a watertight roof proved difficult (6:123).

After four days of continual but fruitless labor, Clark concluded that
"Scerce one man in camp can bost of being one day dry Since we landed at
this point" (6:125). Under these circumstances, with only rudimentary
tools to turn trees into manageable boards, the scantily provisioned party
tried to erect usable living quarters. After some experimentation the Corps
"found a kind of timber in plenty, which splits freely," but their need for
boards outstripped their production capacity; in despair, Clark dispatched
Sergeant Pryer "with 8 men" to seize the lumber from "an Indian house
which had been abandoned" (10:182 and 6:133). By combining the pilfered lumber with their own puncheons, the Corps finished their huts on
December 24. Proud and hopeful, they moved into their new winter quarters in time for a Christmas celebration. Their relief was short-lived
because they had neglected to build chimneys (except on the captains'
hut). As Gass observed, the men soon found their huts "smoked," making
breathing difficult if not impossible (10:184). The fires they built to dry
their sodden clothing drove them out into the open air. Once more the
captains assigned the party to construction details. Finally, on December
30, with newly forged chimneys in place, Gass was able to record with satisfaction that they had "completely finished" the "fortification" (10:185).

Lewis and Clark named the promontory near where they built Fort
Clatsop *Cape Disappointment*, because they had reached the Pacific Ocean
without discovering a waterway that linked the western coast of the continent with the Mississippi. The water highway that Jefferson had hoped
would connect the Mississippi to the valuable fur trade of the Pacific
Northwest simply did not exist, a discovery that damped the imperial and
commercial ambitions that fueled the expedition. Worse than that frustration was the recognition that the Corps would have to spend the winter of
1805 in the dreary and foggy area in which they found themselves. They
would not be able to cross the Bitterroot Mountains until the spring thaw
made them passable. Morale had never been lower; their mission—but
not their journey—was over. Whatever Lewis and Clark may have
thought about the successes and failures of the expedition, the more
pressing concerns of food and shelter dominated the daily *Journal* entries.
With their gaze firmly focused eastward (for the first time in almost two
years), they were much less attentive to the issues of commerce, politics,
and ethnography.

Historians have typically focused on themes of mobility and discovery
in their discussions of the Corps of Discovery.[75] Readings that situate the
Journals within an imperial narrative habitually focus on the outward journey, often neglecting both the Corps' retrograde movement and the stasis
of their encampment at Fort Clatsop. Yet "the fixation upon epic ambition

(and dashed hopes)," Thomas Hallock argues, "obscures how" the Corps "processed and came to know their surroundings."[76] Recently, spurred by the bicentennial of the expedition, critics have begun to reexamine the traditional historiography of the Corps. This new critical turn examines the *Journals* themselves as, in the words of Thomas Slaughter, "contestable terrain."[77] Engaging the *Journals* as less stable than "indisputable facts," and imagining Lewis and Clark as more than "a latterly example of sinister conquerors or agents of empire," as Kris Fresonke suggests, is to begin to appreciate the complexity of the voyage's second act.[78] In motion, the Corps was in flight from the ambiguity that plagued them when at rest. At Fort Clatsop they were stationary, becoming less nomadic at the same time and in the same place where they first encountered Native American tribes that were not predominantly migratory. On the continent's western frontier, the Corps found the experience of house building vastly different from that of exploration. This change in subject position unsettled their enterprise. Similar to the ways in which Bartram and Brown present the difficulties attendant to homesteading as altering preconceived notions about the cultural and racial hierarchies, Lewis and Clark, in the expedition's *Journals*, refigure their experiences after occupying the role of house builders.

The experiences of the Corps of Discovery while garrisoned at Fort Clatsop betray how operant structures of thought and feeling were challenged by an encounter with the architectural and cultural practices of the Native Americans of the Pacific Northwest. At Fort Clatsop the behavior of the Corps shifted in regard to Native Americans: for even as they became increasingly bitter about what they perceived as the savagery of the Clatsops, the Corps also understood their own dependence on them for survival. Simply put, without access to Clatsop goods and foodstuffs the Corps would have rotted away in the dreary climate of Cape Disappointment. Even as the Corps denigrated Clatsop behavior, they unabashedly pilfered Clatsop lumber. Eventually, as the Corps prepared to decamp, they stole a Clatsop canoe because of their own incapacity to legitimately procure one. By examining how the Corps naturalized these thefts and their own prejudices toward the Native Americans inhabiting the area, a discernible record emerges of how the material conditions at Cape Disappointment inflected the ethnographic observations contained in the *Journals*. Like Brown's *Edgar Huntly* and like Bartram in *Travels*, the Corps of Discovery encounter evidence of Native American settlement histories, and this discovery shifts their hopes for national expansion and settlement. Coming across architectural evidence of prior possession unhinges preconceptions about cultural development in each of these texts, and collectively they chart the ways in which the nation was continually obsessed with the consequences of discovering houses that exhibited the domestication history of the wilderness. Embedded in the Fort Clatsop entries of the *Journals* exists a complex register of the superiority of Clatsop material culture. Lewis and Clark's recognition of the Clatsop skills conjoins a previously unseen (within the *Journals*) racism aimed at denigrating the tribes native to the area in which the Corps were forced to spend the winter of 1805. During the entirety of their twenty-eight month journey, it was only during their relatively short four-month winter garrison at Fort Clatsop that the Corps felt the need to isolate themselves or to steal from the Native Americans they encountered. Even as they neglect to deeply examine their own behavior, Lewis and Clark continually describe the Clatsops and Chinooks as itinerant thieves and intruders, as if by highlighting their own supposed mistreatment they can explain away their own ungenerous behaviors.

Although Fort Clatsop was the Corps' third winter headquarters, circumstances there were very different from those of their previous posts. At the first two winter stops, *terra nova* lay ahead. Shortly after they embarked in 1803, the Corps built their first winter quarters, Camp DuBois, near St. Louis. At Camp DuBois they were still in semi-regular contact with federal authorities and were involved primarily in procuring provisions for their journey. Then, in 1804, after months of traveling, the Corps of Discovery built their second encampment, Fort Mandan on the upper Missouri River. Here, the Corps was visited by French trappers and agents of British trading companies, and Lewis was able to send back a report and specimens to President Jefferson. During these early bivouacs, the Corps understood they had not yet fully engaged their mission. They leisurely prepared documents to be sent back east and held reasonable expectations that such documents would reach their destinations. Although in uncharted territory, the Corps of Discovery passed the winters of 1803 and 1804 in anticipation of what was to come.

When they built huts to survive the rainy winter of 1805, the Corps recognized that their eastward voyage would involve retracing their own footsteps. Their previous camps had been pauses, berths to wait out the weather before continuing west. In 1804 plummeting temperatures signaled when the Corps needed to establish a winter camp, and as the river began to freeze they sought the company of native informants so that they could spend the winter gathering information. In short, the Corps left the river in 1804 when they had determined they had moved as far west as could be reasonably expected. At Fort Clatsop, they confronted a much different set of choices, all of which involved painfully forestalling their own pronounced desire for retrograde movement.[79] They could try moving inland before building a winter camp, positioning themselves as far east on the return path as possible. They might build near the coast and hope to encounter a trading vessel willing to transport specimens and notes. Using the letters of credit President Jefferson had given them, they might even negotiate return passages for the entire party. No longer concerned with extending their western reach, they had to decide where to position themselves to return east.

Clark describes the location that Lewis selected for the construction of Fort Clatsop as "Certainly the most eligable Situation for our purposes of any in the neighbourhood" (6:114). Yet unlike the winter encampment at Fort Mandan, which was located close to the Mandans, the Corps established Fort Clatsop at a relative remove from any surrounding Native settlements. More significant than simply living in close quarters with the Mandans is the fact that the Corps operated as the Mandans' loosely affiliated allies during the winter of 1804, exhibited by such activities as joint buffalo hunts, frequent visits between the two groups, and an expansive New Year's Day celebration during which the Corps (particularly York) delighted the Mandans with their dancing.[80] The association of the Corps and the Mandans during the winter of 1804 provided Clark with valuable assistance as he drafted, revised, and completed the comprehensive "Estimate of the Eastern Indians." No such comparable document concerning the Native Americans of the West emerged during the Fort Clatsop winter. Indeed, the Corps' "Estimate of Western Indians" reads as more of a catalog of unexamined data, an index of numbers, than as an ethnographic study.

In juxtaposing the differences in placement of the 1804 and 1805 winter quarters, James P. Ronda notes that "if Fort Mandan was set at what geographer John Allan has aptly termed 'the keystone of the upper Missouri region,' Fort Clatsop was isolated in a cultural backwater."[81] Even as they were aware of substantial Chinook villages to the north and several larger, more permanent Tillamook settlements to the south, Lewis and Clark decided to establish their winter camp at a significant distance from any Native American town. Indeed, there was, as Ronda notes, "only one small Clatsop village within easy walking distance" of the eligible spot Lewis had decided on.[82] In essence, Lewis and Clark elected for an emplacement that poorly positioned them to undertake any ethnographic observations, to conduct commercial activities, or even to negotiate political treaties. If the goal of the winter pause was to establish the entry of the United States into the northwestern fur trade, the Corps of Discovery could not have picked a worse location from which to undertake that task. In essence the Corps stayed home and attempted to hibernate during the winter of 1805. Unfortunately, the scarcity of game in the area and the dampness of the weather (which severely hampered the Corps' ability to preserve meat) significantly curtailed the Corps' hopes for self-sufficiency.

Having exhausted the possibility of moving west, the Corps found that their relation to American nature had altered. No longer transients, they had become short-term residents in a well-established native community. Indeed, the Corps of Discovery had never operated in virgin terrain. Even if their maps showed great stretches of blank space, their travel had been rich in Native contact. In the farthest reaches of the Pacific Northwest, they found themselves dwelling in the midst of tribes well established in the landscape. The Clatsops, Chinooks, and Tillamooks were sophisticated traders, well settled in permanent lodges. Skilled carpenters and craftsman, they produced intricate woven baskets so finely constructed that they were "watertight without the aid of gum or rosin" (6:215). The Corps, whose own clothes were flea-infested tatters, marveled at the Clatsops' ability to weave "nearly waterproof" hats out of bear grass, which Lewis was convinced were more durable than those made of "chip or straw" (6:221). Comparatively, the leaky huts of Fort Clatsop must have seemed quite primitive. Life at Cape Disappointment dealt a final blow to U.S. preconceptions about the West; indeed the very roof over the Corps' heads testified to the capabilities of those who had preceded them in this so-called *wilderness*.

The representations of Pacific Northwest Native American building and manufacturing practices contained in the *Journals* encode a more generalized anxiety about the viability of the American experiment. Far from finding an unoccupied landscape, Lewis and Clark encountered a landscape replete with houses and with ruins. Lewis and Clark's reactions to the import of Native American architectural practices implicitly register how unsettled their models for identity construction (on both personal and national levels) became after encountering the superiority of Clatsop material practices. Thomas Hallock argues the *Journals* continually record how "experiences in the field were negotiated alongside—and scarcely eclipsed by—Jeffersonian preconceptions."[83] By unpacking how the *Journals* represent (and repress) these negotiations, we can begin to tease out the multivalent meanings of the expedition. "The *Journals* change after November 1805, when Lewis and Clark begin to plan the retreat," Kris Fresonke argues, noting how, at this juncture, "the nostalgia for civilization is more poignant, and the experience of the unknown is less susceptible to paraphrase."[84] While the *Journals* differ in tone during the Fort Clatsop period, this shift results less from agitation over a return voyage than from the Corps' disturbing experiences among the Clatsops. If there is any extended period of time in the *Journals* that exemplifies the tensions Hallock points toward, it is surely the winter of 1805. During their residence at Fort Clatsop, the Corps suffered from having to confront the fact that their own abilities as craftsmen proved barbaric compared with those of the Native Americans surrounding them. This realization only further served to demoralize the Corps, already impatient to leave the Pacific Coast and return to the civilized confines of the United States.

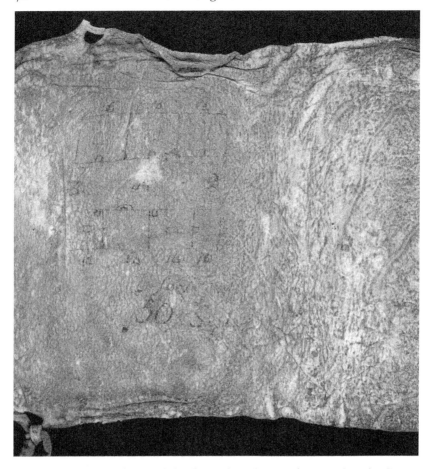

Figure 4. Clark's sketch of the floor plan of Fort Clatsop. Photo by Cary Horton, courtesy of Missouri Historical Society, St. Louis.

A rude, walled encampment, Fort Clatsop contained seven rooms and some hastily constructed furniture. The design of the compound followed traditional blueprints for frontier fortifications. Clark's sketches of the design of the fort, traced on the cover of his field book, depict two buildings (see fig. 4). The western building was divided into three rooms, the eastern into four. The fronts of the buildings faced each other; a series of crudely hewn palisaded fences, lashed to the frames of the buildings, enclosed the space. A parade ground roughly twenty by forty-eight feet separated the two buildings, forming a quad in the middle of the fort. The eastern building housed Lewis, Clark, Sacajawea, her husband, and infant son in one room, with the two remaining rooms devoted to the Corps' communal purposes. The three rooms in the western building were the shared quarters of the remaining men. Cramped to be sure, the fort mirrored many rudimentary outposts built by the U.S. Army in *unsettled* areas; as such, it demonstrates that rather than adapting to local circumstance, Lewis and Clark were committed to what they deemed *civilized* prerogatives and to the preservation of military hierarchies.

As soon as the compound was complete, Lewis and Clark "issued an order for the more exact and uniform discipline and government of the garrison" (6:152). Drafted by both Lewis and Clark, the order decreed:

> At sunset on each day, the Sergt. attended by the interpreter Charbono and two of his guard, will collect and put out of the fort, all Indians except as may specially be permitted to remain by the Commanding offercers, nor shall they be agin admitted untill the main gate be opened the ensuing morning. At Sunset, or immediately after the Indians have been dismissed, both gates shall be shut, ad secured, and the main gate locked and continue so untill sunrise the nest morning. (6:157)

As well as instituting a practice of ejecting all visitors at dusk, this mandate included instructions for building "a Sentinel Box" to house an around-the-clock guard (6:146). Such practices flew in the face of native hospitality, and marked the first and only time during the expedition that the Corps so rigidly entertained such polices. While the Clatsops were at first offended by the Corps' behavior (Clark records that the Clatsops were "very impertenant and disagreeable" when initially asked to leave), Lewis and Clark persevered (6:146). Given the distance of Fort Clatsop from any Native settlements, the order virtually assured a decrease in the interaction between the two groups. The racial curfew stands in stark contrast to the Corps' practices at Fort Mandan, where they frequently allowed overnight visitors. As the winter wore on, Native American visitors came to the compound with much less frequency, presumably put off by the Corps' rudeness. The Clatsops and Chinooks were, according to James Ronda, "accustomed to considerable freedom in dealing with white traders, [and] they could only resent the suspicion directed toward them from the fort."[85] When Lewis and Clark authored the racial curfew, they effectively undercut their own ability to gather information about the Native communities of the area.

Perhaps it was mere meteorological coincidence, but Clark declared the first day that the Corps was able to "shut the gates at Sun Set" to have been "the fairest and best we have had since our arrival at this place," even though they suffered through "three Showers" (6:146). Given the reality of his own atmospheric recordings, Clark's pronouncement concerning the day's success seems less a by-product of the weather and more a result of the Corps' newfound capacity to achieve enforceable isolation. With the boundaries between the Corps and the Clatsops blurred, Lewis and Clark became more insistent on lines of demarcation. The captains may have been wary of their men contracting venereal diseases and of pilfering, but they also believed that they needed to reinscribe presumptive hierarchies. By shutting the gates at sunset, Lewis and Clark created the illusion that they had marked off a portion of the region as U.S. territory. The racial curfew allowed the Corps to imagine that they were a normally function-ing military unit garrisoned in an unsettled environment, even as the *Jour-nal* entries from this period demonstrate just how strained their notions of inside and outside were at Fort Clatsop.

The Clatsops and their neighbors, the Chinooks, were not simply two more of the many tribes encountered by Lewis and Clark. The Clatsops had traded with fishing and commercial vessels for many years, and this exposure to European commerce had inured them to the colored beads and shiny medals the Corps of Discovery had to offer. Moreover, the Corps' transcontinental journey had exhausted the bulk of their trading stores, leaving them in the unenviable position of desperately needing favorable rates of exchange just as they found themselves interacting with Native Americans well acquainted with Euro-American manufactured commodities. Accustomed to yearly trading visits from both English and American traders, the Clatsops, Chinooks, and Tillamooks had acquired all kinds of knowledge from these annual rites of exchange. In unpacking just how attuned the Chinooks were to the trading practices of Anglo-Americans, James Ronda writes that "the Chinook trade jargon was amply filled with salty English words and phrases."[86] More than just having learned to curse, the Native Americans of the Pacific Northwest had acquired a confident knowledge of the laws of supply and demand well before the Corps arrived on the scene.

The Corps' residency at Fort Clatsop was a disappointment, not just because it signaled the inability to find a direct waterway across the West, but because it destabilized their presumptions about racial and cultural hierarchies. As the remaining barter they brought with them proves to be of little value, Lewis bemoans the fact that "we have not been able to keep anything dry for many days," blaming the "excessively great" "humidity" of the area for damaging their wares (6:169). To explain his inability to secure favorable rates of exchange, Clark declares the Clatsops "great higlers in trade" and charged them with "an avaricious all grasping dispo-sition" (6:165). While Lewis and Clark's inability to keep themselves or their possessions dry hardly positions them to attack Native American material culture, they nevertheless scorn the craft and behavior of the

Clatsops. Even as he acknowledges that the Clatsops manufacture their clothing and pattern their style of dress to suit the damp environment of the coastal region, Lewis declares that "I think the most disgusting Sight I have ever beheld is those dirty naked wenches" (6:436). While Lewis understands that the Clatsops are "obliged to be frequently in the water," a circumstance that "renders" many "articles of dress inconvenient," he still denigrates their behavior while registering how they adapt their material practices to the dictates of their environment (6:436). The disdain Lewis displays toward these habits of dress is almost unrivaled in its venom within the *Journals*, suggesting the deep-seated nature of his frustration with the situational and environmental adaptability of the Clatsops.

These negative sentiments are framed by numerous passages that record Lewis and Clark's respect for the cultural practices of the Clatsops. In many *Journal* entries, they express regard for the Clatsop baskets and the Chinook cooking vessels, containers so impermeable that they are able to "boil their fish or flesh" in them (6:215). Tribal government also elicits admiration. "The creation of a chief depends on the upright conduct of the individual," Clark writes: "his ability and disposition to render Service to the community, and his authority and deference paid him," stem from "the popularity or voluntary esteem he has acquired among the individuals of his bands, or nation" (6:223). Power is not transferred or inherited but is a matter of popular sovereignty. While Clark stops short of calling Clatsop government democratic, he notes that the tenure of chiefs is dependent on their ability to provide for the people under their care. "Their Laws," Clark observes, "like all uncivilized Indians consist of a Set of Customs which has grown out of their local Situations" (6:223). What makes these tribes uncivilized—even from Clark's retrospectively racist perspective—is hard to fathom. They build homes and band together in self-selecting political confederacies. Indeed, Clark's description of the Clatsops' government parallels Jefferson's vision of a social order governed by a communal moral sense. Instead of reflecting on how the political customs of the Clatsops might compare favorably with U.S. models, Clark retreats from his observations and reifies a Jeffersonian preconception about Native American cultural mores. At other moments during the westward movement of the Corps, Clark often moves to draw connections between Native American practices and his own sense of the frontier, but at Fort Clatsop even that measured sense of ethnographic observation seems missing. In other words, Clark denies the weight of his experiences and fails to successfully navigate a cultural divide. These abortive acts of cultural translation uneasily parallel the material shortcomings of the Corps themselves; and while the *Journals* register an appreciation for Native American material production, they stop short of overtly acknowledging how Clatsop tradition might inform the Corps' own practice.

Perhaps the most difficult act of negotiation between Lewis and Clark's field experiences and the Jeffersonian preconceptions they carry with them involves Clatsop building praxis. In January 1806, Lewis writes an extended entry on the architecture of the tribes of the Pacific Northwest. Notably, he *discovers* that Native American building techniques are superior to those which the Corps deployed in erecting Fort Clatsop. Unlike the nomads of the plains, the Clatsops and Chinooks construct dwellings larger than necessary for the present population. Made of "timber altogether," these houses, Lewis writes, "are from 14 to 20 feet wide and from 20 to 60 feet in length" and can "accommodate" several families at once (6:218). Similar in their framing to the mortise and tenon houses that Thomas Jefferson rails against in *Notes on the State of Virginia*, the Clatsops' houses are, in Lewis' words:

> constructed in the following manner; two or more posts of split timber agreeably to the number of divisions or partitions are furst provided, these are sunk in the ground at one end and rise perpendicular to the hight of 14 or 18 feet, the tops of them are hollowed in such a manner as to receive the ends of a round beam of timber which reaches from one to the other, most commonly the whole length of the building, and forming the upper part of the roof; two other sets of posts or poles are now placed at proper distances on either side of the first, formed in a similar manner and parrallel to it; these last rise to the intended hight of the eves, which is usually about 5 feet (6:218).

With this wooden skeleton of the house raised, the Clatsops then take "smaller sticks of timber" and place them "by pares in the form of rafters, resting on, and reaching from the lower to the upper horizontal beam" and "attached at either end with cedar bark" (6:219). The size of these houses demonstrates an investment in labor that underscores the Clatsop commitment to creating lasting settlements. The Clatsops, in short, conceive of their dwellings as permanent homes that root them in the landscape; as such they are almost incomparable to the rough huts of Fort Clatsop. Solving the problem that frustrated the Corps, Clatsop house builders cover their roofs "with a double range of thin boards, and an aperture of 2 by 3 feet [is] left in the center of the roof to permit the smoke to pass" (6:219). The rising warm air and smoke emanating from the sunken hearth create an updraft that prevents the rains from pouring into the room. Weatherproof and well ventilated, these houses are, as Lewis clearly understands, everything that Fort Clatsop is not.[87]

Although one massive hall, built in the Clatsop manner, might have been more functional for the Corps than the huts of Fort Clatsop, Lewis and Clark held fast to customary design and belief. The captains' desire to architecturally frame notions of hierarchy by dividing public from private space reflects the same impulse that led them to establish the racial curfew. By walling off their private space from their enlisted men and by barricading U.S. "territory" from the surrounding wilderness, Lewis and Clark sought to embody within the frame of Fort Clatsop a semblance of federal authority. Perhaps, realizing how their situation curtailed their ability to construct that authority, the Corps chose to hold fast to artificial boundaries. Such a decision would explain why they limited their exploration of the surrounding area, as if their alienation from the environment caused them to feel secure only within the confines of Fort Clatsop. As they navigated between Jeffersonian preconceptions and their own experiences at Cape Disappointment, Lewis and Clark became poignantly aware of the fragility of their endeavor, and this realization only fueled their desire to "proceed on" once again.

In preparation for their departure, the Corps begin mending their goods and seeking to procure additional canoes from the Clatsops. For the cost of Lewis' "uniform laced coat and nearly half a carrot of tobacco," Sergeant Pryor is able to purchase one canoe (6:426). Lewis' anger over the high cost of this canoe is only exasperated by the Corps' dire need for more than just one, a situation complicated by the realization that they have almost nothing left to barter. Faced with this dilemma, Lewis and Clark decide to "take one from them in lue of the six Elk which they stole from us in the winter" (6:426).[88] Lewis and Clark justify their larceny by rewriting the expedition's history, suggesting that the theft of six elk, which were left behind by one of the men after a hunt on 6 February 1806, entitles the Corps to a canoe. What this accounting leaves out is the fact that a Clatsop chief made restitution by giving the Corps three dogs as payment on 12 February 1806. By invoking the privilege of selective memory, Lewis and Clark forget that they have already been remunerated for the theft. The incident is further indication of the difference between the relationship the Corps has with the Clatsops and the one they had with the Mandans; during their joint buffalo hunts with the Mandans, the Corps came to accept that any animal not immediately claimed by a hunter was going to be treated as free and unclaimed game.[89] Even if Lewis and Clark do not equate three dogs with six elk, their actions display an utter lack of patience with the Corps' manufacturing skills and a strong desire to finally proceed on from the Pacific Coast.

"Altho' we have not fared sumptuously this winter & spring at Fort Clatsop," Clark writes on 20 March 1806, "we have lived quite as comfortably as we had any reason to expect we should" (6:442). Having accomplished "every object which induced our remaining at this place except of meeting with the traders who visit the entrance of this river," the Corps prepares to depart (6:442). Curiously, after noting that many of "our men are still complaining of being unwell," Clark predicts that the start of the journey will heal the sick, for movement "has always had that effect on us heretofore" (6:442). Clark's sense that continual physical exertion will make the unwell healthy also suggests that the Corps functioned better when they acted within the clearly defined roles of exploration. In motion, they were explorers traveling through foreign territory, reassured by their rootlessness that their home lay elsewhere. At Fort Clatsop they were stationary, laboring as builders, traders, and hunters, like the tribes from which they wished to differentiate themselves. In stasis, they were also forced to acknowledge—even if only as a muted undercurrent within the *Journals*—that the Native Americans they encountered were far more skilled than the Corps at occupying all those subject positions.

Prior to abandoning the fort, Lewis records with some pride that the Corps has made a bequest of "our houses and furniture" to the chief who has been "much more kind and hospitable to us than any other in the neighborhood" (6:444). A courteous gesture, certainly, but one of relatively little value; it is hard to imagine that the Clatsops would have had much use for the ramshackle fort, built—after all—from remnants of their own abandoned houses. Given the superiority of the Clatsop artisans and woodworkers, the Corps' detritus probably had even less appeal than Lewis is able to imperially project. Indeed, Lewis appears to be laboring to make a virtue of necessity. By casting the Corps as gift givers, Lewis reasserts the racial hierarchies that the Clatsop experience has unsettled, somehow trying to promote the Corps' abilities over and against the material evidence. As settlers, as house builders, the Corps of Discovery could no longer operate as a military expedition, particularly since they had fulfilled their charge. While in residence at Fort Clatsop the Corps ceased being explorers and became instead isolationists; as they broke camp, they were filled with hope that they would soon return to terrain where they felt more comfortably orientated.

William Cronon has argued that our received conception of wilderness as "the natural, unfallen antithesis of an unnatural civilization that has lost its soul" is tautological.[90] A "dream of an unworked natural landscape," Cronon maintains, "is very much the fantasy of people who have never themselves had to work the land to make a living."[91] The unraveling of the dream of a self-yielding earth reoccurs across Bartram's *Travels*, Brown's novels, and the Corps' *Journals*, as each text accounts for how the question of settlement demystifies any operant preconceptions post-Revolutionary Americans might have about the wilderness as a blank slate. At Fort Clatsop, the Corps has to work the land if they are to survive, and the change in subject position (from explorer to settler) unnerves them. As soon as an inkling of spring arrived, the Corps is anxious to proceed on. The Clatsops advise against a hasty departure, knowing that the deep snows have yet to melt and that the still-blocked passes through the mountains will prohibit the Corps' movement back east. But Lewis and Clark refuse to heed their warnings. They are "determined," Lewis writes on 22 March 1806, "to set out" regardless of the atmospheric conditions. Unfortunately for the Corps, they fail yet again in the art of waterproofing. Lewis ends his journal entry for the twenty-second by noting that they will "stop the canoes temporarily with Mud and halt at the first fair day and pay [repair] them" (6:444).

3

"Home Bred Virtues and Local Attachments"

New York and the Evolution of the American Home

Washington Irving ventured to England in 1815 to help his brother Peter manage the trading firm of P. & E. Irving and Company. The War of 1812 had disrupted the transatlantic flow of commerce, but Peter Irving assumed that peace would reignite the American appetite for foreign luxury items. Undeterred by the obvious instabilities of the postwar economies of both England and America, Peter optimistically began using credit to purchase vast quantities of merchandise. For his own part, Washington Irving was equally sanguine, writing to his friend Henry Brevoort on 23 August 1815 that "our business I trust will be very *good*—it certainly will be very *great*, this year, and will give us credit, if not profit."[1] Unfortunately, the brothers' shared hopes for the restoration of a thriving transatlantic trade were ill-founded. Peter sorely misjudged the American marketplace, in large part because he failed to account for how the virtual suspension of international commerce had hastened the development of native U.S. industries.[2] In the midst of these restless fluctuations, Peter kept purchasing merchandise without realizing any returns, hoping against hope, like so many of his fellow merchants, that one stroke of luck would changes his fortunes. Throwing good money after bad, Peter only made the problem worse. "It was my lot," Washington Irving was to observe years later, "almost on landing in Europe, to experience a reverse in fortune, which cast me down in spirit, and altered the whole tenor of my life."[3]

The enthusiasm that had buoyed Washington Irving on his move to Liverpool rapidly vanished as he realized the ramifications of Peter's overly confident speculations, and "the humiliation of the firm's failure," as Stanley T. Williams observes, "lacerated him."[4] Despondent and depressed after the firm declared bankruptcy in 1818, Irving decided "to return to my pen, not so much for support, for bread & water had no terrors for me, but to reinstate myself in the worlds thoughts—to raise myself from the degradation into which I considered myself fallen."[5] The collapse of P. & E. Irving effectively, as Jeffrey Rubin-Dorsky notes, "forced" Irving "to confront the issue he had been avoiding since the publication of *Knickerbocker's History of New York* in 1809: could he risk declaring himself a professional author and succeed where no American previously had?"[6] Irving's life—and in particular his decision to return to writing as a career—has been overly sentimentalized, a trend fueled by Irving's own romanticized history of the construction of *The Sketch Book of Geoffrey Crayon, Gent.* (1819).[7] Far from being a "diffident tourist" traveling across England to satiate "his fancy for aristocratic culture amidst the finery of the Old World," as Rubin-Dorsky suggests, Irving was actually a disillusioned businessman intent on recouping his losses.[8]

Irving's move to England was about risk and the public sphere from the outset, and his decision to market his writing instead of dry goods signals more of a change in commodities than one of purpose. *The Sketch Book* is fully informed by what Irving learned about supply and demand, a series of lessons that taught him the utility of having a firm grasp of your audience before putting a product before the public. Andrew Jackson's victory at New Orleans, against the very same British regiments that had defeated Napoleon, spawned a previously unseen nationalist fervor across the United States; many Americans viewed the battle as a watershed that confirmed the nation's prowess and sense of purpose.[9] This nativist isolationism, which Peter Irving had not accounted for, informed the rejection of British manufactured goods, and Washington was determined not to replicate his brother's mistakes. Far from being a politically disengaged text, *The Sketch Book* addresses the problems engendered by this restless nationalism head-on, seeking to reestablish bonds of association between the United States and England to ensure a transatlantic audience for the volume. Rampant speculation and rootlessness had caused the collapse of P. & E. Irving, and *The Sketch Book* redresses these systemic problems by fabricating a tradition of commonality. By marking a series of domestic customs as the foundation of English history and culture, Irving creates a blueprint for Americans to adopt and adapt them for the construction of their own cultural forms. In *The Sketch Book*, Irving argues that England and America are imagined communities constructed, in Benedict Anderson's terms, for specific political and social ends.[10] This figuration of community serves to place the United States on a par with its European precursors in terms of cultural production.

Recent critical treatments of *The Sketch Book* have focused more directly on the ways in which Irving's experiences as a failed speculator affected the collection. In considering "the twin specters of credit and debit" that haunt *The Sketch Book*, David Anthony argues that the volume offers a nostalgic retreat to "a period predating the modern period of commerce and credit."[11] In examining how Irving reconciled his sketches to suit the tastes of both English and American audiences, Alice Hiller proposes that rather than become "politicized or radical" after his own bankruptcy, Irving sought to "deny" the "traumas" of "the post-war economic climate" by portraying only "picturesque and unthreatening characters, who felt only goodwill towards America, unlike the bankers and merchants reluctant to help out the struggling Irving firm."[12] Reading *The Sketch Book* through the lens of postcolonial theory, Richard V. McLamore proposes that the volume encodes Irving's attempt to consider how "culturally transmitted resources" conjoin to "form images of a *possible* cultural identity that could transcend stringently defined political, economic, or cultural boundaries."[13] Defending Irving against long-standing charges of "genuflection before the altar of English tradition," Bryce Traister contends that "Geoffrey Crayon can be viewed as something of an imperializing tourist, whose genteel designations of 'authentic' English identity announce that a lowly American possesses sufficient cultural authority to both criticize and idealize English society."[14] Each of these critics emphasizes the importance of reading *The Sketch Book* in the context of Irving's complex biographical history. In so doing, they highlight how Irving's nostalgic construction of an imagined England advances the overall argument of the volume. Building upon these critical foundations, this chapter maps how *The Sketch Book* counterbalances postwar restlessness by inventing traditions that bridge the supposed transatlantic divide.[15]

Irving's strategic deployment of nostalgia does not necessarily indicate a retreat from an engagement with contemporary cultural concerns. Within *The Sketch Book*, Irving seems less invested in denying traumas or retreating from sociopolitical contexts and more concerned with rescripting them. He does so narratively, by adumbrating a set of traditions and practices that will anchor community development despite the fluctuations of transatlantic trade. In his intriguing article "Irving's Posterity," Michael Warner suggests, "anachronism is the contradictory apprehension of history through which Irving attempts to remediate modernity."[16] Following the line of Warner's argument, Irving seeks to reconcile the present to the past by fictionalizing history, folding past disruptions into a generative narrative that allows him to create an England that is not exceedingly different from America. Rather than figuring Irving as denying the traumas he encountered, we might more profitably consider his articulation of how domestic practices offer a buffer against the precariousness of transatlantic trade. In an effort to reduce the differences between these two imagined communities, Irving harks back to a style and a subject matter that predates the political divide of England and America. In one of the harshest reviews of *The Sketch Book*, William Hazlitt describes Irving's writings as "literary *anachronisms*."[17] Hazlitt dismisses Irving as an incompetent imitator of eighteenth-century prose because of his inability to represent the realities of early-nineteenth-century England. Ridiculing Irving for naively interpreting the social world before him, Hazlitt disregards the possibility that Irving's style is a strategic choice.[18] By imitating eighteenth-century English writers, Irving replicates a narrative voice that represents an agrarian social order that had more in common with Irving's Republic than with industrial England, and Irving's pointed borrowing of these styles and concerns allows him to circumnavigate the transatlantic divides posited by later generations of writers.

From the outset of the volume, Irving demonstrates how the cultural order of England resides in its vernacular architecture, a tactic which implies that Americans could replicate the same structural environment within the United States. In essence, Irving employs a nostalgic gaze not to avoid the complexities of his own cultural context but rather to highlight areas of commonality between the two nations. Instead of cataloging the usual litany of ruins and monuments one would expect of a tourist on a European grand tour, *The Sketch Book* indexes architectural sites that could easily be located on either side of the Atlantic. In "The Author's Account of Himself," Irving casts Geoffrey Crayon as a restless wanderer. More than a mere "lover of fine scenery," abundant in America, Crayon seeks "the charms of storied and poetical association."[19] He hopes "to tread," in Europe, "in the footsteps of antiquity—to loiter about the ruined castle—to meditate on the falling tower—to escape in short, from the commonplace realities of the present, and lose [him]self among the shadowy grandeurs of the past" (9). Yet in the volume that follows, Crayon pays little attention to ruins and monuments. By avoiding architectural markers of difference, Crayon foregrounds a structural landscape of similarity. Following his "idle humour" away "from the great objects studied by every regular traveler," Crayon creates a book "crowded with cottages" rather than with monuments and shrines (9–10). Conventionally, nineteenth-century European travelers figured the westward transatlantic crossing as a startling journey from a highly developed structural environment to a primitive one. Crayon deflates this cliché by reversing its terms: the prospect of entering "the land of promise" exhilarates Crayon as he approaches England (14). Reconnoitering the shoreline for signs of a human presence, Crayon recounts how his eye fell "with delight on neat cottages with their trim shrubberies and green grass plots" (14). The site of humble cottages and not storied ruins greets Crayon upon his arrival in England, and his gaze remains fixed on houses as he undertakes his tour.[20]

Continuing to demonstrate the commonality between the two nations, Crayon roots British character in nature, effectively countering restlessness by planting national cultural firmly in domesticated landscapes. In England, Crayon notes, "even the inhabitants of cities born and brought up among brick walls and bustling streets, enter with facility into rural habits and evince a tact for rural occupation" (50). Operating from this premise, Crayon adopts a rationale to "go forth into the country" to understand England. Such a practice parallels the strategies of a host of European tourists who traveled to the United States and sketched the American character. To best understand America, ethnographers on both sides of the Atlantic advocated that a visitor must experience its farmhouses and frontiers, a literary trope dating back at least to J. Hector St. John de Crèvecoeur's *Letters from an American Farmer*.[21] Crayon turns that injunction around in his attempt to grasp English life, anachronistically turning away from the rootlessness of modernity by retreating into rural landscapes. By clouding the reported dissimilarities between English and American citizens, Crayon moves to remodel cultural development by providing an alternative to the hustle and flow of unreasoned expansion. "The rudest habitation; the most unpromising and scanty portion of land," Crayon writes, "in the hands of an Englishman of taste, becomes a little paradise" (52). Praising the English for this practice, Crayon promotes constant cultivation as a source of social stability. Instead of readily converting the natural into disposable products, Americans should commit themselves to the labor of rooted domestication. Paradise is to be found not by lighting out for the territories, but by properly tending to the garden one already inhabits.

The attention to landscaping, Crayon argues in "Rural Life in England," creates social stability by promoting community. An attachment to the land breeds associations between the classes. "Rural occupation" may be "simple and rough," but it is never "vulgar"; "the man of refinement, therefore, finds nothing revolting in an intercourse with the lower orders in rural life" (53). "The great charm," Crayon notes, "of English scenery is the moral feeling that seems to pervade it" (54). This custom leads to the "hereditary transmission of home bred virtues and local attachments" (54). By viewing nature in more than just utilitarian terms, the English appear less restless than Americans. The "sweet home feeling" pervading the English countryside results not from the rigidity of development but from how the English view landscapes and buildings as capable of being redefined by the present population (54). In each successive generation, the English reaffirm their connection to local nature by intimately involving their environment in their lives. By refashioning their relationship with buildings and with nature, Americans, Irving implies, could create the same enduring regional attachments. Instead of relying on the ceaseless fluctuations of the marketplace to forge their identities, Irving advocates the idea that Americans could secure a better cultural foundation in the domestic residences already dotting the nation's landscape.

Crayon stresses that a generational attachment to the landscape does not overly determine social behavior. Indeed, individual taste and style flourish within a historical context. Residual architecture does not constrain the present population but functions as a fluid source of connection. A staid monument can be expressive of contemporary needs and desires. Crayon vows, for example, that even an "antiquated" parsonage has been "repaired and altered in the tastes of various ages and occupants" (54). Crayon employs architecture as a register of the flexibility that occurs naturally when individuals commit themselves, and their progeny, to a particular region. The past does not need to be demolished or abandoned, for Crayon demonstrates how his contemporaries can easily remodel their structural inheritances to suit their present needs. The continual occupation of a region is made possible by the regenerative power of architecture; since buildings are imagined as adaptable, they repeatedly reroot inhabitants to the spaces they inhabit. Ruins do not constrain the development of social order; rather, Crayon celebrates how the plasticity of vernacular structures enhances social equilibrium.

Crayon continues to question the effects of the structural environment on character development in the "Christmas" section of *The Sketch Book*. While tradition appears "obliterated by modern fashion," Crayon discovers that customs still linger like "picturesque morsels of Gothic architecture" in rural districts (148). "Partly dilapidated by the waste of ages," Crayon writes, "and partly lost in the additions and alterations of latter days," these domestic customs live on (148). Metaphorically linking architecture to cultural practice, Crayon implies that neither functions as a rigid systematizing influence. In Britain buildings appear capable of being reinvented by their inhabitants so as to reposition their meaning. Because they are able to redefine the meanings of structures, the English treat their inherited environment as mutable rather than constricting. Crayon challenges the notion that Americans lack the historic grounding of Europe by portraying how English ancestral habits have been reinterpreted to meet the demands of the present. The fusion of architecture with cultural practice indicates by inference that ancient piles provide only the illusion of history; because history is understood to be a narrative, the present, and not past, occupants of these buildings construct there meanings.

The importance of being able to redevelop and sustain previous architectural constructions is a theme that dominates the "Christmas" section of *The Sketch Book*. By rooting holiday traditions within the frame of the house, Irving explores how domestic architecture shapes cultural practice. In England the Christmas season calls for a return to "the paternal hearth" by "the children of a family, who have launched forth in life, and wandered widely asunder" (149). English children, like their republican cousins, leave their birthplace; the holiday allows them, as it might Americans, to return home. Centered in the home, the holiday functions as a celebration of communal connection, an occasion for everyone to recall the importance of the domestic. In *Christmas in America: A History*, Penne L. Restad displays how the American post-Revolutionary calendar was bereft of holidays, with few communities even officially recognizing Christmas, Thanksgiving (outside New England), or New Year's Day.[22] Restad unwraps how Irving was among the first American authors to write extensively about a particular holiday, leading her to conclude that Irving saw in Christmas "the potential to bind society together and to provide an antidote to the ills of modern society."[23] Shared holiday traditions, for Irving, served to reify kinship connections and other domestic traditions.

At the heart of the "Christmas" section resides Bracebridge Hall, the edifice that Irving deploys to prove the benefits of an invented tradition. "An irregular building of some magnitude," Bracebridge Hall seems to be composed "of the architecture of different periods" (161). With elements that are both "evidently very ancient" and with "the rest of the house in the French taste of Charles the Second's time," the estate is an architectural mosaic (162). Crayon echoes this external feature by noting how the interior decorations are equally comprised of random bits and pieces. While Squire Bracebridge claims that the paintings and armor on display are the cherished possessions of an ancestral crusader, they in fact bear "the stamp of more recent days" (181). Not an heirloom, the armor was actually found "in a lumber room" and subsequently "elevated to its present situation" by the squire (181). At Bracebridge Hall, and by implication in all England, historical authenticity exists as barley more than a carefully manufactured illusion. Squire Bracebridge did not inherit a storied history, so he invented one to suit his need for a domestic history. Overall, the "Christmas" section of *The Sketch Book* proves the benefits of imagining that the domestic narrative roots cultural development because of its adaptability. Bracebridge is not restricted by the binding decisions of previous authors or architects; rather he proves that simply by having an expansive imagination, one can adapt the works of the past to serve contemporary needs.

The question of architectural adaptability dwells at the heart of two of *The Sketch Book*'s most famous American tales. "Rip Van Winkle" and "The Legend of Sleepy Hollow" have been read consistently as nostalgic celebrations of the social traditions of pre-Revolutionary America.[24] Almost always considered as solitary productions and rarely figured as informed by their original publication contexts, they have been regarded as registers of the restlessness of the early national period. Impatience flows through the center of each tale, but it is important to note that these tales are meditations on *post*-Revolutionary American society. Moreover, all too often readers submerge the original textual setting of these tales; reading them against *The Sketch Book*'s overall concern with architecture and domesticity provides a very different frame for understanding Irving's preoccupation with houses as he considers the consequences of rampant rootlessness on national development.[25]

In *The Sketch Book*, Crayon claims that "Rip Van Winkle" was "found among the papers of the late Diedrich Knickerbocker," an ethnographer of Dutch traditions (28). Crayon introduces "Rip" by calling attention to the emblematic status of domesticity. Crayon writes that whenever Knickerbocker's research led him to a Dutch family, "snugly shut up in its low roofed farm house," Knickerbocker studied both house and family "with the zeal of a bookworm" (28). By reading houses and their occupants as texts, Knickerbocker created, with "scrupulous accuracy," a "history of the province" (28). Knickerbocker's "historical researches" were not "so much among books, as among men," for it was amid the inheritors of tradition, among those who still lived within the frames built by the past, that he found "true history" (28). The inclusion of Knickerbocker allows Irving to have Crayon create a meta-narrative within his text, a narrative disjunct that both testifies to and authorizes the idea of reading houses in order to register cultural stability.

Many critics have read "Rip Van Winkle" as a sentimental meditation on the costs of the Revolution, yet as Jay Fliegelman notes, "Irving's tale in its stress on domestic politics is more historically acute than has perhaps been realized."[26] One of the most curious threads in "Rip Van Winkle" is that all the figures of the tale's earlier period are duplicated in the world of the Republic. Indeed, Rip Van Winkle seems much happier after his wife's death than he was when living under her "petticoat government" (40). After the initial shock of his readjustment wears off, Rip quickly resumes "his old walks and habits" and is revered as "one of the patriarchs of the village" (40). Mourning any of Rip's "former cronies" appears pointless, for they all have their post-Revolutionary proxy. Just as King George has been replaced—locally, by a few strokes of the sign painter's brush—by General Washington, Rip's "termagant wife" mirrors the "bilious" and "haranguing" orator presiding over the election (30, 37). Mr. Doolittle echoes Nicholaus Vedder as the silent patriarch of the town's public lodging. Rip's daughter, Judith Gardenier, radiates the same generosity of spirit that Rip's female neighbors do before the war. Young Rip shabbily stands as a "precise counterpart of" his father (38). This continual doubling proves that both social structures easily accommodate divergent personalities. As Richard V. McLamore suggests, the villagers can reembrace Rip because he symbolizes "family relationships and [a] noncommercial heritage," traditions they elect to cling to despite "the 'self-importance' of the political culture in the early United States."[27] Substantial changes do occur in the village, as its built environment undergoes a more lasting transformation than the shift in political orders appears to have wrought. In recording these architectural changes Knickerbocker registers a profound sense of loss, and it is this final melancholic turn that contains the heart of Irving's mediation on post-Revolutionary life.

The pre-Revolutionary village, founded by Dutch colonists, still contained "some of the houses of the original settlers," which had been "built of small yellow bricks from Holland" with "latticed windows and gable fronts" (29). "In one of these very houses" (albeit one "sadly time worn and weather beaten") Rip lived prior to his twenty-year slumber (29). Rip reawakens to discover that the "very village" is "altered," for not only is it "larger and more populous," but there are rows of houses he has "never seen before, and those which had been his familiar haunts" have "disappeared" (36). Elsewhere in *The Sketch Book* Crayon figures the strength of English rural customs as stemming from their situational adaptability. Sadly, no such architectural preservation has occurred in the post-Revolutionary United States. Even Rip's "old resort, the village inn," has been demolished and replaced by a "large, rickety wooden building" with "great gaping windows, some of them broken, and mended with old hats and petticoats" (37). In their desire to remake their environment, to formulate a more democratic architectural aesthetic, the villagers have neglected their inheritance. Steve Blakemore advances that the deterioration of the Union Hotel reflects the dilapidated state of Rip's own home, and that this mirroring suggests that within "Rip Van Winkle" change "is merely superficial and that (sub)versive repetition is really the story's secret theme."[28] Blakemore's focus on Irving's use of architecture as a measure of cultural change misfires because he neglects the melancholic tone by which Irving figures the differences between the pre- and post-Revolutionary environments. The fact that the ramshackle Union Hotel replaced the rustic inn of the past as the village center unsettles any reading that promulgates the idea that nothing has changed since the Revolution. Even Rip's own home emerges in worse shape after the war, but more importantly the public house at the village's center has gone from a site of fixity to a decrepit structure, a transformation that dramatically registers a sense of loss. As Robert Ferguson argues concerning the world Rip reawakens to find, "because they believe that they have created a new world, the first citizens in the new nation dismiss the immediate past and everyone associated with it."[29] Indeed, more tragic than just dismissing history, these first citizens actively labor to overwrite and demolish previously treasured legacies.

The villagers' attitude toward their shaped environment even caused them to reduce "the great tree, that used to shelter the quiet little Dutch inn of yore" into a Liberty Pole, "a tall naked" staff bearing a "fluttering flag on which was a singular assemblage of stars and stripes" (37). Thus the very symbol of the post-Revolutionary comes at significant cost to the town's natural environment. The new residents of Rip's old village destroy their past, unveiling a troubling attitude toward the nation's structural history. Gathered to hear an anonymous orator trumpet nameless "heroes of seventy six," the villagers have forgotten their own immediate connections to the past (37). When Rip asks the whereabouts of several of his contemporaries, who (unknown to Rip) left the village to serve in the war, the crowd cannot give him any answers. Rip eventually does learn that the venerable Nicholaus Vedder, the former patriarch of the village during Rip's day, has died and been memorialized with a "wooden tombstone," so neglected that it has almost completely "rotted" away (38). The republican villagers seem to have a quite distant relationship to their own immediate, regional history. Rather than commemorating the specific accomplishments of local inhabitants, creating ironclad markers of their contributions, they have folded the deeds of the village's former inhabitants into a faceless national narrative. The nation of the future appears, Knickerbocker implies, too caught up in the present. Whereas their ancestors had imported bricks from Holland, literally to cement their connections to the past, in the short course of twenty years the newly minted citizens of the United States have abandoned their forefathers. They make no effort to curate their history, and in their rush for architectural change they undertake no efforts of preservation or maintenance.

Knickerbocker's other American tale, "The Legend of Sleepy Hollow," was originally positioned as the concluding tale of *The Sketch Book*.[30] Far from complementing Rip Van Winkle, Ichabod Crane directly threatens the stability of Tarrytown. Rip's circulation (in both time periods) finds him working to shore up or restore community, even to his own detriment. Crane moves only to procure superfluities, traveling far and wide to swallow "a supernumerary dish of cakes or sweetmeats" (276). Noting that Crane's mouth has all the "dilating powers of an Anaconda," Knickerbocker regards him as a snake in the garden (275). As Michael Warner, David Greven, and David Anthony have recently argued, Crayon's presentation of Crane in "The Legend of Sleepy Hollow" reverberates with early-nineteenth-century questions about masculinity and identity construction.[31] Collectively, these essays offer some of the most suggestive readings of "The Legend of Sleepy Hollow" (particularly Warner's) in some time. In their focus on how Crane's masculinity encodes Irving's bachelorhood, these essays read the presentation of the conflict between Brom Bones and Crane as the most important element in the tale. While I find these readings informative, my own interest in "Sleepy Hollow" resides in how it continues to consider how domestic structures inform community construction.

A Connecticut Yankee in New York, Crane has no historic attachments to the landscape. Knickerbocker stresses Crane's rootlessness by noting both his *foreign* birth and his itinerant status; many, he writes, have easily "mistaken him for the genius of famine descending upon the earth" (274). Crane's financial dependence keeps him moving from one farmer's house to another's, and this constant mobility blinds him to the benefits of association. Because he cannot see the possibility of collaboration, Crane willingly believes that "all the witches in the country" turned his schoolhouse "topsy-turvy," rather than realizing that Brom and his comrades were responsible (283). Knickerbocker's exacting, detailed description of the schoolhouse, designed by the architect "Yost Van Houten," notes that the "low-building of one large room, rudely constructed of logs," was secured by limiting access to its interior (274). "A withe twisted in the handle of the door, and stakes set against the window shutters," prevent any thief from leaving the building even as he might "get in with perfect ease" (274). Knickerbocker assumes that Houten "borrowed" the design "from the mystery of the eelpot" (274). Contrived to trap eels that swam into them, eel pots allowed easy admission but prevented the possibility of escape. The design of Houten's security system, however, thwarts only an individual thief; anyone with an accomplice outside the building could easily overcome the design. When Crane discovers that his schoolhouse has been vandalized, he assumes that only a supernatural agent could be responsible. Conversely, the villagers all know that when "any mad prank, or rustic brawl," occurs in the vicinity. "Brom Bones and his gang" are invariably the culprits (282). Crane fails to comprehend that his rival would have partners in his mischief making. His blindness to the possibilities of community leaves him unprepared to interpret the clues offered by the architectural design of the schoolhouse.

Crane's attraction to Katrina Van Tassel also demonstrates his lack of interest in fostering civic association. Old Baltus Van Tassel imagines his house as a site for communal pleasure. His only line of dialog is a "pressing invitation" to his myriad guests that they should "fall to, and help themselves" (287). Comparatively, Crane dreams that his "inheritance" of the Van Tassel property—after Katrina marries him—will allow him to "snap his fingers in the face" of any "niggardly patron," and kick "out of doors" anyone "that should dare to call him comrade!" (287). His affection for Katrina grows after he has "visited her paternal mansion," for "his imagination expanded with the idea" that the Van Tassel "domains" might "be readily turned into cash, and the money invested in immense tracts of wild land, and shingle palaces in the wilderness" (279). For Crane, the picturesque lands of the Hudson River Valley exist only as an opportunity to cat-alog "sweet thoughts and 'sugared suppositions'" (286).

As Knickerbocker suggests, and as Crayon argues throughout *The Sketch Book*, "local tales and superstitions thrive best in these sheltered, long settled retreats" and are "trampled under foot, by the shifting throng that forms the population of most of our country places" (289). This rest-lessness imperils more than just legends; local customs and connections are endangered by those seeking to commodify nature. If Crane takes pos-session of the Van Tassel home he will carve it up into saleable parcels. In essence, Crane longs to take what has functioned as a communal gathering place and transform it into subdivisions. If he becomes "the lord of all" the Van Tassel property, the disease of social mobility, coursing through Crane's veins, will infect the town and drastically alter its history (289). Knickerbocker's comic disdain for Crane also registers his distaste for fig-uring that the parts are more valuable than the whole.

Van Tassel's estate promotes social stability by housing local history and legend. Under Van Tassel's roof, the community gathers to share stories of Revolutionary history, as farmers embellish their actions till each is "per-suaded that he had a considerable hand in bringing the war to a happy ter-mination" (289). Unlike the amnesiac villagers Rip awakens to discover, Van Tassel's home and his hospitality ground the community in its history. Knickerbocker's pronouncement that in the "little retired Dutch valleys" of New York "population, manners, and customs, remain fixed" describes the actions and narratives of Van Tassel's guests. Crane's ambition omi-nously threatens the dissolution of that stability.

Rejected by Katrina, the "desolate and chopfallen" Crane leaves the Van Tassel home "with the air of one who had been sacking a hen roost" (291). But this humiliation bears little responsibility for removing the dan-ger from the community. Rather, the resurgence of local legend hastens Crane's departure. Whether Brom Bones or the apparition of the Headless Horseman chase Crane hardly matters, for they signify the same thing. Either Brom adopts the guise of a local legend, or the ghost reappears to protect the village from dissolution. History is invoked to drive away the harbinger of change. David Greven notes how immediately upon Crane's disappearance the community performs a "ritualistic blaze of cleansing," burning all his abandoned possessions seemingly in the hopes of annihilat-ing any trace of his existence.[32] Since Crane has no real connections to the community, its members appear unconcerned about the fact that he has simply vanished. Crane embodies, as David Anthony writes, "a kind of radical alterity, one that represents a theft of enjoyment—a way of life—to both Sleepy Hollow and to 1819 America more generally"; his expulsion from the town ensures the survival of the older order that Van Tassel and his farmhouse represent.[33]

Crayon's inclusion of these American tales in *The Sketch Book* allows him to explore the prospects of American social development in the context of rural English culture. The practices toward nature and architecture Crayon admires in the English, he implies, can easily be transported to the United States. In both "Rip Van Winkle" and "The Legend of Sleepy Hollow," architectural and cultural traditions anchor cultural life. Irving argues that by preserving rural history, through the fruitful readaptation of previous built structures and practices, Americans have the opportunity to establish rooted and stable communities. Irving continued to explore the connections between domestic architecture and community formation (both the construction and preservation of local and national histories) across the length of his career, but perhaps most explicitly embraced these themes when he returned to the United States and began to undertake the construction of his own home.

Washington Irving returned to New York from his lengthy European stay as a conquering hero in 1832. The international success of *The Sketch Book* had more than restored the financial losses caused by the collapse of P. & E. Irving, and transformed Irving into the most prominent American author of the Jacksonian Era. Immediately upon his arrival, Irving was feted by the social and political elite of the nation. A series of seemingly endless dinners was held in his honor, culminating in a public ball hosted by the City of New York. "The return of Geoffrey Crayon," Philip Hone observed, "has made old times and the associations of early life the leading topics of conversation."[34] Hone was far from alone in blurring Irving's identity with those of his creations; and, indeed, Irving's shock upon his return caused him to be as bewildered by his native city as the reawakened Rip Van Winkle was by his. In very little time, Irving realized, New York had become a vastly different city.

After a seventeen-year absence, Irving was filled with misgivings about what New York had become. "I would fancy myself arrived in my native city, but the place would be so changed that I would not recognize it," Irving wrote in his 1835 preface to *A Tour of the Prairies*. As he first "stepped upon land," Irving's apprehensions were confirmed because as he "passed through places that ought to have been familiar" he found "all were changed." The structural landscape of the city had altered. "Huge edifices and lofty piles had sprung up in the place of lowly tenements," Irving observed; "the old landmarks of the city were gone; the very streets altered." Stunned, Irving suffered the "saddening conviction" that he was "a stranger in my own home!" Irving had left New York in 1815, and by 1832 the city had indeed become a "splendid metropolis." In the intervening years the Erie Canal had assured the city's economic supremacy, and Irving returned to a dramatically altered landscape. New York "had outgrown my recollection from its very prosperity," Irving noted, "and

strangers had crowded into it from every clime to participate in its over-
flowing abundance."[35]

As Christopher Mulvey argues, most antebellum British travelers were
as "knowledgeable about America as they were about Fairyland."[36] While
the American mind might have possessed, in the words of Henry James, a
"latent preparedness" for England, the reverse was certainly not true: thus
"the Englishman was, then, more bewildered by America than the American by England."[37] Irving had left a colonial city and returned to find a
rapidly expanded economic capital captivated by pretensions of becoming
a metropole. European travelers, however, generally regarded New York's
claims to being the most European of American cities as naive and preten-
tious. All too often, European travelers failed to account for how varying
social systems inevitably generated different architectural schemes. No
palaces would ever be built in New York, because there was no aristocracy
to inhabit them. Instead of trying to compare the houses of each nation's
emerging capitalist elite, Europeans sought more residual frames of reference and looked for aristocratic mansions when they read New York's
structural environment.[38] They compared grand republican homes with
feudal estates, and not with bourgeois English homes. Irving's experience
was quite different. While he had not witnessed the city's growth from
seed to sapling, he could recognized finite changes. Moreover, as Irving
had argued throughout *The Sketch Book*, English pride in the historical
density of its structural and cultural landscapes masked the fact that they
were founded by acts of imagination. Upon his return to New York, Irving
began to plan the purchase and design of a home of his own, and as he
undertook this project he recalled his early experiences in England, particularly the visit he had paid to Sir Walter Scott's house in 1817 during the
period in which he was beginning to plan *The Sketch Book*. In *Abbotsford*
(1835), Irving's reflections on Scott's domestic life, Irving continued his
deconstruction of the myths attached to Europe's historic homes.

II

Irving's *Abbotsford* represents two important moments in his career. The
sketch describes a journey Irving undertook after the collapse of P. & E.
Irving and during the period in which he turned to writing to dig himself
out of financial ruin. He drafted and published *Abbotsford*, his recollection
of this experience, after his triumphant return to the United States, and in
the midst of his plans to build a new home for himself. The narrative's
connection to these two flash points makes it an interesting record of Irving's evolving sense of the prospects for American domestic architecture.
Within the text, Irving offers portraits of Scott and Abbotsford, while

simultaneously indexing the possibilities of attaching storied sensibilities to the domestic sphere. The connections between Scott and Irving are well known and are perhaps best summarized by Alice Hiller, who notes how Irving "viewed Scott as a professional role model as well as an exemplary friend and father figure."[39] While much critical attention has been paid to Scott's influence on Irving's writing career, very little consideration has been afforded to Irving's portrait of Scott's domestic life.

As Irving tried to hatch his embryonic plans for *The Sketch Book*, he traveled to Scotland in 1817 intending to gather material for his projected volume but, more importantly, to meet Francis Jeffery, the editor of the *Edinburgh Review*, and Sir Walter Scott, the internationally renowned author of the Waverly novels. After spending some time in Edinburgh with Jeffery and his circle, Irving made his pilgrimage to the "mighty minstrel of the north."[40] Irving arrived at Scott's estate bearing letters of introduction on 30 of August 1817 and stayed for several days. Scott's hospitality and his admiration for *A History of New York* (1809) raised Irving's wilting spirits. By the time Irving drafted his sketch of Scott for publication in 1834, his own popularity nearly equaled that of his subject's. Returning to America in late May 1832—after a seventeen-year absence— Irving was crowned with numerous civic laurels. America embraced Irving as the author who had internationally championed U.S. culture. He had also managed, perhaps as a direct result of his prolonged absence, to avoid the kinds of literary squabbles plaguing James Fenimore Cooper. Prior to undertaking a western journey, recounted in *A Tour of the Prairies* (1834), Irving began looking for a permanent American residence. He focused his attention on Tarrytown, New York, an area he had admired since his boyhood. His success as an author liberated him from the economic dependency that had caused him to leave America in the first place, and now, like Scott, he wanted a home of his own.

During his search for a new residence, Irving reimagined his first visit with Scott, perhaps, as a means of working through his own questions about what he wanted to accomplish with the purchase and design of his home. Furnished with this heightened sense of authority, and focused on his own building plans, Irving undertook a depiction of Abbotsford, a celebrated architectural blend of Old World style and modern convenience (see fig. 5). Irving begins his portrait by recalling the somewhat chaotic state of a house under construction. Scott's "snug gentleman's cottage," which had "something rural and picturesque in its appearance," was in the initial stages of conversion into a "huge baronial pile" (125). "Masses of hewn stone" cluttered the "court yard" as Scott labored over the "birth" of his home (125). Irving depicts Scott as just starting to remodel a small house into an elaborate architectural site. The faux-medieval residence that Scott was erecting was not so much an antiquarian renovation project

Figure 5. James Johnston, *North Distant view of Abbotsford,* **from** *History and Antiquities of Melrose, Old Melrose and Dryburgh Abbeys* **by John Bower.** General Research Division, The New York Public Library, Astor, Lenox and Tilden Foundations.

as it was an exercise in historical invention. Irving notes how "Scott pleased himself with picturing out his future residence as he would one of the fanciful creations of his own romances," further linking the tasks of fiction and house building (143). Thus, he opens his text by detailing that Scott built a manor house and had not inherited one, a move which emphasizes that such a project would also be possible even within the "un-storied" confines of the United States. This tactic locates his portrait chronologically; for just as the house had not yet assumed its final shape, Scott, in 1817, was not the monumental figure that he would become by the 1830s. Retrospectively, Irving advances that he, Scott, and Abbotsford have greatly changed in the intervening period.

Abbotsford was both famous and infamous by the time Irving drafted his recollections. Renowned as an architectural marvel, and blamed as the source of Scott's economic ruin, Abbotsford, like Monticello, was a house that consumed its proprietor's imagination and his resources. The cottage Scott had purchased in May 1812 was so small that Scott wrote his brother-in-law, "on the whole we live as if we were on board ship."[41]

Almost immediately, Scott set about reshaping the house and its grounds to suit his ambitions. Deciding "to plant & to improve," Scott aspired "to make Abbotsford a very sweet little thing in the course of a few years."[42] To achieve that end, Scott requested that friends send him acorns from historic gardens and forests, envisioning a great sculpted landscape, replete with romantic associations.[43] "Where no one else can see anything but fallow and broom," Scott declared, "I am anticipating lawn and grove."[44] By the time of Irving's visit, Scott had commenced his second major overhaul of the house. The first renovations had failed to create an adequate space, either for Scott's curios or the ever increasing number of guests who called on him, and he had to expand.

Scott's renovation plans included the incorporation of relics and fragments of storied ruins into the walls of the house, a design element that delighted Irving, for it proved the possibilities of inventing a tradition based on the incorporation, or co-option, of local customs into contemporary practices. To achieve his goals, Scott directed the pilfering of masonry from nearby ruins to cover Abbotsford with gray stone, and hired foragers whose mission was to acquire anything "within thirty miles" that might be useful.[45] Scott hoped, by virtue of these borrowed materials, to embody within the house "all the most attractive features of medieval architecture."[46] Like a nineteenth-century William Randolph Hearst, Scott strove to build a house that would look like a "castle" on the outside but would be thoroughly "modern" in its interior.[47] He focused enormous attention on the exterior of the house to achieve the effect of an antiquated Abbotsford. In addition to seizing regional antiquities for ornament, Scott commissioned plaster copies of sculptures from nearby ruins to decorate his facade.[48]

Scott supplemented his interior decoration with more legitimate antiquarian acquisitions. Purchasing beams from the site of William Wallace's death, Scott had a chair made "as a memorial of our most patriotic hero," modeling it after another he had admired at Hamilton Palace.[49] Appropriating every type of artifact he could, Scott directed his builders to fit the relics into the scheme of his house, including forming his kitchen doorway with stones taken from the Bastille of Edinburgh.[50] Abbotsford's illusions and chicanery did not enthrall all of Scott's guests. One visitor noted with disgust that "the furniture had little copper plates with inscriptions affixed" detailing each item's history, adding to the museum-like quality of the house.[51] Scott's curatorial impulses denote Abbotsford as a pedagogic space, designed to both conserve and create a national tradition. A jumble of old and new, and with a great many fictionalized additions, the estate Irving visited was carefully manipulated to create a historic sensibility where nothing historic had existed. Not inheriting a house with storied associations, Scott unabashedly manufactured one. Throughout *Abbots-*

ford, Irving highlights Scott's fabrication of a domestic history and celebrates Scott's positioning of Abbotsford as if it were an ancient dwelling
rather than a modern construction. Irving's preference for reshaping historic structures and artifacts so that they would be of use in the present
made Scott's boldness enormously attractive. Scott, it seemed to Irving,
had blended fiction and material fact into a house that testified to the narrative nature of history: Abbotsford embodied the idea that history was a
narrative constructed by the present in order to house its imagined past.
By attempting to build Abbotsford as a monument to Scottish culture,
Scott also erected and stabilized a Scottish history.

In designing Abbotsford Scott incorporated "various morsels from the
ruins of Melrose Abbey" to give his house an air of historical importance
(143). Scott had a particular affection for Melrose Abbey, Irving registers,
for it contained "such rich bits of old time sculpture for the architect, and
old time story for the poet" (144). From the ruins of Melrose Abbey, Scott
created a viable source for both fiction and his home. In effect Scott mined
the abbey twice: once for intellectual property, and then—literally decon-
structing it—by materially incorporating it into his architectural designs.
Scott's writing—from his first important work, *The Lay of the Last Minstrel*
(1805), to novels such as *The Monastery* (1820) and *The Abbot* (1820)—registers the importance of the site, calling attention to the neglected ruin and
making a case for its historical significance. With the profit Scott made
from the ongoing literary enterprise of *inventing* a Scottish history, he paid
for Melrose Abbey to be broken down into spare parts that he could then
incorporate into his own design projects. The products of the past were
not untouchable artifacts but malleable elements to be blended into ser-
viceable material. Ruined structures served as architectural junkyards,
sources of all manner of literal and fictive projects. Indeed, Irving records
with barely suppressed glee how "the fictions of Scott had become facts"
with even the older residents of the area (129). No longer sanctified sites of
historical consequence, residual structures were transformed by Scott's
practices into storehouses waiting to be plundered. This commodification
of ruins suggests, just as Irving would contend in *The Sketch Book*, that in
Europe ruins were not sacred sites but repositories for current needs.
Scott's practices mimic, at least in Irving's reformulation, the argument
about house building that Irving would, shortly after his departure from
Abbotsford, articulate in *The Sketch Book*.

Irving "quotes" Scott as endorsing the idea that America has the same
resources, for fiction and building, that Scotland has. "At Leith," Scott
once saw "an immense stick of timber, just landed from America. It must
have been an enormous tree when it stood on its native soil, at its full
height and with all its branches" (135). Scott gazed at the timber "with
admiration," for "it seemed like one of the gigantic obelisks which are now

and then brought from Egypt, to shame the pigmy monuments of Europe" (135). "In fact," Scott continued, "these vast aboriginal trees, that have sheltered the Indians before the intrusion of the white men are the monuments and antiquities" of America (135). Irving has Scott refigure historical monuments and ruins, architectural sites of cultural history, as commodities for both fiction and building. Americans need not be concerned by their own *diminutive* cultural achievements, for as both *Abbotsford* and Abbotsford suggest, *history* is a by-product of narrative framing. Nothing prevents America from creating a national identity and an architectural legacy at least equal to, if not greater than, those of European nations.

Immediately after expressing admiration for the New World, Irving's Scott praises a poem by Thomas Campbell, "Gertrude of Wyoming," for demonstrating "the poetic materials furnished by American scenery" (135). Irving transcribes Scott as positing that the ancient trees of America provide a source both for poetic inspiration and for the construction of an edifice worthy of an author who assembles such an imagined past. Around the grounds of Abbotsford, Irving discovers that Scott has used his neighbors as models for characters in his novels. An old man who works in the quarry cutting stone for Scott's building projects strikes Irving as the prototype for a character in *The Antiquary* (1815), as "his ruddy yet rugged countenance, his grey hair, and an arch gleam in his blue eye, reminded me of the description of Edie Ochiltree" (132). Irving represents Scott as a master craftsman, fabricating the life that he envisions out of rubble, ink, and imagination. For Irving, Scott's experience proves how the lines between the author of a usable national past and the architect of a "historic" home are intertwined. Almost as if to underscore this recurrent thread in the sketch, Irving relates an extended conversation with Scott about a very particular "small antique monument " (138). The memorial bears an inscription "in Gothic characters," translating as "Here lies the brave Percy" (138). Thinking the marker must "be the tomb of some stark warrior of the olden time," Irving questions its origins (138). Sidestepping the issue, Scott proclaims it simply a "nonsense" monument (138). Irving lets the matter drop, learning only later that the site memorializes not deeds of historical importance but "a favorite greyhound"(138). Irving feigns disappointment over the tombstone incident, turning it into a cheery expression of Scott's devotion to his pets. More than just suggesting the depths of Scott's humanity, Irving carefully manipulates the episode to display Scott's inventiveness in creating a domestic environment marked by an invented tradition. Like Irving's fictive Squire Bracebridge, Scott cultivates a fictive history for his estate, elevating the commonplace into a site of memory and importance. Irving's tone in this episode connects his portrait of Scott's domestic life, *Abbotsford* (1835), to *The Sketch Book*. Both texts celebrate attempts at enriching the present built environment by cultivating (and harvesting) historical associations.

For an American audience captivated by Scott's writings, Irving's message is clear: Scott forges his fictions out of artifacts he salvages from his daily life. Scott's use of local artifacts authenticates Irving's use of his native environment as the setting for his own work. If Scott can find Edie Ochiltree in his local quarry, why can't Irving find in his native environment a minor figure for use in "Rip Van Winkle" or "The Legend of Sleepy Hollow"?[52] By speculating on the process through which Scott develops his artistry, Irving lays a foundation for his own fiction and house-building ambitions. Throughout Irving's career, the greatest burden facing American authors was the perception, both at home and abroad, that America lacked the necessary materials on which to ground a national literature. By uncovering how Scott finds his inspiration in contemporary materials, Irving implies that Americans are not hampered by inhabiting a young nation. Irving's biographical sketch of Scott argues that those problems are illusions, and thus serves to clear the ground for Irving's own architectural and literary ambitions.

The desire to build a home that would rival "one of the fanciful creations of his own romances" led Scott to the brink of economic ruin. As Irving notes, "the great pile of Abbotsford with the huge expense it entailed him, of servants, retainers, guests, and baronial style, was a drain upon his purse, a task upon his exertions and a weight upon his mind that finally crushed him" (143). While it might be tempting to reduce imagined "air castles" into "solid stone and mortar," Irving also realizes that this can become an all-consuming impulse (143). *Abbotsford* embodies the burden, both physical and economic, that construction placed upon Scott. Perhaps as an exercise in self-discipline, Irving's text probes the nebulous relationship between imagining a cultural history and embodying one.

Washington Irving held many of the same Anglophilic aspirations that Scott did. Both struggled throughout their lives for approval from English cultural sources. Moreover, Irving overtly acknowledged the same multivalent cultural connections between his "colonial" society and Britain that Scott did.[53] Irving's first major work of fiction, *The Sketch Book of Geoffrey Crayon* (1819), was drafted while Irving was living in England and traveling in the same social circles as Scott. The influence of Scott on Irving was deep-seated, and shaped the ways in which Irving decided to pursue his life and his craft. For both Irving and Scott, reimagining the past rerooted the connections that bound England and its former colonies. By clarifying what the mystic chords of memory and fresh political wounds might have blurred, they suggested rewriting history to highlight allegiances and commonality.

As Crayon's and Knickerbocker's tales argue, the steadiness of a rural habitat could anchor a culture at risk of dissolution. For Irving, Scott had manufactured such a stabilizing force in Abbotsford, an example that had an America application. In June of 1835, just a month after *Abbotsford* was published, Irving purchased, as he described, "ten acres, lying at the foot of Oscar's farm, on the river bank," a "beautiful spot, capable of being made a little paradise."[54] Irving had been eyeing this particular parcel of Tarry-town land since November of 1832. After acquiring it, he immediately began to refashion it. Irving happily undertook the remodeling of the little cottage, as well as the entire reshaping of the grounds and foliage. Like Scott, Irving sought to create an elaborate "history" for the land and its structures.[55] In short order, Sunnyside obsessed Irving as much as Abbots-ford had Scott, and the writing of *Abbotsford* must have reminded him that his task—both the physical remodeling of his actual house and the writing of it into a historical continuum—was going to be arduous labor.

III

"With characteristic taste," Andrew Jackson Downing judged, Washing-ton Irving had selected "one of the most delightful nooks on the banks of the Hudson" for the site of his "permanent residence."[56] The author of numerous widely successful landscaping and architectural guides, and the consummate arbiter of antebellum American domestic design, Downing praised Irving's Sunnyside as "the beau ideal of a cottage orné"[57] (see fig. 6). "Charmingly covered with ivy and climbing roses," Sunnyside was, according to Downing, "embosomed in thickets of shrubbery."[58] The ivy—still clinging to the house's walls—was a signature element of Irving's design scheme. He had imported the plant, at considerable expense, from the ruins of Melrose Abbey. Like Scott, Irving aspired to transform a dilapidated vernacular house into an architectural site of consequence. Purchasing an abandoned, two-room "small stone Dutch cottage," Irving fashioned it, by pen and pocketbook, into the preeminent antebellum architectural shrine in America.[59] In many ways Sunnyside stands as the culmination of Irving's recurring concerns over the links between literary and cultural production and the possibilities of domestic architecture.

By the middle of the nineteenth century Irving's Sunnyside had become as famous as its tenant. "Sunnyside functioned," as Kathleen Eagen John-son argues, "as 'America's Home' and was widely illustrated in commercial art."[60] Sunnyside was, Oliver Wendell Holmes noted, second only to Mount Vernon as "the best known and most cherished of all the dwellings in our land."[61] In the intervening years between Irving's purchase of the ten acres near Tarrytown and Downing's praise, the idea of an American

Figure 6. Sunnyside, Residence of Washington Irving, Esq., near Tarrytown. Illustration from *A Treaty on the Theory and Practice of Landscape Gardening* by Andrew Jackson Downing. Collection of The New-York Historical Society (negative number 79718d).

home creating cultural permanence, imperiled in the restless climate of Knickerbocker's fictions, no longer seemed so improbable. Sunnyside, and Irving's quest to invent a tradition for his home and its environs, played a pivotal role in that shift. This development indicates both a continuation and a democratization of a cultural embrace of architectural imagery as a source of identity formation. In many ways the popularity of Irving's fictions about the secluded houses of the Hudson River Valley region had prepared the American public for considering a vernacular domestic architecture as having national significance. His previous catalog had whetted the American appetite for history and had grounded it in the very region in which he now sought to build his own home. Moreover, Irving labored continually after he moved into Sunnyside to ensure its reception as a modest, yet culturally significant, house.

The humbleness of Sunnyside, as carefully crafted as the solidity of Mount Vernon, argued that a properly fashioned home was possible for any citizen in the Republic. Indeed, as Joseph T. Butler writes, Sunnyside

"was seen throughout most of the century as an Irving creation as significant and admired as Rip Van Winkle or Ichabod Crane."[62] Like his celebrated characters, Irving's house became emblematic of the possibilities of
American vernacular culture. Just as Irving's literary production provided a
foundation for a developing national literature, Sunnyside became a prototype for the emerging American taste for domestic architecture. Andrew
Jackson Downing's burgeoning career was based on the premise that any
American could inhabit a house of consequence, and Irving's Sunnyside
became a national symbol of that very ideal. Irving understood that his
popularity was tied to his various folk persona, and he sought to fabricate a
house that could easily have been occupied by Crayon, Knickerbocker, or
Rip. A simple cottage, Sunnyside was not an unattainable or foreboding
architectural site but rather a model home that could be built anywhere
and occupied by anyone.

Irving first conceived of Sunnyside as "a nest, to which I can resort when
in the mood."[63] Originally he did "not intend to set up any establishment
there," and as a result planned only to "put some simple furniture in it."[64]
Near enough to New York City—a few hours by boat, and but half a day by
coach—Irving fancied Sunnyside a country retreat, available to him when
the pressures of the city became too great. But his intentions changed
when he experienced the regenerative possibilities of a rustic home. During the late summer of 1835, Irving lived at John Jacob Astor's house, Hell
Gate, organizing Astor's papers in preparation for writing *Astoria* (1836).
Located in the sparsely populated upper east side of Manhattan, Hell Gate
was far removed from the bustle of lower Manhattan. Irving found this
"bachelor hall" the most "delightful nest" he had experienced since returning to America.[65] Life at the secluded Hell Gate was "sweet"; it afforded
Irving unfettered access to "pure air, agreeable scenery, a spacious house,
profound quiet, and perfect command of my time and space."[66] In "consequence," Irving recorded, "I have written more since I have been here than
I have ever done in the same space of time."[67] For Irving, cultural production flowed from the stability of a genteel domestic environment. Devoting
early 1835 to *Abbotsford* and in the summer enjoying the liberty of Astor's
Hell Gate, Irving decided to reconfigure Sunnyside as a permanent home
so that he could continue the leisurely productively he had found as a by-
product of his domestic location.

In early October 1835, Irving broke from work on *Astoria* to check on
progress at Sunnyside. With a bemused pride he wrote to his brother that
the cottage was "in a considerable state of forwardness."[68] In the six weeks
since his last visit, Irving noted that the new additions to the cottage had
"risen from the foundation," and he expressed hope that his design would
yield a "quaint, picturesque little pile."[69] Irving also admitted, à la Scott,
that he "intended to write a legend or two about it and its vicinity, by way

of making it pay for itself."[70] Irving's admission of his desire to commercialize his house (after penning a market for its significance) echoes his presentation of Scott at Abbotsford. A week after Irving's confession about his literary ambitions, he wrote to his brother about how he was impatiently awaiting the arrival of an "inscription stone" he had commissioned for placement over the south entranceway.[71] This tablet bore an engraving in Dutch, which translated to "Erected in the year 1656. Reconstructed by Washington Irving in the year 1835. Geo. Harvey Architect."[72] On Sunnyside's west side (the river side), Irving added the date 1656 in imitation of "the dated wrought iron tie beams found on many colonial New York dwellings."[73] The fictitious 1656 date, inscribed on the house in two places, exemplifies Irving's desire to antiquate and historicize his house, by announcing that it was a seventeenth-century production, a remnant of the careful settlement that "Rip Van Winkle" and "The Legend of Sleepy Hollow" had endorsed. In actuality, there was more new construction at Sunnyside than architectural preservation; very little would remain of the dilapidated, humble farmhouse that Irving had purchased. Yet Irving did everything he could think of to camouflage the idea that Sunnyside was not a pre-Revolutionary farmhouse that he was simply renovating. The inscription stone was the first authorial attempt to "authenticate" the history of Sunnyside, but it was far from the last. In his remodeling Irving strove to make the house reflect residual building practices, so that he could embody in the house an argument about Sunnyside's historical origins.

Following Scott's plans at Abbotsford, Irving altered the roof's pitch to sharpen it, ordered the addition of stepped gables, and clustered the chimneys in imitation of English rustic styles. Furthermore, the windows of the cottage, consistent with romantic architectural tradition, were irregular both in placement and in shape to provide an intricate exterior to the house. These stylistic alterations were homages to Abbotsford's Gothic and Tudor arrangement and echoed the early Dutch houses of Irving's boyhood Manhattan. Irving actively borrowed what he wanted from a broadly defined architectural lexicon; disliking the appearance of fieldstone on his house's facade, he covered the walls with stucco. Like George Washington at Mount Vernon, Irving had the plastering scored to create the illusion that Sunnyside was a cut stone building. This simulated facade was far cheaper than actual cut stone, an economy that revealed itself only on close examination. Irving made Sunnyside into an argument about the narrative possibilities of historical stability. Sunnyside had endured since well before the Revolution, Irving argued, and thus it was in houses and not in political systems that the real traditions of the nation resided. This house had survived to provide the present, his illusions aimed to suggest, with a tangible legacy that could be inhabited and thus preserved.

To crown his roof Irving rescued several Dutch-style weather vanes from demolished buildings in New York and Albany. Just as Scott pilfered ruins for objects to incorporate into his home, Irving gathered materials for Sunnyside aimed at exhibiting his curatorial vision of Hudson River history and culture. So, Irving invented a tradition for his weather vanes, claiming in the *Knickerbocker Magazine* that one had "battled with the wind on the top of the Stad-House of New Amsterdam, in the time of Peter Stuyvesant," while embellishing the actual history of another, boasting that it was "once the weather-cock of the great Vander Heydan Palace of Albany."[74] Irving thus positioned his house as a repository for the colonial Dutch history of New York, and as a monument to the entirety of the region's cultural heritage. Weather vanes that had once adorned the first governmental buildings and mansions of a pre-Revolutionary history now dignified Sunnyside, signaling it as the inheritor of these traditions. Moreover, he made this imagined history a public facet of his private life. As such, these fictions also served to domestic the pre-Revolutionary history of the United States, and fabricate a tradition of preservation that sought to cultivate an appetite for markers of historical meaning. If Americans embraced such a practice, they might find themselves as rooted by their structural environments as Irving figures the English are throughout *The Sketch Book*.

Irving paid as much attention to the design of the interior of his house as he did to its exterior. Outlining his intentions for the master bedroom in a letter to Harvey in November 1835, Irving explicitly detailed his plans.[75] He based his blueprint on the recollection of "an irregular attick room" he had seen in France and included in his letter several rudimentary drawings to convey his vision (see fig. 7). Irving wanted "a recess made at the end adjoining the small centre bedroom" (the room's interior wall), and "the other end of the room left with the natural pitch of the roof." This design would "hide the slope of the roof at the angle made by the front and rear building" and allow Irving "to gain to the room the full height, up to the beams." His arrangement disguised the defect caused by the intersection of the roof beams at such an odd angle and allowed him to fit a bed within the recess. This placement of furniture maximized the room's potential, suggesting an airiness otherwise unattainable. Irving further directed that the outer wall of the room (farthest from the recess) be "papered with striped paper, so as to resemble the curtain of a tent." The interior decorations effectively furthered the illusion of roominess despite the limitations imposed by the house's exterior design.[76]

Irving also directed that a skylight—a novelty in nineteenth-century America—be placed in the house's eastern roof face. The skylight provided a cheap source of illumination to the attic storage area, the second-floor hallway, and by the innovation of a sliding shutter (located within the

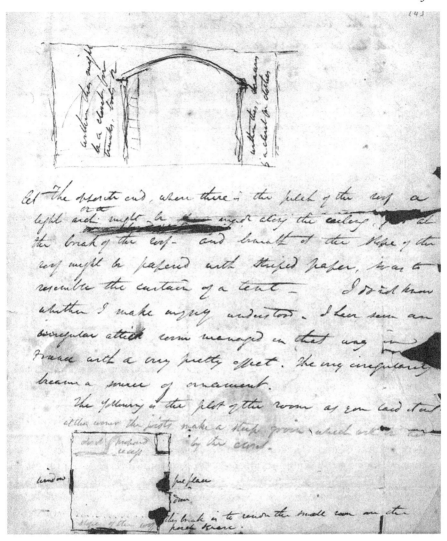

Figure 7. Detail from Washington Irving's November 23, 1835 letter to George Harvey. Courtesy of Historic Hudson Valley, Tarrytown, NY.

house on the hallway wall) to his "tented" bedroom as well. Each detail of Irving's orders records his obsession with perfecting his nuanced vision. Like Scott, Irving blended interior innovations within an overall argument about the venerable status of his home. Each was motivated by the desire to join comfort with stability, novelty with a manufactured tradition. Hav-

ing cast Scott as a master builder, capable of constructing a house and a
lens through which to interpret it, Irving positioned himself as Scott's
architectural heir, seeking to replicate in America what he had witnessed
being fabricated in Scotland.

In the "Letter to the Editor of the *Knickerbocker Magazine*," where
Geoffrey Crayon brags of his weather vanes, Irving weaves a web of
mythic associations for his cottage. Crayon boasts that the cottage that *he*
recently purchased and restored was "one of the most ancient and historical mansions in the country" and that it had served as the base of opera-
tions for Diedrich Knickerbocker's now famous "ransacking" of old Dutch
homes during the creation of his *History*.[77] This letter was the first in a
series of thirty sketches that Irving wrote for the *Knickerbocker Magazine*
from March 1839 to October 1841. Like many of the sketches that followed, it served double duty: Irving profited from its literal publication,
while the popularity of the fiction increased Sunnyside's property value. As
he had argued in *Abbotsford*, the author who found material in his immediate environment understood the true meaning of natural resources. If a
true history for Sunnyside did not exist, Irving felt perfectly willing to
manufacture one, and he understood such an endeavor as a natural element of his remodeling.

The "Letter" registers Crayon's delight in reclaiming "the historic pile
from utter ruin" and in having "repaired and renovated it with religious
care, in the genuine Dutch style." Crayon declares the cottage as noteworthy, for it contains "sundry reliques of the glorious days of the New
Netherlands" and even artifacts of Knickerbocker's personal property,
including "his elbow chair, and his identical old Dutch writing desk."[78]
Just as Scott had sought to blur fiction and fact at Abbotsford, Irving
undertook this same task at Sunnyside. His writings gave Sunnyside a new
history, making it a landmark of enormous cultural interest. In addition,
these later sketches connect his earlier writings more directly to a national
tradition. Irving had been chastised by American reviewers of *The Sketch
Book* for focusing too much attention on British subjects; he domesticated
this uneasiness by having both Knickerbocker and Crayon become tenants
of the history of Sunnyside.[79] Thus, Irving sought to make his construction of a home into an act of preservation, a move that positioned him as a
caretaker of historical legacies rather than just another new builder.

In "Wolfert's Roost," Irving again employs the Crayon persona to fashion more "historical" associations for Sunnyside. "Wolfert's Roost" com-
prises three short sections, each enumerating a different epoch in the
history of Sunnyside's ownership. The first section is set in "a little old-
fashioned stone mansion, all made-up of gable ends, and as full of angles
and corners." The tale recounts the adventures of a renowned "medicine-
man" who lived on the shore of the Hudson and ruled an extensive empire

from his seat at Sunnyside. The section concludes with the erection of a house on the land by Wolfert Acker, "one of the privy counselors of Peter Stuyvesant." The second section tells the story of Jacob Van Tassel, relative of *The Sketch Book*'s Baltus, a Revolutionary War hero, who conducted a series of "legendary" raids against Tory strongholds from Wolfert's house, which he came to own. "The house was sacked and plundered" by the British, seeking revenge against Van Tassel, "and remained a melancholy ruin" with only "its stone walls and brick chimneys" standing at the owner's triumphant return after the war.[80]

Van Tassel rebuilt the cottage, and after "years and years passed over the time-honored mansion," Diedrich Knickerbocker, who admired the "exterior of the eventful pile," settled into it while investigating the history of the region.[81] Full of architectural details, "Wolfert's Roost" presents Sunnyside as an important local historical site. Irving manages both to antiquate the house, to date it back to the original Dutch settlement of New York, and to argue that Sunnyside memorializes American Revolutionary heroism. The original stone walls have been preserved, he suggests, across the length of the nation's history. These surviving walls testify to the resilience of the republican project. Home to a Native American medicine man, an important seventeenth-century Dutch diplomat, a Revolutionary War hero, and a famous literary figure, Sunnyside is transformed by Crayon's tale into a contiguous site of architectural importance. Sunnyside becomes a testimonial to the Republic's own history, and to cultural and architectural heritages that predate the birth of the nation.

By December of 1840, Irving's Sunnyside residence had "attracted others," as he wrote to his sister Sarah Van Wart: "cottages and country seats have sprung up along the banks of the Tappan Sea, and Tarrytown has become the metropolis [of quite] a fashionable vicinity."[82] What had been "a mere hamlet" had evolved and now boasted of "its hotels and churches of various denominations."[83] This transformation occurred prior to the completion in 1848 of the railroad along the Hudson's banks, and stemmed from Irving's presence in the area, his literary efforts, and the broad-based celebration of his architectural and landscaping designs. Irving had made fashionable in America the very rural lifestyle that he found so admirable in *The Sketch Book*. In effect, Irving's popularization of Sunnyside furthered his hope that Americans would mirror the sustainable developmental practices he had praised the English for having in 1819. His actions serve to mark the construction of Sunnyside and his later writings as continuations of the argument he had begun in *The Sketch Book*.

"There is something about the cottage, as about himself," T. Addison Richards wrote in *Harper's New Monthly Magazine* in 1856, "an air of reserve, without coldness, which while cordially inviting approach, creates

instinctively and willingly a respectful deference."[84] House and man, Sunnyside and Irving, were by 1856 so synonymous that Richards could suggest that "the sweet, sunny sentiment of his home is ever seen in his genial
smile, and his kindly and benevolent nature in its aspect of cheerfulness
benignity."[85] By midcentury Irving's popularity as a writer was in decline,
but the reputation of Sunnyside as the pinnacle of genteel cottage life was
still soaring. The notoriety of the Hudson River School, the works of the
landscape architect and tastemaker Andrew Jackson Downing, and the
increasing cultural interest in the work of the architect Alexander Jackson
Davis all contributed to the ongoing celebrity of Irving's cottage. Richards'
"meticulously detailed account" of Sunnyside, with its "reverent tone," as
David R. Anderson has argued, expresses an avid "interest in the minutiae
of Irving's domestic arrangements."[86] This intense interest advances the
notion that for antebellum Americans homes had an enormous cultural
resonance.

   Nestled in a sculpted landscape, Sunnyside was shielded from the working portions of the farm on both the land and the river approaches, so that
the house would appear, like Jonson's Penshurst, as a leisurely rustic paradise. Sunnyside's prominence fueled a trend of trying to blend European
architectural styles and genteel traditions harmoniously within the American landscape. Ostensibly built prior to the Revolution, it reminded the
new nation of the stability it could find in its own architectural history, not
by rushing to embrace change and relocation, but by remodeling and con-
serving previously built structures. Richards' *Harper's* article lovingly
describes the landscape and the architectural features of Sunnyside, often
reporting Irving's fictitious accounts of his house as fact. Moreover, it
credits Irving with having made rural residences popular, suggesting that
"when Mr. Irving first took up his abode at Sunnyside, he was all alone by
himself, yet now every inch of the adjacent country is gardened, and
lawned, and villaed."[87] Far from objecting to this transformation of the
landscape, Richards argues that development offers the region a "sweeter
charm," because it has been conducted by "many of those gifted ones
whose genius and works have endeared their names to our imaginations
and hearts."[88] Cataloging the admirable figures who have made the Hudson River environs their home, Richards composes a lengthy list, including
Martin Van Buren, James Kirke Paulding, Samuel B. Morse, Andrew Jackson Downing, Asher B. Durand, Henry Kirk Brown, Nathaniel Willis,
Susan Warner, Gulian C. Verplanck, and John James Audubon. Among
these Hudson River inhabitants Richards focuses on Thomas Cole, of
whom he writes: "It was in a beautiful home, directly overlooking the
Hudson, and commanding the grand panorama of the Catskills, that the
lamented painter Cole lived, and labored and died."[89]

IV

"I have been reading Irving's *Abbotsford*," Thomas Cole recorded in his journal on 4 June 1835, and it "gave me real pleasure."[90] Cole's reading might have prompted him, later that same summer, to propose to Irving that they jointly undertake a project to visually and textually represent the glories of the Hudson River region. Irving rejected the idea, fearing that the book would prove "monotonous."[91] Enjoying enormous popularity and engaged with building and historicizing Sunnyside, Irving more likely did not want to be disturbed by the work of collaboration. While the two never did form a partnership, their careers are closely linked. Irving's pen and Cole's brush promoted the Hudson River Valley as America's most picturesque region. Firmly tied to the artistic and publishing communities of Manhattan during the 1830s, both migrated from the city, during the same period, to live farther north along the Hudson.[92]

Cole's desire to collaborate with Irving, America's most celebrated author, is not surprising. Cole needed a way to mass-market his work to liberate himself from the constraints of patronage. Still, that he considered such a partnership while in the middle of his most ambitious series, *The Course of Empire* (1836), is somewhat startling. Perhaps Cole felt from his reading of *Abbotsford* that Irving was absorbed with the same themes his series was exploring. Cole's sequence questioned the fate of American social development in terms of its relationship with European precursors. Irving's writings continually questioned the consequences of importing foreign models even as they examined the links between architecture and cultural order. Although more apprehensive about the issue, Cole also probed the complex question of architectural transplantation by reversing Irving's terms: instead of looking for domestic resonances in Europe, Cole portrayed the consequences of transplanting difference. Serially, *The Course of Empire* exhibits a deep-seated fear about the use of classical architecture as a frame for American subjectivities. Within these paintings Cole questions how such imported forms will affect the social composition of American life.

The Course of Empire consists of five oil paintings, four of which are the same size. Collectively they depict a cyclical vision of a landscape that becomes "civilized" by human occupation. The sequence moves from a prehistoric, presettlement wilderness to the decadent ruins of a culture that has burned itself out. The first canvas, *The Savage State* (fig. 8), depicts a windswept wild scene, with the few visible figures dressed in furs and animal skins and lodged in primitive tents. The second canvas, *The Pastoral State* (fig. 9), shows the area after it has been rudimentarily domesticated.

The snarled wilderness has been cultivated and calmed; the occupants tend a flock of sheep and dwell in humble vernacular structures. The third and largest canvas, *The Consummation of Empire* (fig. 10), displays the same landscape after it has undergone a massive reconstruction. The greenness of nature, so dominant in the previous two canvases, has been superceded by a predominance of stone and marble and the rich pastels adorning the figures in the triumphant parade. This frame overflows with imposing buildings, monuments, and a parade of lavishly dressed figures, while the gentle harbor is overcrowded with trading vessels. The fourth canvas, *Destruction* (fig. 11), records a scene of riot and excess: raging fires consume the city as the buildings and bridges crumble and mobs rape and pillage; the colorful palette of the earlier canvas is supplanted by darker hues. The fifth canvas, *Desolation* (fig. 12), portrays the landscape after it has been deserted by its former inhabitants. Nature reasserts itself as ivy clings to the few battered columns not completely ravaged, but the colors also suggest a twilight scene, for the resurgence of nature is portrayed in gray tints rather than rich greens. Arranged with the first and second canvases grouped on the left and the four and fifth canvases on the right, with the larger third canvas centrally positioned, these paintings collectively form a single exhibit, *The Course of Empire.*

After three years of work, Thomas Cole finished *The Course of Empire* in October of 1836 and arranged for an exhibition at the National Academy of Design. As America's foremost landscape painter, Cole enjoyed a widespread critical acclaim; still he worried that his series would not find a sympathetic audience. The reaction to *The Course of Empire* was far from what Cole had anticipated. As Ellwood Parry records, in just "eight and a half weeks, from October 17th to December 15th, 1836, the exhibition of the series grossed one thousand two hundred and ninety-three dollars."[93] Admission to view the five canvases was priced at fifty cents, so in all probability over two thousand people attended the exhibit. So large an audience for a series of five paintings was unprecedented in the United States.

In her discussion of Jacksonian imagery in *The Course of Empire*, Angela Miller argues that the series' successful reception resulted from a "collective denial of Cole's real subject—America in the 1830's."[94] Miller argues that the audience viewed the paintings as an allegory of Old World history, and avoided "acknowledging any parallels between Cole's imaginary empire and [their] contemporary America."[95] Disagreeing with Miller, Alan Wallach contends that "if anything, the series was too well understood."[96] Noting a repetitious dismissal of Cole's cyclical version of history, Wallach suggests that reviewers faithfully believed that "democracy and material progress" freed the United States from this terrifying trajectory depicted in Cole's series. Miller and Wallach both maintain that the widespread cultural optimism concerning America's future prospects made

Figure 8. Thomas Cole, *The Course of Empire, Savage State,* **1836.**
Collection of The New-York Historical Society (negative number 1858.1).

Figure 9. Thomas Cole, *The Course of Empire, Pastoral State,* **1836.**
Collection of The New-York Historical Society (negative number 1858.2).

Figure 10. Thomas Cole, *The Course of Empire, Consummation*, 1836.
Collection of The New-York Historical Society (negative number 1858.3).

Figure 11. Thomas Cole, *The Course of Empire, Destruction*, 1836.
Collection of The New-York Historical Society (negative number 1858.4).

Figure 12. Thomas Cole, *The Course of Empire, Desolation*, 1836.
Collection of The New-York Historical Society (negative number 1858.5).

reviewers skeptical of the idea that the United States could suffer cultural annihilation. But Cole's understanding of the contemporaneous state of U.S. culture was, perhaps, more nuanced than his critics have suggested. The cyclical paradigm held enormous currency in Jacksonian America, evidenced by the successful "vogue" of "protoromantic" artists such as Gibbon and Volney.[97] The idea that the United States was at a crucial turning point in its history was a commonplace in Jacksonian Era rhetoric, and that Cole should seize on the notion of a cyclical vision of history to engage this idea is hardly surprising.[98]

The Course of Empire opened a month before the hotly contested 1836 presidential and New York mayoral elections would be decided. With Jackson set to leave office after eight years, many Americans saw both of these elections as crucial. Vice President Martin Van Buren positioned himself as Jackson's heir, essentially running on the promise to stay the course with Jackson's polices. For Cole, who mourned the results of continual expansion and feared the social upheaval generated by the Jacksonian appetite for unending change, the future stability of the United States was imperiled by Jacksonian policies. Locally, New Yorkers were equally concerned about the direction of the city. In short, at stake in these elections, for many Americans including Cole, was the future course of the

United States. According to Marvin Meyers, "by contemporary standards New York was relatively mature in social and economic development," thus making it a site "of serious competition for support" among the parties.[99] News of the national election dominated New York culture, particularly since its eventual victor, Martin Van Buren, was a former senator and governor of the state whose power base was rooted in Manhattan. Manhattan's mayor, Cornelius Van Wyck Lawrence, linked his campaign to Van Buren's in an effort to forge party loyalty and ensure that everyone on the Democratic ticket remained in power. For both the city and the nation the issue of the day was whether the Republic would continue in its embrace of Jacksonian ideology or turn away from its tenets of political spoils and unregulated commerce. The mayoral election played out the same questions on the local stage, as boisterous party factions struggled to drown out the concerns of their foes.[100] Mirroring the acts of the national Jacksonian party, Tammany Hall promoted itself as the party of the working classes, even as it endlessly catered to merchants and bankers. The local party held enthusiastic celebrations for its candidates that its opponents characterized as riotous excesses, and the unruly distresses of partisan politics festered throughout the campaign season. Several events of the mid-1830s demonstrate in New York City a significant degree of civic unease with Jacksonian polices and their local inflections, which Cole, splitting time between Manhattan and Catskill, witnessed firsthand.[101]

Sean Wilentz has characterized 1836 as "the year of the strikes," because of the massive economic protests held in Manhattan that year.[102] In June of 1836, "a gigantic evening rally drew nearly thirty thousand workingmen—roughly one-fifth of New York's adult male population—to City Hall Park," where they burned the effigy of a local judge to protest recent legal decisions.[103] This protest was not a singular example of the social unrest in New York City. A panic-inducing 1832 cholera epidemic and several brutal riots in 1834 further suggest the fragility of the city's order. A devastating 1835 fire necessitated a massive rebuilding of the city, and continual construction further disrupted its social fabric as most of lower Manhattan was reconstructed in a short period of time. Most major New York newspapers were in the hands of the Jacksonian Democrats, or at least businessmen with a vested interested in Jacksonian politics. As news of the national and local elections dominated daily life, New Yorkers endlessly debated the direction of the city and the nation. In this context, the idea that viewers failed to recognize Cole's series as a mediation on 1830s New York does not seem as far-fetched as it might first seem. To do so would have meant that they had to recognize, in what looks like a depiction of ancient Greece or Rome, the instability of their own positions.

Historically, New York comprised buildings of disconnected architectural styles. The city's economy was not tied to the actual production of goods or the cultivation of natural resources; rather it was defined by speculation and transportation, and the dominance of mercantilism affected its architectural development. The completion of the Erie Canal in late 1825, which transformed the Hudson River into the main trade artery of the nation, cemented New York's position as the economic center of the United States. As Charles Sellers argues, the canal "cut shipping costs between Lake Erie and New York City from $100 to under $9 a ton, and eventually as low as $3 for some commodities."[104] In just a few months after the canal's opening, Sellers records, New York was receiving "twice the amount" of freight of New Orleans.[105] Consequently New York harbor became the most important port of call in the Republic. The canal's ceremonial opening, a "grand Festival of Connection," was marked by an enormous parade in which, as the historians Edwin G. Burrows and Mike Wallace note, "over one hundred thousand people—nearly two-thirds of the city's entire population"—participated.[106] By the middle years of the 1830s, after two terms under Jackson, the economy in New York, led by vast speculation, was flourishing. As Burrows and Wallace argue, "stoked by a tremendous expansion in the availability of credit," merchants, businessmen, bankers, and speculators centered in New York fully embraced Jacksonian capitalism.[107] As a result of this commercial boom, New York was an evolving metropolis on the verge of reinventing itself architecturally. Manhattan's social evolution magnified the problems inherent in the larger cultural narrative about American domestic arrangements; for, in effect, New York was the antithesis of the Jeffersonian ideal of the United States as a nation of autonomous farms.[108] Manhattan's appearance was dictated by commercial and not agricultural concerns, and as a result New Yorkers resided in close proximity. Moreover, the geographical constraints of Manhattan Island created a dramatic juxtaposition of wealth and poverty, and this enforced association turned the city into a testing ground for the relationship between architectural style and cultural identity. New York's houses were not fashioned as independent, isolated sites that radiated social stability; in Manhattan, buildings were crammed together, with homes and warehouses sharing common walls. As such, New York presented a more urban, more quasi-European landscape than any other American city. If the house was to be a center for identity formation, then New York illustrated the consequences of the market revolution for the formation of a republican citizenry.

   While New York was the Republic's largest city, according to the first federal census, it was only barely so.[109] Its population doubled by 1800, and quadrupled (from its 1790 figure) by 1820.[110] While the city's population rose exponentially, very little attention was paid to its architectural development. In practice, the city expanded haphazardly to accommodate the influx of new residents. Buildings were thrust up—wherever they would fit—with little thought given to qualities or consequences of design. Yet, even as its population skyrocketed, the city clung to the southern portion of the island. In 1811, however, the New York State legislature passed a bill laying out the area above Fourteenth Street into, roughly, its current grid system.[111] The state could do so in part because the city had not really expanded north of Fourteenth Street. Prior to 1811, the city was a chaotic sprawl of irregular streets containing a mélange of architectural styles. Buildings of vastly different sizes, constructed from a variety of materials and designed for divergent purposes, abutted one another. This architectural cacophony also created a hazardous environment, as a ravaging fire on 16 December 1835 was to prove. Freezing temperatures, which plummeted as low as seventeen degrees below zero, hampered the ability of firefighters to contain the blaze, which had started in a warehouse on Merchant Street, and before the fire was extinguished almost seven hundred buildings were totally destroyed. "The sky was lit so brightly," historians Burrows and Wallace relate, "the glow could be seen in Poughkeepsie, New Haven, and Philadelphia."[112] As the fire jumped from street to street, firefighters used explosives to demolish buildings and create a firebreak to curtail the spread of the fire northward. Recounting the fire in his diary, Philip Hone proclaimed it "the most awful calamity which has ever visited these United States."[113] In the aftermath of the fire, looters openly defied attempts to stop them as the city reeled from the effects of the blaze. Eventually, both tempers and buildings cooled and order was restored in lower Manhattan, but while the embers had burned the city was on the brink of total disaster. As contemporary illustrations suggest, such as William James Bennet's aquatint *View of the Great Fire in New York, December 16 & 17, 1835* (fig. 13), the blaze had turned lower Manhattan into an architectural wasteland.

After the embers cooled, the remaining husks of the scorched buildings in the area were demolished to make way for new structures. While the insurance industry was bankrupted by the effects of the disaster, the Jacksonian economic order seized on the destruction of the fire to reimagine the city in classical terms. Constant expansion and remodeling meant that 1830s New York was a city continually under construction. The architectural style that dominated the era was classical in character. Architectural historian Talbot Hamlin has argued that "the decade of the thirties was essentially the era of the triumph of the Greek Revival in New York." While "Greek detail began to appear spasmodically in the late twenties," it firmly took hold of the cultural imagination in the 1830s.[114] The embrace of the Greek style was a result of several factors. In the architecture of republican Greece, many Americans thought they had discovered a style whose form embodied their political ideology.[115] Second, the boom economy allowed for more costly construction, making stone and marble build-

Figure 13. *View of the Great Fire in New York, December 16 & 17, 1835,
as seen from the top of the Bank of America, corner of Wall and Williams
Streets,* **hand-colored aquatint/etching, by William James Bennet.**
Collection of The New-York Historical Society (negative number 50114).

ing more feasible. Further, the noncombustible nature of stone buildings
would prevent the spread of fires. The material protections offered by
stone buildings made sense in the aftermath of the 1835 fire, but the dras-
tic alteration of the architectural style of the city was shocking.

Cole feared that the embrace of laissez-faire capitalism, and the erection of buildings meant to embody that new order, was severing Americans
from nature. The widespread adoption of Greek Revival architecture
seemed out of tune with national mores, and Cole feared that the city was
blindly locking itself into a delusory structural environment. As Angela
Miller notes, Cole was "skeptical of party politics," and "Whiggish in
political sympathies and strongly anti-Jacksonian."[116] Cole lamented, in
August of 1835, that Americans were "too fond of attributing [their] great
prosperity" to the government "instead of seeing the source of it in the
[nation's] unbounded resources." In adopting a Greek Revival aesthetic for
commercial buildings, New Yorkers was building a series of temples to
commerce, rather than embracing the chance to reimagine lower Manhattan in some more appropriate way. Dismayed, Cole anticipated "the down-
fall of this republican government" and feared that "its destruction will be

a death blow to Freedom, for if the Free government of the U[nited] States cannot exist a century[,] where shall we turn?" In such an event the "hope of the wise & the good will have perished, and scenes of tyranny & wrong, blood & oppression such as have acted since the world was created, will be again performed." Cole's doleful prediction would not have shocked his contemporaries in 1830s Manhattan, for Jacksonian New York was a turbulent world of civil unrest, natural catastrophes, and economic collapse.[117] The city had survived the devastation of the raging fire and the riotous plundering that followed in its wake, but it was not unscathed by these disasters, and it would not have taken a leap of faith to see New York's recent history recorded on Cole's canvases.

If "scenes of tyranny & wrong" were destined to consume the United States, the blame, for Cole, resided in Americans turning away from nature as a source of cultural inspiration. Cole worried that if Americans modeled their public buildings on foreign models, they would be importing forms connected to social codes incongruous with a democratic culture. Cole believed that architecture should reflect the social order and environment of a community, and he was troubled that America had failed to develop a style to parallel its unique political and social forms. By simply copying previous styles, Americans were too readily also adopting foreign customs and practices. Arguably, Cole not only had Jacksonian America in mind in crafting *The Course of Empire* but, more immediately, the experiences of 1830s New York. Several facets of the canvases themselves, as well as contextual material, imply that the landscape depicted in the series was topographically inspired by New York. The oddly angular rock formation topping the background mountain of each painting signals that all these canvases represent the same area. Moreover, the foreground bay and background ocean suggest that this capital is a port city. The Palisades on the western bank of the Hudson River, across from northern Manhattan, might not contain such a singular rock formation, but they create the same rugged background. Indeed, Cole continually figured the hills of the Hudson River region as craggy and sharply angular.

In the eleven years between the opening of the Erie Canal and the exhibition of Cole's canvases, New York's economy was increasingly tied to trade and speculation. Popularly, New York was associated in the minds of European travelers with Venice, because of its supremacy in water trade.[118] The iconography of the third canvas, *The Consummation of Empire*, suggests a sea-trading nation fixated on wealth, so much so that its citizens have overwritten their immediate environment in celebration of their economic prowess. The exquisitely gilded statues, the draped garlands, and the two fiery beacons at the mouth of the harbor suggest that this capital is a mercantile center. The vernal landscapes of *The Course*'s first two canvases have been replaced in *Consummation* by Greek-style buildings. This deforestation matches Cole's observations about the Hudson River Valley. In his "Essay on American Scenery" (1835), which he was preparing for publication while working on the series, Cole continually worries about the destruction of America's natural resources. Pointedly, in an 1836 letter to his patron Luman Reed, Cole writes: "They are cutting down all the trees in the beautiful valley on which I have looked so often with a loving eye. This throws quite a gloom over my spring anticipations."[119] The natural environment of the Hudson River Valley and the greater New York City area was being attacked by "dollar-godded utilitarians" intent on commercializing the area. While this evidence does not prove a direct correlation between the paintings and the real Manhattan, it does indicate that Cole conceived of the two locations in similar terms. More striking evidence resides in Cole's description of his inspiration for the buildings so central to the argument of the third canvas.

Writing Reed about the slow progress of the series in September of 1835, Cole explained that he "had to tear down some of the buildings [on the third canvas] that were nearly finished, in order to make improvements, a la New York."[120] Cole was likely referring to the effects of the devastating 1835 fire. Thus what, on first impression, seems an architectural style that distances *The Course of Empire* from its local contemporary context in fact express the current state of Manhattan's structural environment. Greek Revival buildings, hardly domestic in their architectural argument, were rapidly replacing the vernacular chaos of old Manhattan with large-scale commercial structures. Instead of purging New York of the problems of speculation, the fire had seemingly paved the way for the city to be reconstituted with an overabundance of classical stone buildings not unlike the architectural landscape of Cole's canvas. Considered in this light, *Consummation* registers the transformation of New York from a vernacular city into a Jacksonian Era landscape dominated by massive Greek Revival temples embodying the triumph of the market revolution.

Perhaps Cole was not as interested in foretelling the future as he was in creating what Raymond Williams has called social art. In defining the social novel, Williams argues that art which fully engages current cultural problems cannot imagine solutions to them without undercutting its claims to realism. To imagine a solution would require an overt act of fiction making akin to trying to will oneself into an unforeseeable future. Williams argues that, as a result, the endings of social novels are chaotic.[121] Social art is less concerned, Williams maintains, with framing solutions to problems than with detailing their causes. Cole's *Course of Empire* displays how architectural design affects the composition of social order. The adoption of certain architectural styles, Cole suggests in the series, is denuding the landscape, wasting natural resources, and detrimentally determining the future course of the nation. Viewing Cole's *Course of*

Empire as a social text suggests a reading that does not judge Cole's vision by its final canvas. Simply because Americans might not imagine themselves rioting and destroying New York does not mean that they could not see themselves represented in Cole's canvases. By reading the series only as a cycle, critics devalue the first three canvases in favor of the dire messages of the last two. But, importantly, for Cole the third canvas was the hallmark of the series.

Larger than the other canvases, *Consummation* was centrally positioned in the exhibition and thus occupied the center of Cole's argument. As Angela Miller has argued, it can also be read as a victorious parade of Jacksonian democrats.[122] Political celebrations not rooted in "the triumph of good principles and the cause of virtue & morality," as Cole wrote in his journal about a joyous "company of Jacksonians," made him very nervous about the current state of his nation.[123] As a result of what democracy had become under the influence of partisan party politics, Cole feared his society was teetering on the brink of the conditions that the third canvas of the series, *The Consummation of Empire*, depicts. Cole dreaded the possible collapse of democracy owing to a misplaced faith in the marketplace. Yet he also understood that while his society may have been precariously hovering on the brink, it had yet to fall. To interpret the series as depicting the inevitable decline of all nations would seem to leave Cole with no hope, and to afford the artist no social agency. Cole's series does not offer an unalterable prophecy for the future but underscores the consequence of continued social mispractice. Given Cole's remarks about the need to venerate American art and to preserve the nation's natural scenery, it is hard to imagine his apocalyptic vision as either fatalistic or as simply allegorical. Rather, Cole's series offers its viewers a warning, serving as a jeremiad aimed at the dangers of Jacksonian fervor for change. If America continues to embrace Jacksonian ideology, then the ruin of *Destruction* and *Desolation* will follow; but change is possible. The series calls for a paradigm shift, a return to the harmony depicted in the second canvas, *The Pastoral State*.

Cole's second canvas depicts a moderately domesticated landscape, evidencing minor human modifications. The wisps of smoke trailing from several background structures suggest houses that blend within their setting. *The Pastoral State*'s houses appear as harmonious in their settings as Irving's Sunnyside. Contrarily, the third and fourth canvases, *Consummation* and *Destruction*, display the natural features of the landscape as overwritten. None of the grandiose architectural sites dominating these panoramas replicate the harmony between man and nature detailed in the early canvases. Gone are the small private dwellings; *Consummation*'s empire city seems to have abandoned any notion of the private sphere. That erasure of the private echoes what was happening in New York. As the city was being transformed by its mercantile spirit, there was less room for private dwellings that might continue to tie citizens to the landscape. Pomp and circumstance were on the verge of dwarfing the culturally regenerative influence of the natural.

Irving's retreat to Sunnyside was also a remove from the social upheaval of Jacksonian America. Cole's series tackles the possible consequences of that restlessness head-on. Irving believed in the possibility of building a "little paradise"; Cole was more apprehensive. Irving argued that the social narratives constructed about buildings helped predict their cultural function, and that social reform could be attained by rewriting architectural narratives. Cole's canvases suggest an unease with thinking that architectural styles could so easily be adapted. The consequences of architectural transplantation remained a complicated debate throughout the period. If New York was the most European of American urban centers, then it was in the most grave danger of succumbing to the darker side of republican ideology. Would the city end in filth and wretchedness (as many had predicted since the shift of the national capital from the city in 1790) or in fire and brimstone, as Cole hinted, or could it become be a commercial center protected by the ordering influences of rural, genteel cottages, as Irving hoped? The question would not easily be resolved, but it was one that fueled the imaginations of generations of New York families, and in particular those of the Cooper family.

4

"The Wants of Posterity"

Community Construction and the Composing

Order of American Architecture

Returning via steamboat to his ancestral home after a prolonged residence in Europe, Edward Effingham, the patriarch of James Fenimore Cooper's novel *Home as Found* (1838), observes how the lower Hudson Valley has changed in his absence. Gazing at the newly constructed houses built along the riverbanks, Edward laments that "nothing but a Grecian temple" is "now deemed a suitable residence for a man in these classical times."[1] The rage for classical architecture had seized the popular imagination by the time the novel was published, and houses like Nevis, James A. Hamilton III's Greek Revival residence built in Irvington in 1835, were sprouting up all over the Hudson River Valley (see fig. 14).[2] Far from admiring such classically styled houses, Edward argues that they seem "better suited to heathen worship than to domestic comfort" (113). Echoing his cousin Edward's sentiments, John Effingham declares that the absurd sight of "smoke issuing, moreover, from those unclassical objects, chimneys," offends a discerning eye (113). Shocked by the state of the nation's design practices, Edward concludes that "an extraordinary taste is afflicting this country in the way of architecture" (113).[3]

The preponderance of Greek Revival houses along the previously rustic Hudson River leads Edward Effingham to conclude that form and function have been separated in American architectural practice. Domestic architecture in America is suffering, John advances, from an adherence to European pattern "books too rigidly" and a tendency to "trust too little to invention" (113). This reliance on imported models is hindering the cultivation of a national architectural style. "No architecture, and especially no domestic architecture," John believes, "can ever be above serious reproach, until climate, the uses of edifice, and the situation, are respected

Figure 14. Engraving of Nevis from *The Hudson, from the Wilderness to the Sea* by Benson John Lossing. Collection of The New-York Historical Society (negative number 79719d).

as leading considerations" (113). Instead of building residences in accord with their environment or patterned after their native political mores, Americans are rushing to erect "mushroom temples which are the off-spring of Mammon" (114). In effect, as John P. McWilliams posits within *Home as Found*, "America's new tastelessness is measured by its buildings."[4] Cooper extends his critique of philistine architectural practices by linking their popularity to the Jacksonian Era appetite for "speculation," cogently collapsing these two trends together to indict the market revolution for dangerously housing Americans in buildings intended for commercial—rather than domestic—purposes (113). Such a practice of replacing vernacular houses with Mammonish temples forces Americans to continually inhabit spaces designed for trade and speculation, a situation that, Cooper believes, encumbers social and cultural development. In short, *Home as Found* concludes, as Eric Sundquist argues, that "the country is bloated by false ostentation," typified, for Cooper and his Effinghams, by the zeal for Greek Revival architecture.[5]

By linking the Jacksonian mania for speculation to the desecration of the American landscape, Cooper's *Home as Found* interrogates how domestic design shapes character formation. The novel takes place in, as William P. Kelly succinctly describes, "a world dominated by expediency and self-interest," a setting that allows Cooper to explore how architectural style reflects and encodes cultural attitudes.[6] Moreover, the novel calculates that the cost of such mispractice will be paid by more than just the present generation. Signe O. Wegener contends that Cooper believed that "in the new republic, the family—and the home—fulfilled the need for perceived traditional values."[7] If Cooper imagined the house as the center of identity formation, then his concern with the failures inherent in classically styled homes evinces more than simply a matter of an interest in aesthetics. The proliferation of Greek Revival houses effectively bound future generations to the design decisions of self-interested Jacksonian Americans. Instead of offering the public an architectural inheritance reflective of a democratic ethos, the builders of these classically styled homes created monuments to capitalism. Inappropriately fashioned Greek Revival houses, like James Hamilton's Nevis, were abominations primarily because they offered delusory models. In their efforts to remodel the nation in the Greek Revival style, Cooper implies, Jacksonian Americans simultaneously refigured national character. One of Cooper's main "objectives," according to Russell T. Newman, "was not only to inform and entertain his readers, but also to instruct."[8] Cooper believed that the average citizen should take his social and architectural cues from his social superiors, and this elitism prompted him to offer, in *Home as Found*, blueprints for behavior and design intended to correct the current state of national mispractice.

As Thomas Cole had observed, Jacksonian New York's architecture was dominated by a mania for classical forms. After returning from a prolonged European sojourn, James Fenimore Cooper similarly discovered that the Republic's cultural development was stunted by a reliance on these poorly chosen models.[9] In Cooper's mind, Americans had haphazardly framed their houses on ill-suited patterns, neglecting to discriminate against aesthetics that competed with the nation's political and social ideologies. In *Home as Found*, Cooper employs the Effingham family as arbiters of taste, and through their judgments critiques the Republic's cultural life. Indeed, the Effinghams in all likelihood function as mouthpieces for Cooper's own personal complaints about American development.[10] Reading the novel as "essentially Cooper's projection of his own preoccupations onto an American landscape," Stephen Railton contends that *Home as Found* registers Cooper's "disenchantment" with "American civilization."[11] Yet, as Donald A. Ringe maintains, more than simply cataloging Cooper's sense of "the failures and excesses of democratic society," *Home as Found* prescribes "what the cure should be."[12] The ostentatious spectacle of a river "lined" with Greek temples was too much for Cooper, or his Effinghams, to bear, for these houses embodied the social dis-ease of the United States.[13] In order for this epidemic to be contained, Cooper proscribes, Americans needed to alter their domestic designs.

Critical assessments of *Home as Found* have long considered it "inept as a novel," as John P. McWilliams writes, only "valuable" as a "social document."[14] Clearly didactic in its design, *Home as Found* might be best understood, as Donald Darnell asserts, as Cooper's "attempt to explain America to Americans."[15] Labeling *Home as Found* "as the sequel to *The Pioneers*," George Dekker figures the Effinghams as "Jeffersonian gentry who make use of their material wealth to cultivate themselves and then spread their culture among their provincial neighbors."[16] For Dekker, Cooper returns to the landscape of *The Pioneers* to reinscribe the importance of America's natural aristocracy—families whose houses and settlements date back to the Revolutionary Era—as cultural anchors for American social development. In so doing, Cooper continually reverts to the theme of architectural design throughout *Home as Found* to question the relationship between houses, as defining locations for communal identity, and social temperaments.

Near the very opening of the novel, Edward's daughter, Eve Effingham, enters into a discussion about the recently remodeled Effingham house in Templeton. With Eve are her cousin Grace Van Cortlandt, the avatar of a patriotic yet unsophisticated American, and Aristabulus Bragg, the quintessential *new* American, fully captivated by the spirit of Jacksonian *goaheadism*. Bragg grouses to Eve that her family has failed to properly embrace "the Grecian, or Roman architecture, which is so much in use in America" (13). Having tried to remodel the Effingham house to better suit its environmental location, John Effingham has, for Bragg, succeeded only in proving that he is "not much of a republican" (13). Bragg barely contains his outrage over the fact that the Effinghams did not consult the public about their designs, since John's choice not to remodel in the Greek Revival style has caused the public to now consider the house "denationalized" (13). Throughout their conversation, Eve ignores Bragg's presumptions concerning the public's control over private affairs and tries to shift the conversation to a more general discussion of American architecture. In response to Bragg's assertions, Eve confesses that she "did not know that the imitations of ancient architecture, of which there were so many in the country, were owing to attachment to republicanism" (13). Eve's coyness punctuates the absurdity of Bragg's associations between Greek Revival architecture and American patriotism. Bragg exposes the faultiness of his logic—a pattern of thinking which blindly rejects anything that fails to reflect a commitment to republicanism—by responding: "To what else could it be owing, Miss Eve?" (14). Quickly, Grace Van Cortlandt interjects, arguing that since the style "is unsuited to the materials, the climate, and the uses" of Americans, it must be "some very powerful motive, like that mentioned by Mr. Bragg," that fuels the trend (14). While Eve pretends to be guileless, Grace's naivete reflects her inability to understand the complexity of Eve's questions. Both Bragg and, to a lesser extent, Grace assume that an adoption of classical forms equals a commitment to republicanism, and that a preference for any other style proves an individual is undemocratic. Throughout *Home as Found*, Cooper examines the subject of domestic architecture to admonish Americans for making myopic connections between the Greek Revival style and democratic mores. Pedagogically, Cooper aims to correct the poor lessons imparted by Jacksonians, like Bragg, who promulgate the idea that Americans should occupy classically styled houses to demonstrate their political dogmatism.

The adoption of Greek and Roman architectural models demonstrated, for Cooper, not a cultural commitment to republican ideology, but an unexamined dedication to the worst kind of fashion. To emphasize this argument in his novel, he has the Effinghams witness the massive fire that decimated lower Manhattan in 1835 (the same fire that drove Cole to recompose the architectural background of *The Consummation of Empire)*. Watching the blaze in horror, the family sees "eight hundred buildings" ravaged "as it were in the twinkling of an eye" (109). Like Cole, Cooper contends, at this point in the novel, that Manhattan missed an opportunity after the fire to properly reimagine its architectural character. While the destruction was tragic, "there was a moment when those who remembered a better state of things began to fancy that principles would once more assert their ascendency, and that the community would, in a measure, be purified" (109). Yet "this expectation ended in disappointment" as "the infatuation" with Jacksonian speculation and an architectural style that encoded the devotion to commercialism was "too widespread and corrupting to be stopped by even this check" (109). Rather than cleansing New York from the stains of the market revolution, the fire only provided an opportunity to build more outlandish Greek Revival buildings representative of the cultural ascendancy of laissez faire capitalism.

As the Effinghams return to Templeton "to breathe the pure air, and enjoy the tranquil pleasure of the country," they gullibly assume that they will leave the problems of the city behind (111). Yet, as they retreat from New York, they observe the influx of country houses modeled on pagan temples, and note how the poisons of the city have infected the countryside.[17] As their hopes are dashed, Cooper shifts focus, turning the narrative toward unraveling the legacies of the nation's architectural heritage. The Effingham house, rechristened the "Wigwam" by John Effingham after he "altered and amended [the] abode," becomes the locus for this investigation (131). The house was constructed under the original direction of Judge Marmaduke Temple, grandfather of Edward and John Effingham and the founder of Templeton, New York (and Cooper's fictionalized version of his own father, William Cooper). Built by the town's founder, the house embodied the connections between the Effinghams/Temples and the town of Templeton. In *The Pioneers* (1823), Cooper recounts the early years of the Templeton settlement, and in *Home as Found* he portrays the village after Jacksonian restlessness has dominated the national mindset. If Marmaduke Temple's house functioned as the patriarchal center of the village, the Wigwam serves as the stage on which the contesting wills of the Effinghams and the new inhabitants of Templeton play out. As Aristabulus Bragg relates, the "majority" of the public in Templeton "think they ought to" have been "consulted about" any changes to the house (14). As misguided as his complaint seems, Bragg's indignation over the lack of consultation demonstrates that he accepts—on the public's behalf—the idea that the Effinghams' house is the paradigmatic center of the village.

Edward Effingham openly scoffs at Bragg's notion that the public should have been consulted about the remodeling of his father's house, insinuating instead that the public should look to the Effinghams, their social superiors, for architectural instruction. Edward falls back on the privilege of his family's connections to the area—Templeton was, after all, founded by his grandfather, Judge Temple—to articulate how his intimate knowledge of the Wigwam's history qualifies him to remodel the settlement's architectural centerpiece. "As my house came to me from my father," Edward suggests, "I knew its history, and when called on for an explanation of its singularities, could refer all to the composite order" (128). Cooper defines the composite order as palimpsestic, a style that allows a modern architect to inscribe his own vision without destroying the work of previous authors. For Effingham, the strength of the Wigwam resides in the fact that it has been preserved and adapted by a consistent lineage of occupants, rather than demolished and remodeled by the whims of the public.

Rather than modify Judge Temple's house into another "Grecian abor-
tion," John Effingham renovates in a "modest" "Gothic" "style" (129).
John's "instructed intelligence" manages to transform "a very ugly
dwelling into one that is almost handsome" (128 and 129). In the Effinghams' collective opinion, the remodeling successfully preserved the familiar interior contours of the house, while offering a better aesthetic exterior
to the community by the corrections to its facade. The Wigwam "had not
a column about it, whether Grecian, Roman or Egyptian; no Venetian
blinds; no veranda or piazza"; rather, "it was a plain old structure, built
with great solidity and of excellent materials, and in a style of respectable
dignity and propriety that was perhaps a little more peculiar to our fathers
than" to "our worthy selves" (151). In their renovations, the Effinghams
attempt to clarify the intent of the original exterior so that the house will
better fit its surroundings.[18] They ambitiously hope that the house will
appear a natural facet of the scene, an aspiration reflected in their co-
option of the term "wigwam," used to signify Native Americanness and thus
to testify to the primacy of their house on this landscape. At a moment in
time when newly constructed houses (like James A. Hamilton III's Nevis) are
being named after foreign locales and when post-Revolutionary settlements
across New York State are being given classical designations (like Athens,
Cato, Carthage, Ithaca, and Rome), the Effinghams, by christening their
house the Wigwam, once again resist modern trends. Instead of attempting to draw connections to foreign locales, the Effinghams undertake an
act of linguistic colonization to legitimate their house as natively and historically important. The appropriation of the name Wigwam intentionally
accentuates the need for Americans to root their current practices in more
local and long-standing traditions. To further their efforts at reestablishing
the house as an antiquated feature of the region, the Effinghams also com-
mission a reconfiguration of the estate's landscaping. In *The Pioneers*, Temple
frames his house with straight rows of poplar trees; in *Home as Found*, the
Effinghams alter the estate's grounds to establish a more "natural" irregularity. This change in landscaping aesthetics speaks to the later generation's
desire to blend the house with the environment, rather than use foliage to
call attention to the structure.

The latter portion of *Home as Found* revolves around restoring the legal
authority of the Effinghams over their own property. The affair of the
point, a thinly disguised fictionalization of Cooper's own legal wrangles in
Cooperstown, serves to reestablish the property rights of the individual as
the foundation, or source, of a stable society.[19] Linked to that assertion is
Cooper's firm sense that in matters of public trust and private interest it is
necessary to clearly understand the wills—both literally and figuratively—
of previous generations to determine how to proceed in the present.
Cooper suggests in *Home as Found* that his fellow citizens need to reaffirm

a connection to the past by appropriately inhabiting and shaping, not destroying, their inherited environment.

James Fenimore Cooper returned throughout his career to the Cooperstown region as a crucial setting in his fiction. He understood the region as representing the varied reflections of the nation's progress. This tendency put Cooper in direct dialog with both the history of national development and, more intimately, the intentions of his father, Judge William Cooper, founder of Cooperstown. Part of Cooper's interest in the region stemmed from an attempt to understand and, perhaps, reaffirm William Cooper's conception of American development. In addition to *Home as Found*, such novels as *The Pioneers* (1823) and *The Deerslayer* (1841) address the relationship between domestic architecture and community construction in the Cooperstown area. These novels very specifically engage in unraveling and reimagining William Cooper's legacy, most directly related in his text *A Guide in the Wilderness* (1810). Susan Fenimore Cooper, James's daughter, also returned to Mount Vision to read her forefathers' conceptions of American development in her texts *Rural Hours* (1850) and "A Dissolving View" (1852). Like her father and grandfather, Susan Cooper uses the frame of domestic architecture to recalibrate American history. Collectively, their individual arguments concerning the centrality of domestic architecture reflect the shifts in opinion, over time, on the importance of a central house within a community as a register of social stability.

Judge William Cooper left several legacies for his son, James Fenimore Cooper, to inhabit, most tangibly his extended essay on the foundation of Cooperstown, *A Guide in the Wilderness* (1810).[20] In *A Guide*, Judge Cooper records his vision for the development of Cooperstown. Seeking to secure the future of the town against alterations in its social fabric, the judge carefully articulates an organizational scheme for the village. Largely unsettled prior to the Revolutionary War, the frontier of western New York State quickly became a testing ground for an emerging U.S. culture.[21] William Cooper personally presided over the development of one of the first post-Revolutionary settlements in western New York. Acquiring a large land grant, he began to build Cooperstown in 1785. As Alan Taylor records, by the dawn of the nineteenth century, "travelers marveled at the rapid development and manifest prosperity of Cooperstown and its hinterland."[22] Full of bluster and self-promotion, *A Guide* registers William Cooper's sense that the time for settlements funded by geographically distant land speculators has passed.[23] The success of Cooperstown, the judge assures his audience repeatedly in *A Guide*, grows out of his continual presence on the scene.

Cooper argues that settlers resent husbanding land that does not belong to them. Believing that such rancor will fester and doom the long-term health of a settlement, Cooper proposes that all land in a given tract be

available for purchase. "The reason is plain," Cooper argues: "the first difficulties are the greatest, and it is only by combination and co-operation
that they can be surmounted" (8). Like the new nation itself, the first
immigrants to Cooperstown have nothing but self-interest to bind them
together. Normally, land speculators would hire workers to clear their
land, or offer harsh terms to those who wanted to purchase plots, while
withholding the most promising tracts. William Cooper believes that true
settlement was possible only if the first laborers were afforded a stake in
future prospects. Such an arrangement, he concludes, allows a settler to
feel himself "as a man upon record" and "his views extends themselves to
his posterity, and he contemplates with pleasure their settlement on the
estate he has created" (11).

Replicating a Jeffersonian vision about the cultivation of a communal
moral sense, Cooper details his methodology for transforming transient
settlers into rooted citizens. By making settlers focus on the future rather
than dwelling on their present difficulties, Cooper contends, he can successfully channel their energy. Initially, a farmer labors to clear "away the
trees, until they, which were the first obstacles to his improvement,
becoming scarcer, become more valuable" (11). Thus, a permanent settler
will "at length" be "as anxious to preserve, as he was at first to destroy"
(11). The only way to orchestrate such a change is to try to ensure that the
first settlers do not want to leave. A farmer thus tied to the community has
his "spirit" "enlivened" even as he "builds a barn and a better habitation"
(11). In accomplishing this sense of commitment to the settlement,
Cooper has effected a type of social control over his leaseholders otherwise
impossible.[24] Instead of worrying about forfeiture and disaster, common
enough occurrences, the residents of Cooperstown sleep "in security," for
they have gotten their land on good terms (11). Free from the "gloomy
apprehensions that seize upon" the minds of less ensconced settlers, the
inhabitants of Cooperstown have prospered (11). Moreover, they have naturally become cautious with the region's resources, thus ensuring the long-
term viability of the community.

By fostering a sentiment of equality among the earliest inhabitants,
Judge Cooper could proudly boast in *A Guide* that, by the close of the first
decade of the nineteenth century, he had "settled more acres than any man
in America" and that "there are forty thousand souls now holding directly
or indirectly under me, and I trust, that no one amongst so many can justly
impute me to any act resembling oppression" (13). Cooper attributes his
success to the "adoption of a rational plan" (13). As Alan Taylor exhibits in
William Cooper's Town, however, the land was far from a barren wilderness
when the judge first arrived, having been the site of both Native American
and Anglo-American settlements. In Cooper's accounting the area is a
blank slate. He makes the landscape virgin, casting himself as the agent

who founded a community in a howling wilderness. Cooper erases the complexity of the area's history so that he can accentuate his accomplishments and promote the idea that it was his philosophy that brought order to this wilderness.

A landlord who "heads" a "settlement, and draws people around him by good plans for their advancement, and arrangements for their convenience," ensures the future of a settlement (20). Such a landowner, rather than just clearing land, actually builds a community. Cooper imagines the duty of the landlord in paternalistic terms, seizing on the contemporary image of the Founding Fathers as benevolent leaders who sacrificed alongside their companions in the struggle for liberty. Cooper posits that he has inherited that Revolutionary mantle, figuring himself as leading his troops in the fields of agriculture as the Republic's citizen soldiers were led in battle. In Judge Cooper's version of American history, Cooperstown is the "first settlement" in the United States "attempted after the revolution" (17). Lacking the aid of a foreign investor, Cooper stresses how his steady hand keeps the community together. By infusing small amounts of capital into the communal coffers, he helps Cooperstown weather the tumult of famine and outlast a rudimentary infrastructure. By never yielding his plans for the future to the whims of the moment, Cooper oversees the construction of a thriving village in the short span of two decades.

From the outset, Cooper has designed the village to structurally represent the interdependence of its citizens. "I hold it essential to the progress of a trading town, that it be settled quickly and compactly," Cooper postulates in *A Guide*, "and the only point in which I would thwart the wishes of the settler, whether merchant or mechanic, would be in the desire" to purchase "a large lot" (26). Cooper defends his dictatorial limiting of the acreage of town dwellers by contending that these limitations promote industry and attention to communal welfare. If a villager divides his time between being "half tradesman and half farmer he will neither prosper as one nor the other" (26). Such a division of attention and exertion would undercut "mutual dependence" between townspeople and farmers (26). If a "mechanic" is allowed, through the sale of large village plots, to devote "his time in any manner to the cultivation of the ground, even to the raising what is sufficient for his own consumption, it is impossible," Cooper writes, that "he should be so active and vigilant in his profession, as he would otherwise be" (26). By limiting the space available to tradesmen, Cooper solidifies the affiliations between town and country, binding them—out of exigency—to mutual interaction.

If "the blacksmith, who has been tilling the ground when he should have been providing himself with coal," fails "to shoe the traveler's horse, or mend the carrier's wagon, it is not he alone then that remains idle" (26). Likewise, if circumstances force a farmer to become a wheelwright, he estranges himself from the practice of husbandry. A "want of punctuality in one man occasions the same in others, and dilatory habits" become "the consequence" for the entire settlement (27). Unchecked, this practice dooms a frontier settlement, for if "there be another village or another market, though more inconvenient or more distant, where every man is to be found at his post," then "such a place will carry off the prize of industry," becoming "the rendezvous of traffic and prosperity" (27). Simply put, Cooper attempts to circumscribe individual attention to job performance by preventing any single settler from occupying more than one social role. Draconian in his settlement plans, Cooper imagines this type of social management as the only way to ensure that Cooperstown will prosper during its initial history.

Small village lots contribute to the rapid growth of civic pride, for in "towns compactly built there is a quicker circulation of sentiment and mutual convenience" (27). This close proximity acts "advantageously upon the manners and modes of life; better houses are built, more comforts introduced, and there is more civility and civilization" (27). By assuring the partnership of town and country, Cooper establishes a more stable social network. Mutually dependent settlers will not quickly abandon their web of associations. Absent such connection, settlers become transients, buying, clearing, and selling land. These itinerant farmers constitute, in Cooper's mind, a grave threat to social stability. He hopes to evade the problem of restlessness by developing an architectural practice (governing the size of house plots) that will foster in a single generation the kinds of relationships that were built across several lifetimes in Europe.

In articulating his design scheme for Cooperstown, William Cooper stresses that every design decision he makes reflects his desire to underwrite the future of the community. His commitment to fostering communal associations at times runs counter to his interests as a capitalist, yet he never wavers. In the end he succeeds in founding a stable community, which is relatively secure from the turbulent fluctuations of the marketplace. Although unable to replicate the success he had in Cooperstown, William Cooper left a structural legacy to his descendants even if he did not leave them a sizable monetary one.[25] As future generations of Coopers, including William's son James Fenimore Cooper and his granddaughter Susan Fenimore Cooper, stood upon Mount Vision, the vista from which William had first "surveyed" his "wilderness" scene, they looked on a landscape that had steadily developed. The view also allowed them to confront the expectations that William Cooper had for American development. William Cooper's conception of community resided in the actual village and homesteads at the bottom of Mount Vision, and these homes allowed James and Susan the opportunity to understand his vision as they struggled to define their own conceptions of the relationship between architectural order and cultural formation.

II

With his third novel, *The Pioneers; or, The Sources of the Susquehanna: A Descriptive Tale*, published in February 1823, James Fenimore Cooper's status as the preeminent American novelist of his day was solidified.[26] Long recognized as a meditation on his father's experiences as the founder of Cooperstown, *The Pioneers* examines the multivalent possession histories of the American wilderness by employing a thinly disguised Cooperstown (Templeton in Cooper's fiction) as a test case. Ever since Henry Nash Smith's groundbreaking reading of the novel, critics have been quick to note the oedipal narratives at play in *The Pioneers*.[27] While these readings are compelling, they often oversimplify Cooper's complex portrait of Judge William Temple. Nash's observation that the novel remains centrally focused on the "issues raised by the advance of agricultural settlement into the wilderness" suffers if we continually attach it to an investigation of Freudian themes.[28] As Susan Scheckel advances, "*The Pioneers* is a book about origins," national as well as personal, and to overly value one thrust of the novel (at the expense of the other) diminishes our ability to fully grasp the force of Cooper's argument.[29] As the novel unfolds, Cooper's sometimes comic treatment of Judge Temple yields to his investigation of frontier community foundation and the interrelationship between Leatherstocking's natural law and the social order embodied in the judge's construction of Templeton. Cooper re-creates contending land claims to "prove" that the order represented by Judge Temple stands as the only one capable of overseeing the growth of a lasting community. Even as Cooper lists the four most distinct claims on the land—those of the remaining Native Americans, of residual Anglo-American squatters, of the returning ousted British gentry, and of post-Revolutionary American purchasers—he also transforms the novel's protagonist, Oliver "Edwards" Effingham (father of John and Edward), into the rightful heir of each of the claimants.

As the literal descendant of the British patentee Major Effingham, the son-in-law of Judge Marmaduke Temple, and the adopted heir of the American squatter Natty Bumppo and the Mohican Chingachgook, Oliver Effingham neatly harmonizes the cacophony of America's contested histories. The novel subsumes possible tensions by restoring Oliver Edwards to his "rightful" position as owner of the lands. By the novel's close, Major Effingham and Chingachgook have both died, and Leatherstocking flees sunlit clearings for the wild; each departure unconditionally ends a possibly disruptive claim. Fiction, unlike the historical record, allows Cooper to make the past a neat narrative, folding away tensions into a single ownership claim. Cooper effectively, as Susan Scheckel observes, "edits out the violence of conflict" in *The Pioneers* by domesticating the violence of both colonization and revolution.[30] By subsuming these contending historical narratives into a seamless past, Cooper foregrounds how the unproblematic "nature" of the Templeton settlement guarantees its sustainability. In detailing the depths of Cooper's conservatism, William Kelly advances that Cooper "turns to the past to reduce anxieties occasioned by a problematic future."[31] Rewriting the possibly contentious past into a harmonious history, Cooper portrays Cooperstown/Templeton—now "pregnant with industry and enterprise"—as a site of cultural stability precisely because of the continuing presence of the Temples and Effinghams.[32]

More than just synchronizing discordant contentions, the novel registers the cultural life of Cooperstown's, or Templeton's, earliest post-Revolutionary settlers. As the first inhabitants to significantly alter the landscape, they are, for Cooper, the first to legally possess the land.[33] As Cooper argues in his 1832 preface to a new edition of the novel, "the incidents of this tale are purely fiction," while "the literal facts are chiefly connected with the natural and artificial objects, and the customs of the inhabitants"(9). It is in the faithfulness of his presentation of the life of the early settlers that Cooper stakes his claims for crafting a realistic text. Embedded within Cooper's defense of the facts dwells the solidification of his position as a historiographer and as an ethnographer of his own father's community. In Clifford Geertz's terminology, Cooper writes "after the fact" of the events that have transpired, even as he is "after the facts" of what life was like then."[34] As Geertz suggests, "there is not much assurance or sense of closure, not even much of a sense of knowing what it is one precisely *is* after, in so indefinite a quest."[35] By implying that his novel accurately portrays the entirety of the environment, both natural and constructed, Cooper foregrounds the settlement process as the preeminent concern of his text.

Cooper ties these two issues together by positioning Judge Temple's organizational talents as that which ensures the community's prosperity. Continually, the novel reaffirms that Judge Temple labored to create a settlement for "the wants of posterity, rather than" for "convenience of the present incumbents" (41). As "there was no part of a *settler's* life with which" he "was not familiar," Temple was the perfect manager for a thriving community (97). Temple makes his most visible argument about how the community should be built in the house he erects. In *Home as Found*, the Effinghams refer to their remodeled home as the "Wigwam," while in *The Pioneers* the original version of that home, Judge Temple's house, is "termed in common parlance" either "the castle" or the Mansion-house (41). In *Home as Found*, the latter generation of Effinghams rename the Wigwam to indicate its age and history; by then, in the chronology of the novels, it remains the only original dwelling still standing in Templeton. In his 1832 preface to *The Pioneers*, Cooper asserts that of all the original buildings constructed in Cooperstown, only his father's house has not "long since, given place to other buildings of a more pretending character" (9). In creating his multilayered fictionalized portrait of Templeton, Cooper similarly marks the Temple house as the only permanent structure of the post-Revolutionary landscape.

While Cooper confesses in his preface to *The Pioneers* that he has taken "some liberty" in differentiating the exterior of Temple's house from Judge Cooper's, he clearly marks it as the village's "principal dwelling" (9). Cooper's 1832 preface thus proffers the Temple house as a key site in the history of Templeton. Some critics have argued that Temple's house, as William Kelly proposes, "is the subject of Cooper's sustained ridicule," but Cooper's treatment of the house need not be read as simply aimed at producing a comic effect. Arguably, Cooper's portrait of the house in *The Pioneers* serves to map the complexities of the settlement process.[36] Although Judge Temple's house might seem unrefined, the fact that he intends his house to testify to his position as founder and caretaker transforms it into a historically important site in Cooper's fictive village. While the Temple house provides a shaky foundation, the novel establishes the fitness of Elizabeth Temple and Edward Effingham to solidify that cornerstone into a more permanent cultural anchor. Far from ridiculing Temple's house, Cooper's portrait of the building casts it as an important legacy that has grounded the village's development. From the outset of *The Pioneers*, Cooper registers his concern with domestic architecture as a register of social practice, and his sometimes comic presentation of the judge's house conterminously advances his arguments about cultural order.

In *The Pioneers*, the structure consistently referred to as "the wigwam" houses several Effinghams, but it does not center the community's ordering schemes. The wigwam of *The Pioneers* is Natty's home. Composed of rough-hewn logs, its interior remains a mystery throughout the novel. In both *The Pioneers* and *Home as Found*, the co-option of Native American architectural terminology defines the oldest dwelling in the area. In *The Pioneers*, the use of the diminutive "wigwam" italicizes the rudeness of Natty's cabin, demarcating it as little better than a shanty; whereas in *Home as Found* the authoritative Wigwam exhibits the historic presence of the Effinghams on the landscape, simultaneously suggesting that they are the inheritors and interpreters of that history. By the end of *The Pioneers*, Natty's wigwam burns down to a dilapidated heap of rubble, and the site later becomes transformed into a graveyard and memorial. By keeping the contents of Natty's hut offstage, Cooper buries its meanings, making it a repository for the uncertainties raised by the pre–Judge Temple history of the area. In unpacking the complexity of Natty's hut, Richard Godden argues that it functions as "a veritable anthology of political iconography," a "charged and semi-prescient image containing the blueprints that were to bedevil political debate for the first four decades of the century."[37] While Natty's hut might prefigure "Harrison's log cabin" and "Webster's coon-skin cap," Cooper does not envision the site as one worthy of architectural preservation.[38] Cooper eradicates Natty's hut, formerly a constant architectural reminder of the community's prehistory, to remind the future that the Effinghams and Temples domesticated the area.[39] The house that preserves and embodies the history of settlement is not Natty's crude hut but the house built by Judge Temple, the house that the Effinghams so carefully remodel in *Home as Found*.

In contrast to Natty's wigwam, Judge Temple's house withstands the social alterations of Templeton. In *The Pioneers*, the Mansion-house regally resides as the centerpiece of the village, and calibrates the rest of the structural environment of Templeton. If *Home as Found* reinvigorates the Wigwam as the hub of social and cultural life, a model for the buildings around it, *The Pioneers* establishes, in the settlement's early history, the house as serving a similar purpose. Cooper maintains that the community's foundation and future link, intrinsically, to the argument that the inhabitants of this house caused the house to make. By preserving the Mansion-house, even though they remodel it, the later generation of Effinghams in *Home as Found* extend the importance of their architectural legacy well into the mid–nineteenth century. While not, in Cooper's eyes, a perfect basis for an American national architecture, the judge's house needs to survive. The house functions as a structural reminder of the community's origins, and its continual presence recalls the debts of the present to the past. In all its guises, the house establishes the central position of the family in this community, as both guardians and residents of its designed legacy.

Cooper opens *The Pioneers* with the return of Elizabeth Temple (grandmother of *Home as Found*'s Eve) to Templeton after a five-year absence in New York City. As her father's sleigh moves down Mount Vision, Elizabeth catches a birds-eye view of the town's "cluster of houses," which lie "like a map at her feet" (46). From this perspective, Elizabeth comprehends that "five years had wrought greater changes, than a century would produce in countries where time and labor have given permanency to the works of man" (46). Stressing both the infancy of the settlement and the dramatic effects of a few years of cultivation, Elizabeth reads the alterations in the valley's structural environment. To distinguish the glen's other houses, "these pretending dwellings," from the Effingham castle, Cooper uses foliage, which marks Judge Temple's superior aesthetic sensibilities (42). "Before the doors" of the town's secondary houses, fashioned as imitations of Temple's Mansion-house, "were placed a few saplings either without branches, or possessing only the feeble shoots of one or two summer's growth" (42). Within these "habitations" live "the nobles of Templeton," whereas "Marmaduke," the village's "king," occupies the more prominent structure (42). "In the midst of this incongruous group of dwellings" rises "the mansion of the Judge," visibly "towering above all its neighbors" (42). Unlike its imitations, the acres of the judge's house are "covered with fruit-trees" (42). These older trees, some "left by Indians," have "already" begun "to assume the moss and inclination of age," forming a "very marked contrast to the infant plantations that [peer] over most of the picket fences of the village" (42). By preserving the residual orchards of earlier inhabitants, Judge Temple has cheated time and positioned his house as a seasoned construction. His trees bear fruit, while those of his neighbors have yet to grow branches. The judge's landscaping serves to both antiquate and authenticate his house as a "presettlement" feature of the region, a fact that dwarfs whatever sustenance he might gain from the trees.

Temple communicates the importance of his house by planting "two rows of young Lombardy poplars, a tree but lately introduced into America, formally lining either side of a path-way," which leads from a gate that opens "on the principal street, to the front door of the building" (42). These trees display Temple's wealth—he has imported them—and simultaneously place his home in a hierarchical relationship with the town. The cultivated rows of poplars formalize the intersection of the house with the public spaces of Templeton. Surrounded by a community populated by loggers, like the novel's infamous Billy Kirby, Temple purposefully cultivates ornamental trees. This act of deliberate landscaping, trees arranged in a straight line, removes the judge's house from the circuit of consumption that dominates the rest of the village. His gardening suggests his house has a different relationship to nature than the houses around him. Temple cares for the environment—he plants instead of chops—because he envisions his descendants as continuing to occupy the structures he builds.

The house itself was "built entirely under the superintendence of a certain Mr. Richard Jones," the judge's cousin (42). Having "commenced his labors in the first year of their residence, by erecting a tall, gaunt edifice of wood, with its gable to the highway," Jones spent the intervening time refashioning the Mansion-house as the centerpiece of village life (42). At best a poor amateur architect, Jones did have the advantage of being able to modify his work to suit the specific climate of upstate New York. Influenced by the itinerant Hiram Doolittle, Jones built the house according to "the composite order" (43). While perhaps less pleasing to an aesthetic judgment, the composite order proved a pliable architectural style. At crucial junctures, Jones and Doolittle were able to recompose even in the midst of construction. The temptation to read Cooper's formation of the "composite order" as laced with derision is understandable. Still, such a figuration neglects Cooper's celebration of the style as uniquely suited to allow the future to dialog with the past without having to dismantle its structural inheritances. While Jones and Doolittle are stock comic figures, the house they fashion is not simply a source of amusement. Carefully supervised by the judge, the two manage to erect a house that, while imperfect, quickly becomes the envy of its neighbors.

"Together," Richard Jones and Hiram Doolittle have "not only erected a dwelling for Marmaduke"; they have "given a fashion to the architecture of the whole county" (43). The prestige of Temple, the overall dimensions of his house, and its imaginative landscaping position the Mansion-house as the central edifice on the architectural horizon. By following "the composite order," an architectural system "composed of many others," Temple's amateur framers employed a style that "admitted into its construction such alterations, as convenience or circumstance might require" (43). As a direct result of the adaptability of this style to the uncertain conditions of frontier life and the environmental dictates of northern New York, "the castle" became "the model, in some one or other of its numerous excellencies, for every aspiring edifice within twenty miles of it" (43). Temple's interactions with Jones and Doolittle demonstrate his dependence on them, establishing that in a frontier settlement even the most well-intentioned house builder had to adjust his vision to the realities of frontier life. Temple's house becomes, as a result of his geographic isolation from other settlements, an amalgamation of his intent and the capabilities of the available workmen.

Although the house represents in part the aesthetics of Jones and Doolittle, they have been instrumentally guided by the chief concerns of their client. Judge Temple insisted on four conditions: that his house be "of stone; large, square and far from uncomfortable" (43). While these mandates might seem insignificant checks on the unsophisticated designers, in fact they regulate most of the major decisions concerning the house. Temple's mandate forces his builders to place utility and continuity at the foreground of the project. The decision to cover the exterior in stone, "a material too solid for the tools of the workmen," creates an "awkward dilemma" for "the two architects" (43). Yet Temple's decrees curb their unhinged enthusiasm and force them to build a seemingly permanent facade. By covering his wood frame with stone, the judge transforms his house into the only nontimber structure in the area. As many of the surrounding wooden houses remain unfinished or in disrepair (a result of the cheapness of wood, which makes these houses, even to their occupants, seem inconsequential), the judge visually removes his house from the market of consumption and waste that his neighbors remain locked in. By further instructing that his house be square, large, and comfortable, the judge plans a house with more room than he needs. The extra space ensures that in the future the house need not be demolished to accommodate his descendants.

Prohibited from having too much leeway in building the house's exterior facades, Jones and Doolittle take "refuge in the porch and roof" as the sites to display their architectural talents (43). The roof becomes "a rare specimen of the merits of the composite order," as it proves the necessity of having a malleable style when building in a new environment. Jones contends that "the ancients always endeavored to conceal" roofs, for they functioned as an "excrescence in architecture that was only to be tolerated on account of its usefulness" (44). Rather than have the roof dominate his creation, Jones has planned to fashion the roof so that it will be "flat, with four faces" (44). But Temple overrules him because this design would collapse under "the heavy snows" that lie "for months" in the area (44). While flat roofs may be appropriate for the milder climates of England or southern Europe, they are wildly irreconcilable with New York's severe winters.

Forced to abandon their initial plans, Jones and Doolittle "effect a compromise" by directing that "the rafters" be "lengthened, so as to give a descent that should carry off the frozen element" (44). However, "some mistake" is made in the "admeasurement of these material parts" and "in defiance of all rule, the roof" is transformed into "the most conspicuous part of the whole edifice" (44). Instead of a tolerated outgrowth, a necessity, the oversize roof becomes the focal point of the Mansion-house. Jones and Doolittle add an abundance of decorative features to mask the prominence of the roof, including all sorts of ornamental carvings. Jones tries no fewer than three different shades of paint—including "sky-blue," "cloud-color," and "invisible green"—to conceal the roof (44). None of these shades camouflages its dominance, obliging Jones to cover the singles with a color that he christens "'sunshine,' a cheap way," he assures his cousin, the judge, "of always having fair weather over his head" (44). The redesign of the roof, and not its coloring, assures the future prospects of the judge, because after the renovations he no longer has to worry about it caving in on his family. Fashioned in the composite order, the capacious roof does not violate any aesthetic principles; rather it is a constant reminder that Americans cannot blindly replicate foreign forms in their new environment.

In time, the roof becomes a source of pride for Jones: within "two years" after its completion, he has "the pleasure of standing on its elevated platform, and looking down on three humble imitators of its beauty" (45).

Cooper's narrator contends that this admiration results from the tendency of the public to render even "the faults of the great" as "subjects of admiration" (45). Yet a "humble" imitation of the roof would still serve the purpose of a covering in this region. Indeed, when John Effingham remodels the house in *Home as Found,* his biggest challenge lies in attempting to refigure the roof in the Gothic style. He quickly realizes that the "castellated roof" he has built is unsuitable for "such a climate."[40] Effingham has to relearn that the turrets and faux battlements he designed ignore the region's climate. Thus, while Jones and Doolittle err with their oversize roof, they do register the primacy of local conditions. John Effingham may later successfully temper the mélange of their composite order on the base of the Mansion-house, but he blunders in remodeling the roof and realizes that in the future it might have to be redone.

The porch of the Mansion-house, originally ill-conceived, testifies to the "advantages" of the composite order as Jones and Doolittle proceed to correct their initial mistakes (60). Resting "on a stone platform, of rather small proportions, considering the size of the building," the porch first consisted of "four little columns of wood" supporting a shingled roof (60). Again, the environment dictated changes. Within a season, the "frost" had undermined the architects' plans, as the contraction and expansion of the ground "had already begun to move from their symmetrical positions" the "five or six stone steps" that were featured as the entranceway to the house (60). These "evils of a cold climate" caused the separation of the steps from "the canopy of this classic entrance," so that the "superstructure was suspended in the air" by its firm attachment to the house (60). As the "base deserted the superstructure," the columns ceased to be "of service to support the roof," leaving an "unfortunate gap" in the "ornamental part" of the design (60). Yet the overarching implementation of "the composite order" allowed Jones and Doolittle to append a "second addition of the base" (60). Refashioned as "necessarily larger" and "ornamented with mouldings," this addition proved to be a flawed corrective as "the steps continued to yield," till finally "a few rough wedges were driven under the pillars to keep them steady" (60). Not supporting the roof, these wedges would "prevent" the pillars' "weight from separating" them from "the pediment" (60).

After the unsightly wedges undermine the aesthetic aspects of the house's front, the composite order allows rectification of the blemish. Since the house does not follow a more rigid architectural order, the steps can be repositioned by adding a larger base to *support* the pillars. Intriguingly, the roof, the one feature designed to accommodate the particular demands of this region, holds fast, preventing a possible collapse. The pillars remain bound to the house, refusing to yield even as their foundation slips away from them. The cracks in the porch base broadcast the expediency of the composite order for American architecture. By demonstrating how time reveals the need for corrections, the cracks confirm that an architectural style that allows for parts to be modified without disrupting the whole best serves the needs of a fledgling community. The adaptability of the house allows it to weather unforeseen difficulties while both its structure and its inhabitants adjust to the landscape.

By foregrounding the importance of the adaptability of a house to its environment in *The Pioneers*, Cooper provides a mirror of the novel's focus on Oliver Effingham. Filled with righteous indignation because he thinks that Judge Temple has stolen property rightfully belonging to his ancestors, Effingham does not attempt to read the real terrain of the community until late in the narrative. In essence, Effingham has to let go of presumptions and learn to decipher the social realities of Templeton. Effingham has to learn that Judge Temple has not "stolen" his rightful inheritance but is holding it in trust for the descendants of the Effingham line. This sense of historical trust coincides with the judge's actions throughout the rest of the novel. Not only does he design the town for "the wants of posterity," but he anchors the community to the landscape by the argument his house makes about *historic* stability. Temple's gardens actively co-opt Native American labor to project a semblance of rootedness. Similarly, his house's stone facade testifies to his intention to have the Mansion-house, no matter who inhabits it, withstand the test of time. Compared with the neighboring houses, whose "unfinished appearance" divulges "the hasty manner of their construction," the Mansion-house appears a long-standing part of the village (41).

Many of the other structures in Templeton remain unfinished, with exposed second stories, "uncovered beams," and "broken windows" in the middle of winter, revealing that "the vanity of their proprietors" has led them "to undertake a task, which they were unable to accomplish" (41). If the frosts and snows have caused so much damage to a finished house, they will surely destroy the untreated and uncovered lumber of these structures; these rooms will deteriorate before they are even occupied. No house with a rotting wood frame and roof will be of service to posterity. Given the cheapness of lumber and the availability of unsettled land, it will be just as easy for these proprietors to demolish their decaying buildings as to remodel them. This lack of architectural foresight breeds an impermanence and transience in the community: unlike Temple, his neighbors fail to create enduring foundations through building, because they have not built houses worthy of preservation. Temple builds not for himself but for the future. The Mansion-house exemplifies his social philosophy, proving that the work of today, if done with care, will serve the citizens of tomorrow. While it is far from a perfect model, the house creates social stability by following a design principle that allows for future occupants to easily amend the structure that they inherit. In effect, the house's elasticity renders it an enduring document, capable of housing the future as well as the present.

As the novel draws to conclusion, and Oliver understands the magnitude of his mistake, he repents and moves to order the future through his marriage to Elizabeth Temple. Critics often read the novel's last chapter as an elegiac conclusion: the dead are mourned, and Leather-stocking prepares to fade into the western forests. But Natty's removal from the stage is not the novel's only exit. Elizabeth moves, at the novel's close, to resolve the plot of Louisa Grant, Elizabeth's rival for the affections of Oliver. Elizabeth orchestrates the Grants' migration to a more settled area of the state. More than just a resolution of loose plotlines, the housing of Louisa Grant acts to create more social stability throughout the region. Elizabeth recognizes that no suitable match for Louisa lives near Templeton, and if she remained there it would mean her sterility. But by having "procured" a position for Louisa's father in "one of the towns on the Hudson," Elizabeth anticipates that Louisa may "meet with such society, and form such a connection, as may be proper for one of her years and character" (449). In moving her out of Templeton, Elizabeth makes sure that Louisa remains in circulation. Elizabeth displays the same sort of concern for posterity that her father does. Louisa's future as another stabilizing domestic influence will engender the same equilibrium that Elizabeth's own marriage ensures for Templeton. The novel ends not with the securing of just the Effingham/Templeton house as a site of lasting social stability; it also displays how soundness in one area, in one house, fosters durability in others.

III

In the spring of 1765, fourteen men crossed Canaderaga Lake, "mistaking it for the Otsego," and then "wormed their way, through the Oaks, into the Susquehannah, descending the river until they reached" their destination.[41] The leader of this expedition, Captain Willoughby, is the patriarch of James Fenimore Cooper's novel *Wyandotté; or, The Hutted Knoll: A Tale* (1843). A retired British officer, Willoughby is searching for his recently purchased patent in western New York.[42] Willoughby secured this grant because it contained an old beaver colony, which had continuously "occupied the place, and renewed the works, for centuries, at intervals of generations" (13). These successive dams flooded an area of over four hundred acres and "killed the trees" and other plants in the district, except for those contained on "an island of some five or six acres in extent" (13). This "rocky knoll," rising "forty feet above the surface of the water" and "still crowned with noble pines," Captain Willoughby decides, is the perfect spot to "build his huts" (13).

Convinced that by demolishing the beaver dams he can rapidly drain the pond and take possession of a richly fertilized clearing, Willoughby orders his axmen to remove the levees. "The first blow was struck against the dam about nine o'clock on the second day of May, 1765, and," the narrator of *Wyandotté* records, "by evening the little sylvan-looking lake, which had lain embedded in the forest, glittering in the morning sun, unruffled by a breath of air, had entirely disappeared" (14). Initially the alluvial soil provides a melancholy vision, leading Willoughby to "almost" mourn "the work of his own hands" (14). Flat, clear, and unmarked, its muddy texture offers the captain, he soon realizes, a blank canvas upon which to paint his own vision for the landscape. The "results of ordinary years of toil" are thus compressed "into those of a single season," allowing Willoughby to promptly overlook the outlines of a "noble farm, cleared of trees and stumps," without having to labor over the process (14). Seizing on the work of generations of beavers, Willoughby does not have to bind his interests to the large number of workers normally required to clear a forest for planting. Needing to hire only a few men to do the work typically performed by a legion of settlers, Willoughby—without much expenditure—rapidly domesticates a sizable farm in the middle of a wilderness. Accomplishing this with employees, instead of having to cast his lot in with other settlers, enables Willoughby to retain title to the entire patent. By co-opting the labor of the beavers, Willoughby avoids the specters of social leveling normally linking a landowner to those who first work the land. In so doing, Willoughby stands in stark contrast with both William Cooper and Judge Temple, who imagine the initial difficulties of settlement as creating a unique bond between founders and laborers, making each a participant in the construction of a joint-stock enterprise.

Wyandotté is a not part of Cooper's cyclical history of Cooperstown, but Willoughby erects his estate in the vicinity of the site that will become Judge Temple's settlement, and thus the novel suggestively offers a pre-Revolutionary counterpoint to Temple's post-Revolutionary project. The difference between the settlement dates in the two locations causes much of the consternation that plagues Willoughby. Although he tries to remain neutral during the Revolutionary War, Willoughby finds himself besieged by misguided "patriots" who use the cover of the American cause to manifest their resentment over his ownership of the entire settlement. The beaver dam so completely alters the labor of domestication that, unlike Judge Temple, Willoughby never conceives of anyone (aside from himself) as having any real stake in the settlement enterprise. With his rocky knoll transformed from floating island to the epicenter of a vast clearing, Willoughby moves—in one day—from being a frontiersman to enjoying the same domesticated landscape as Judge Marmaduke Temple. Without the natural advantages of the beaver dam, such an accomplishment would have been impossible. By virtue of his being able to clear hundreds of acres so rapidly, Willoughby avoids sublimating his interest to the concerns of other settlers.[43] Instead, his patent can remain an estate, rather than a community, with those who live with the family remaining employees and not ever becoming independent farmers.

Donald A. Ringe, among others, interprets Willoughby as essentially another version of Judge Temple, figuring both as "honest landowners who were entrusted in Cooper's novels with the direction of society."[44] Such a reading misaligns the two founders. Judge Temple labors to build a settlement through hard work and civil law, perhaps best demonstrated by his honorary title, a designation intended to project his commitment to legal equality. Capt. Willoughby, as his formal title suggests, does not operate from the same foundational premise. Never having worked to establish civil law, Willoughby suffers because he imagines that, as John McWilliams writes, his own "self-imposed moral laws" will inculcate themselves in those around him.[45] Willoughby operates, in effect, as the quintessential opposite to Natty Bumppo, hoping somehow to create a situation governed by natural law that still respects the rights of property owners. As the novel draws to a conclusion, events force Willoughby to confront the lawlessness of demagoguery, the extreme version of self-justification writ large. Cooper's disdain for mobocracy flows consistently throughout the novel, but Willoughby's settlement plan—embodied in the castlelike fort he builds for his family to occupy—serves to incubate such behavior. In his recent reading of *Wyandotté*, Russell T. Newman suggests that the beaver dam allows Willoughby to avoid having to "adapt" his "needs to what the land offers"; instead he "destroys" the dams "and reaps the benefits."[46] In effect, Willoughby commodifies the wilderness and constructs his settlement on a feudal, rather than democratic, model. As such, *Wyandotté* (like both *Home as Found* and *The Deerslayer*) privileges the same type of settlement construction undertaken by Judge Temple.

Unlike Judge Temple and his fellow settlers, Willoughby does not face the hardships normally associated with domesticating a frontier. Without having to struggle to clear fields for cultivation, Willoughby quickly plants crops that rapidly yield abundant "fodder for the ensuing winter" (15). This harvest allows him to leave the settlement after directing his employees to commence building his home. His experiences as a career military officer inform his blueprints, for Willoughby believes that his remote location demands that security be his paramount concern. Taking advantage of the foliage remaining on the rocky knoll, Willoughby decides to build on the oasis the beavers left behind. By situating his house within the only cultivated landscape, albeit by beavers, he attempts to create a sense of permanence and gentility in the region. During his winter retreat to Albany, Willoughby directs his laborers "to commence a house for the patentee," to begin building "a few bridges," to "clear out a road or two" and build a few outlying "sheds" as well as a "log barn" (15). Willoughby leaves with the desire of discovering on his return a habitable estate, commissioning laborers to work on his behalf while he hibernates in civilization. From the outset, Willoughby figures himself as landlord and not as a community builder. This is, perhaps, best expressed by his architectural plans, for the house that Willoughby designs has more in common with medieval fortresses than it does with domestic houses. Willoughby's "impenetrable walls," as Wayne Franklin notes, seem less designed to offer domestic comfort than to carve out a place in which his family can "hide themselves."[47] While the Willoughbys strive to turn their hut into a communal center, their fundamental and structural remove from everyone else begins to breed discontent. Whereas Judge Temple's house functions as a cultural anchor to his community—a model home, mimicked by others—Willoughby designs a dwelling that will always be distinct from those around it. While the Willoughbys initially appear happy with the design of their home, the argument that the house makes in terms of social arrangements effectively guarantees the failure of Willoughby's settlement experiment.

When the Willoughbys return to the patent after their winter residence in Albany, Mrs. Willoughby gasps in surprise that so much has been accomplished in so little time. The labor of only a year has done "a vast deal for the place," she notes, finding the denuded landscape just "irregular" enough "so [as] to be picturesque; while the inequalities" are "surprisingly few and trifling" (30). Mrs. Willoughby's reaction reveals that she was prepared for a more unpolished scene and again trumpets how rapidly Willoughby has transformed the landscape. "Accustomed to witness the slow progress of a new settlement," Mrs. Willoughby has "never seen what might be done on a beaver-dam," and to her all the progress appears "like magic" (30–31). The winter wheat is stacked on the driest portion of the field, and the sown grass flows like "two wide belts of verdure" on both banks of the stream, "giving" the year-old farm "an air of rich fertility" (30). Such a scene of cultivated progress would have been an extreme rarity in western New York during the 1760s; moreover, that it has happened in so short a period of time is remarkable.

Willoughby's positioning of his house in a "place of difficult access" follows the logic of "ordinary prudence" (31). Even after the pond was drained, the rocky knoll upon which he first hutted "had great advantages" both "for a dwelling and for security" (31). Choosing an "almost inaccessible" site, Willoughby "directed the men to build a massive wall of stone, for a hundred and fifty feet, in length, and six feet in height" adjacent to a massive rock outcropping to secure the perimeter of his house (31). As the hill itself was "covered with heavy stone," all the building materials that the men required were readily at hand (31). By using the natural features of the landscape, Willoughby enclosed "an area of two hundred, by one hundred and fifty feet, within a blind wall of masonry" (31). To this outer wall Willoughby admitted only "a single passage," which he intended to secure with two massive gates of oak in "the centre of its southern face" (31).

Behind the stone walls he customized "a building of massive, squared, pine timber, well secured by cross partitions" (31). Willoughby's architectural designs have more in common with military fortifications than they do with domestic homes, yet his use of stone and finished lumber display his determination to take root in the area. Instead of using unfinished, bark-encrusted logs, Willoughby's workmen have milled and planed their timber. This expense has yielded a more pleasing effect and indicates Willoughby's intentions to manufacture a permanent building. Still, the absence of windows or apertures on the exterior facade of the building have furnished it with a "somber and gaol-like air," more "barracks" than "an ordinary dwelling" (32). Between the sheer faces of the natural rock formations and the intricately laid retaining walls, Willoughby's house is nearly impenetrable. As the domestic center of a settlement, Willoughby's earthen castle is almost as out of place as a Greek Revival house would be, evincing his determination (even though he is not confronted with any obvious danger) to have security rather than aesthetics guide his designs.[48]

The interior of the house, while not as flawless as its exterior, is "plain" but "comfortable," plastered and whitewashed with an abundance of "space" (38). The house is split into two halves, with the eastern wing designated as private space. The western wing is devoted to storage and an "eating room and divers sleeping rooms for the domestics and laborers" (38). The interior of the house strives to appear less like a barracks and marks its pretensions to be a manor house. The clear separation of the public and familial spaces indicates that the interior is modeled after traditional genteel homes. Unlike typical frontier architects, Willoughby does not allow the lines of social hierarchy to spatially bleed into one another in his domestic arrangements.

Distant from other pacified districts, the house serves a variety of purposes, and thus Mrs. Willoughby accepts that defensive principles should decide architectural decisions. "Part house, part barrack, part fort, as it is," she resigns herself to be "hutted for life" (39).[49] With its interior presenting "the odd contrast between civilization and rude expedients, which so frequently occur on an American frontier," the Hutted Knoll offers enough comfort for "persons educated in refinement" so as to allow Mrs. Willoughby to envision it as a fortuitous seat for the family. Carpets, rare in America "in the year of our Lord 1765," cover the centers of several rooms, and a hodgepodge of furniture "collected in the course of twenty years' housekeeping" makes the building an enviable house, given its remote locale (40). This is the first real home that the Willoughbys have ever had. As a result, when Mrs. Willoughby surveys the contents of her new house, she takes pride in the collection of all their possessions together for the first time: she now sees "many articles that . . . belonged to her grandfather assembled beneath the first roof that she could ever strictly call her own" (40). Constructed not only for the future prospects of family members and their present necessities, the house allows them to assemble the objects of their pasts, collectively, for the first time.

Form follows function in the design of the Willoughby house. Even though the house approximates a barracks, it is conceived as a manor house. Unlike Judge Temple, Willoughby does not cultivate a democratic village around his house; rather, he fashions an estate, which will be the only significant dwelling in the area. Similarly, Willoughby does not assume a semi-legitimate legal title to identify his role in the community, as Judge Temple does, but retains his military rank. Although untitled, he builds an aristocratic estate house.[50] By sustaining his privileges through his refusal to sell or lease any of his land, Willoughby ensures that the Hutted Knoll remains the unquestionable center for all the activities that give purpose and meaning to the community. He builds, in effect, a feudal estate in the pre-Revolutionary American wilderness. Jeffrey Walker reads Willoughby's architectural decisions as embodying the captain's desire "to protect his garden-wilderness from" the dangers of the "encroachment of civilization or the cyclical pattern of nature."[51] While Walker's contention that Willoughby seeks to isolate himself as much as possible makes sense, it seems overdetermined to suggest that he removes himself from the encroachment of civilization. Willoughby is more naive than nihilistic, and the problems he faces stem from his ambitions to transform the patent into a quasi-European estate where all the other "settlers" are really retainers. Cooper's inability to imagine the Hutted Knoll as a sustainable model demonstrates, regardless of his distaste for social leveling, that he cannot imagine a narrative for American settlement that does not unfold according to the reasoned plans laid out by Judge Temple.[52]

The novel is set against the tumultuous backdrop of the Revolutionary War, and during the course of the conflict Willoughby's house is besieged. The political motivations of the invaders are murky at best. Although he served in the British army and his son is a major in that army, Willoughby's political allegiances, as far as he betrays them, are with the insurgent colonials, with whom his son-in-law (Colonel Beekman) is a prominent officer. Not having committed any energy or support to the Crown, Willoughby is an odd target for the wrath of the insurgents. It quickly becomes clear that the rebels surrounding the Hutted Knoll are more interested in Willoughby's property than his politics.

Echoing his message in such volumes as *The American Democrat* (1838), Cooper's argument, architecturally, in *Wyandotté* is that it is possible to favor maintaining privileges based on wealth and talent and still be committed to democracy. Willoughby believes in the cause of American independence, but he vigorously asserts that his ownership of the land is just. Seeking to establish his independence from the whims of others, Willoughby manages his estate as "an isolated establishment" (42). "Thus it was that he neither sold nor leased," meaning that "no person dwelt on his land, who was not a direct dependent, or hireling, and all the earth yielded he could call his own" (42). Willoughby's sole interaction with outside markets is his yearly conversion of fattened cattle for young calves and necessary supplies. For all intents and purposes, Willoughby has achieved the self-sufficiency that the colonies sought in the War for Independence: he has severed his dependencies on foreign sources by living off the abundance of a well-managed estate. Yet he has done nothing to actually found a community, and his independence relies on his employing retainers. The island in the wilderness that Willoughby claims as his own capsizes in the tumult of the Revolution, for, although he has declared his independence, he has done nothing to establish a network of mutual support.

Everyone around him envies Willoughby's independence. In particular, Joel Strides, an employee who leads the desertion of Willoughby's men and sides with the insurgents, resents Willoughby's position. A native of New England, Strides finds it "distasteful" to "see a social chasm as wide as that which actually exist[s] between the family of the proprietor of the Knoll and his own, growing no narrower" (264). As a result of his sole ownership of the land, Willoughby can slow economic mobility in the immediate vicinity. For Strides, the wealth of the Willoughbys is not offensive in itself, but he abhors the idea of a class distinction based on education, manners, and morals. Cooper blames this rancor on Strides' origins. The "social conditions" of New England, since its settlement, have bred within "the interior of the New England provinces" a "social equality so great" as to "almost remove the commoner distinctions of civilized associations, bringing all classes surprisingly near the same level" (261). "The results of such a state of society are easily traced," the narrator concludes, as "habit" takes "the place of principles," and people become "accustomed to see" all questions, private or public, as matters fit to be judged either by the church or by "public sentiment" (261). Willoughby hopes to circumnavigate this by denying the presence of a public in his company town, and while he is filled with disdain for social leveling, Cooper falls short of suggesting that Willoughby has constructed a sustainable foundation for future growth. Unlike the settlers of Templeton, the retainers of the Hutted Knoll cannot envision that their labor will ever allow them to change their social position on the patent. Such a rigidly hierarchical social order cannot withstand the structures of thought and feeling that coalesce with the Revolution.

By situating *Wyandotté* amid the backdrop of the Revolution, Cooper argues that the aim of the Revolution was not, and should not be reimagined as, eliminating social distinction. Rather, the struggle aimed to divorce the Republic from the constraints of dependency, a situation that Willoughby's land management does not allow for. While Willoughby does not tax or levy his tenants unjustly (for he has none), his philosophy denies everyone else the possibility of self-sufficiency. Without a personal stake in the settlement, as William Cooper argued, "settlers" will either resent the landowning class or simply decide to abandon them. Strides is an employee, free to leave the estate when he chooses, but such a practice will result only in constant geographic mobility, a phenomenon that J. F. Cooper, like his father before him, blamed for eroding cultural stability. By the end of the novel it becomes clear that neither Strides' coup nor Willoughby's isolationism will prove generative. Willoughby's assertion that he has not denied any of his employees their freedom is technically true, yet his social order is also fundamentally undemocratic and therefore seemingly cannot survive the Revolution.

The deserters and their Anglo-American allies flee upon the arrival of the real Continental Army. This retreat proves that the marauders who first attacked the Hutted Knoll have no legitimacy, and demonstrates that their actions were only a thinly veiled attempt to place "themselves in the way of receiving fortune's favors" (359). Realizing that their "merciless deeds and selfish acts" would deny them any "claim" for "patriotic service," they scurry to "conceal their agency in the transaction" (359). Instead of heralding their supposed Continental Army allies, the marauders spot them and end their siege of the Hutted Knoll. Thus the narrative legitimates the Revolution's aims as terminating foreign control of the nation, and not as ending social distinction within the colonies. Yet the conclusion of the novel also signals the failures of Willoughby's model as a sustainable one. None of Willoughby's self-justifications can outlast him, and when he is murdered (by Wyandotté, a Native American he beat savagely years earlier), the Hutted Knoll becomes an empty shell of his vision for wilderness settlement.

After the uprising and the murder of Captain Willoughby, "the Knoll was to be abandoned, as a spot unfit to be occupied in such a war," for "none but laborers, indeed, could or would remain" behind as caretakers (364). The captain's son, Major Robert Willoughby, still enlisted in the British army, cannot safely remain on his deceased father's estate, nor can the captain's widowed son-in-law, Colonel Beekman, who has arrived as leader of the Continental regulars, dwell at the scene of his wife's murder. Without a resident owner there is no point in having employees remain on the patent, since it was designed as a self-sustaining farm and not as a profit-making enterprise. The estate is resigned to the care of "nature, for the few succeeding years" (364). Thus Captain Willoughby's attempts to secure an estate upon the Hutted Knoll fails as a result of an attempt to erase distinctions in social class. The manor house fails to survive not because of the actual causes of the Revolution but as the result of an envious mob seeking to eradicate difference. The insurgents who unhut the family do so not because of their attachment to the cause of independence but because they willingly deny any definition of republicanism but their own.

As the novel closes, nineteen years after the Hutted Knoll was abandoned, the narrator reminds us that "the ten years that elapsed between 1785 and 1795, did wonders for all this mountain district" (368). During this post-Revolutionary period, towns such as Cooperstown, "for years the seat of justice for several thousand square miles of territory," literally "sprang into existence" and generated the stability in the region that pre-Revolutionary establishments had failed to erect (368). During the nineteen years that separated the desertion of the Hutted Knoll by the Willoughby family and the return of Robert and Maude Willoughby to their ancestral American home, the remoteness of the locale kept it concealed from human visitors (369). They are not surprised to discover "the Hut . . . exactly in the condition in which it had been left" (370), abandoned and boarded up. Cooper ends the novel by eviscerating the house of any future potential. Without being continually occupied, the Hutted Knoll becomes a doomed relic of possibility, rather than a monument to real social experience.

Despite his desire to fashion a feudal estate by willfully inscribing his presence on the landscape, the wilderness reabsorbs Willoughby's house. So why did Willoughby's vision fail to sustain itself? In *Wyandotté*, Cooper offers us another vision of how the pre-Revolutionary history of American settlement is littered with failed patterns. These deserted houses fail to solicit a lasting order, and are inherently doomed, because of their unsound foundations. Fundamentally dissimilar to William Cooper or Judge Temple in his refusal to bind tenants to his community through the sale of land, Willoughby imagines his neighbors as employees, as soldiers in his own private army. Such a vision stands as antithetical to the management of a new community. Joel Strides' actions are understood as representational of an American character that judges all matters as if they are of public interest. While Cooper has not shifted in his abhorrence of such behavior, as he registers in *Home as Found*, he does seem resigned to its continual recurrence. Through their policy of selling settlers an interest in the community, by allowing them to envision their own property as tied to a larger order, Judge Temple and William Cooper both create a public interest tied to the private realm. The exterior arrangement, the outer facades of buildings around which communities are centered, best communicates a founder's sense of social order to the surrounding settlers. By refusing to have his house embody a more democratic aesthetic, Willoughby builds a structure that cannot survive, except as a relic of failure, in post-Revolutionary America.

As William Cooper understood, and as James Fenimore reiterates in *Wyandotté*, the greatest obstacle to founding an enduring community is social flux. Willoughby offers no challenge to the fleeting promise of mobility, and thus he and his house are abandoned. If Strides, and the mob that follows him, felt that their possessions and houses were also threatened, they would not have resented the protection and stability that the Knoll offered them. Judge Temple never faces such an insurrection, because the people of Templeton feel a connection to him that is not based solely on contractual employment. As William Cooper took pains to argue, an architect of a community must build structures that ensure mutual dependency. Willoughby rejects this idea, believing he can found a house that can flourish as a floating island unmoored to other structures.[53] William Cooper cast himself as benevolent founding father, and molded Cooperstown with an eye toward future concerns; his fictional representation, Judge Temple, does the same thing. In contrast, Captain Willoughby decides not to intertwine the future of his community to anything outside his private concerns. Such personal projects will never create stability, because they fail to yoke settlers to the land. Plotting America's past, James Fenimore Cooper again underscores which narrative of community construction, which architectural model, will support the needs of both his contemporary circumstances and those of the future.

IV

In her best-known work, *Rural Hours* (1850), and in a complementary essay, "A Dissolving View" (1852), Susan Cooper calls for the development of uniquely American cultural forms reflective of the nation's democratic doctrines. Intimately linked to this appeal is her description of nature as essential nourishment for the national imagination. Implicit in her argument is a second call, the necessity of preserving this resource. By becoming familiar with their native environment, Americans will discover foundations for institutions in harmony with the landscape around them. Susan Cooper charges Americans to stop imitating European cultural models, urging her generation to form a new national identity grounded in American nature.[54] Within these two texts, which need to be considered in tandem to appreciate fully her conception of American development, she argues that while Americans have not yet devised cultural forms to embody their democratic values, they have also not irrevocably altered their environment.

Susan Cooper firmly believed that cultural values were products of the material culture (the entire shaped human environment) and the landscapes in and on which they were fashioned. Petitioning Americans to pause before making further mistakes, she contemplates, in *Rural Hours*, the cost on American social development if the nation fails to rectify its current architectural practices. She proposes the scrutiny of new building plans prior to construction, for "there is a certain fitness in some styles of architecture which adapts them to different climates" (297). By obscuring the negotiation between man and his specific environment, architectural failures threaten the stability of the culture. She teases out meaning on a local level, confining her examination to Cooperstown to illustrate her vision of national amelioration. Susan Cooper transforms Cooperstown into a "city upon a hill" to decry current cultural practice, arguing, as her father and grandfather did before her, that it mirrors much of the nation in economic and social progress at midcentury.

Susan Cooper's connections with her locale were deeply rooted; she understood that the natural environment and social development of Cooperstown were tied directly to her familial history. Susan was the third Cooper to describe the natural and structural environment of central New York State. The views expressed by these three authors, writing of the same region over a forty-year period (1810–1850), document significant shifts in the history of American attitudes toward nature and toward the question of how optimally to arrange a stable population within that wilderness. William Cooper held a primarily utilitarian vision of wilderness, and his writing details how his own sense of architectural arrangement will help fashion a mutually dependent and, thus, stable society. James modified his father's vision by questioning his predecessors' interactions with nature, while simultaneously claiming the wilderness as containing the multivalent settlement history of the nation. Susan infused her writing with a protoscientific consciousness absent in her forefathers' writings. Thus the progression from William to Susan Cooper mirrors developments in American natural history and community planning while also suggesting the great depth of her rootedness in the Cooperstown region. The movement further records the shift over time of the importance of a central house within a community as a register of social stability. Like her father, Susan returns to a primal scene—prior to her grandfather's inscription of architectural order on the landscape—to display that his reasoned approach to building for the posterity of tomorrow is the only viable approach to American development.

As a post-Revolutionary settlement, Cooperstown represented the social conditions of many western American settlements. By recording its developmental history, Susan Cooper hoped to teach others to respect the demands of the environment so that they might optimally arrange the human presence. Fashioned as a seasonal journal, *Rural Hours* catalogs the attempts of individuals in Cooperstown to inhabit their environment. The wealth of natural observations collected in *Rural Hours* functions as source material for her more pointed arguments in "A Dissolving View."

In the "Autumn" section of *Rural Hours*, Susan Cooper considers the impact of the American wilderness on the writing of natural history. She describes a process of cross-pollination through which Europeans have reconceived their environment in light of a new respect for American scenery, asserting "that all descriptive writing, on natural objects, is now much less vague and general than it was formerly; it has become very much more definite and accurate within the last half-century" (208). Cooper notes the popularity of landscape painting and the propensity for a "natural style in gardening" as possible causes of this transition (208). But, she contends, social patterns are rarely altered by discrete factors: "It is seldom, however, that a great change in public taste or opinion is produced by a single direct cause only; there are generally many lesser collateral causes working together, aiding and strengthening each other meanwhile, ere decided results are produced" (208). Cooper's caveat forestalls reading cultural trends reductively, and it emphasizes her concern with how "causes" combine to produce change.

Susan Cooper employed the languages of both natural history and domesticity to probe the current state of her society. American social maturation was, for Susan Cooper, intrinsically tied to the production of indigenous architectural forms. She believed that the Republic's social structures had grown out of the management of its natural resources and that the manner in which the constructed environment was envisioned would dictate the cultural growth of the nation. Cooper's nuanced understanding of the "collateral causes" that collectively shape "public taste" exhibits her attempt to refine various disparate narratives in circulation. In *Rural Hours* and "A Dissolving View," she promulgates the notion that American cultural behavior, both in practice and in planning, ought to take into account and somehow represent America's environmental uniqueness. Familiar as she was with nineteenth-century natural histories, her own work deploys these source texts, and ideas derived from them, to deliberate America's social, architectural, and cultural practices.[55]

Cooper's conception of nature and the patterns nature offered represents a paradigm shift in the way natural history writing was understood in the early nineteenth century. This shift emancipated treatments of American nature from the confines of eighteenth-century European descriptions of the New World. Liberated from the restraints of such residual practice, Susan Cooper demanded that Americans, in order to define themselves, turn toward nature rather than continue to reject its primacy. The advent of gentility in America during the mid–nineteenth century was, as Richard Bushman notes, yoked to a "beautification campaign," which insisted that "everything from houses to barns to village streets was to be made beautiful; every scene was to be turned into a picture."[56] In *Rural Hours*, Susan Cooper argues for the congruence of interiors and exteriors by unearthing "how large a portion of our ideas of grace and beauty are derived from the plants, how constantly we turn to them for models" (316). Look at "all the trifling knick-knacks in the room," Cooper directs, "and on all these you may see, in bolder or fainter lines, a thousand proofs of the debt we owe to the vegetable world" (316). Cooper urges the incorporation of interior decorations that match America's exterior environments, rather than relying on foreign models. While Cooper's remarks recall the tenets of European *Naturphilosophie*, they are more properly read as a careful adaptation of that doctrine. Susan Cooper shuns the idealization of nature, insisting instead that Americans adopt realistic forms from their immediate environment.[57]

A major influence on Susan Cooper's conception of landscape aesthetics was Andrew Jackson Downing, whose widely celebrated *Treatise on the Theory and Practice of Landscape Gardening, Adapted to North America* (1841) was the first American work devoted to landscape design.[58] In Downing's work Susan Cooper found a voice counseling patience and the cultivation of nature as the optimal means of advancing American cultural development. Promulgating the cultivation of gentility, Downing argued that as nature could be shaped and husbanded so too could social practices, and that alterations in the landscape would provoke shifts in cultural habit. In an editorial in the *Horticulturist*, a journal Downing edited from 1846 until his death in 1852, he advised that "to live in the new world" meant leaving foreign preconceptions behind.[59] Downing called for moderation in the modification of the landscape and assailed the gospel of *goaheadism*. If America was to develop a refined native culture—autonomous, yet comparable to European society—then its citizens must proceed with caution. For Downing, landscape and social structure were directly linked. The cultural institutions Americans created must be grounded in an interior and exterior architecture that represented the democratic tenets of the Republic; for as Downing advanced in *The Architecture of Country Houses*, "different *styles* of Domestic Architecture" were "nothing more than expressions of national character."[60]

America's foremost popularizer of the Picturesque, Andrew Jackson Downing defined that aesthetic mode as "an idea of beauty or power strongly and irregularly expressed," as opposed to "the Beautiful," which was "calmly and harmoniously expressed."[61] In creating a picturesque scene, Downing observed, "everything depends on *intricacy* and *irregularity*."[62] He was aware that nature was not inherently picturesque but required arrangement and embellishment so that picturesque scenes could be formed, and that this shaping "springs naturally from a love" for the terrain.[63] To express a wild yet cultivated nature, landscape gardening must be tailored to local conditions. In America the progress of landscape gardening was not impeded by a lack of resources but by a failure to adapt European ideals to the demands of America's geographical and historical particularities.[64] Downing's equation of regional differences in attitude toward nature with sociopolitical values demonstrates how closely linked were these seemingly divergent agendas. A landscape aesthetic must reflect the demands of a given environment while representing a nation's heritage.

In *Rural Hours*, Susan Cooper investigates American social mores as an extension of the Republic's relationship to its natural environment. In a pivotal essay that appeared two years later, she advances her argument more specifically, mapping the historical terrain of American architecture and its connection to the landscape. In "A Dissolving View," Susan Cooper entreats readers to emancipate themselves from received practice, to imagine their own location in nature as the central experience of their lives. In so doing, she recapitulates residual conceptions about American social evolution and considers how emerging interests in natural history and landscape aesthetics departed from that inherited tradition.

Susan Cooper situates "A Dissolving View" in Cooperstown during autumn. Her choice of season grounds her essay within (as she conceives it) the paradigmatic American season. Beginning in *Rural Hours*, Susan Cooper argues that America's autumnal palate offers unrivaled vistas. "Our native writers, as soon as we had writers of our own, pointed out very early both the sweetness of the Indian summer, and the magnificence of the autumnal changes," which uncovered, Cooper continues, "the precise extent of the difference between the relative beauty of autumn in Europe and in America: with us it is quite impossible to overlook these peculiar charms of the autumnal months," whereas in Europe "they remained unnoticed, unobserved, for ages" (209). The explosion of color during an American autumn affords a spectacle unfamiliar to Europeans. These diverse tints are the most difficult to reproduce, for "there is no precedent for such coloring as nature requires here among the works of old masters, and the American artist must necessarily become an innovator" (215). Autumn is, Cooper argues, an unworked genre, delivering American artists from the constraints of unfavorable comparisons with the artistic conventions of Europe. Representing American autumn requires painstaking attention to fleeting scenery. The best vantage point a seeker of picturesque scenes can have is in "the hanging woods of a mountainous country" where the "trees throwing out their branches, one above another, in bright variety of coloring and outline" sufficiently frame the intricacy of the scene (211). Susan Cooper's narrator occupies such a position at the opening of her meditation on the development of Cooperstown. Moreover, this seat on Cooperstown's Mount Vision also has direct familial associations. It is the spot from which William Cooper reportedly first saw Lake Otsego and from which Elizabeth Temple reads the development of her native village at the opening of Fenimore Cooper's *Pioneers.*

Susan Cooper opens "A Dissolving View" with a familiar account of the beauty of the autumnal American landscape. That rendering is complicated when she describes autumn as protean. During fall an observer is unbalanced, never knowing "beforehand exactly what to expect," for "there is always some variation, occasionally a strange contrast" (80). Yet Cooper quickly reveals that it is the human modification of the multihued landscape that generates the picturesque: "I should not care to pass the season in the wilderness," for while "a broad extent of forest is no doubt necessary to the magnificent spectacle," there "should also be broken woods, scattered groves, and isolated trees" (82). For, she continues, "it strikes me that the quiet fields of man, and his cheerful dwellings, should also have a place in the gay picture" (82). Fall contains "a social spirit," drawing attention to the human presence in the landscape (81).

Cooper locates her narrator on the trunk of a fallen pine tree, which overlooks the country "for some fifteen miles or more," framing her field of vision and enabling her perception of the picturesque (81). A nearby "projecting cliff" and some oaks whose branches overshadow the narrator's seat, creating a natural Claude glass, guide her vision, imparting a graduated scale to the objects in the background (81).[65] Situated within the forest, Cooper's narrator overlooks a cultivated landscape, which figures the progressive development of American settlement: "the lake, the rural town, and the farms in the valley beyond, lying at our feet like a beautiful map" (81). From this topological position, the favorite perch of the Hudson River School, Cooper's narrator witnesses—and records—the history of American social evolution, while ruminating on the consequences of all human development.[66] She concludes that, although "the hand of man generally improves a landscape," there is a danger that terraforming projects partake of the hubristic (82). In such work man "endeavors to rise above his true part of laborer and husbandman," assuming "the character of creator" (82).

For Cooper, this hubristic inclination has contaminated architecture since its advent. Europe is replete with architectural projects that compete with nature rather than harmonize with it: "Indeed it would seem as if man had no sooner mastered the art of architecture, than he aimed at rivaling the dignity and durability of the works of nature which served as his models; he resolved that his walls of vast stones should stand in place as long as the rocks from which they were hewn; that his columns and his arches should live with the trees and branches from which they were copied; he determined to scale the heavens with his proud towers of Babel" (84). While such "imposing" ancient piles stir up wonder, they also recall the combative cultures out of which they arose.[67] The "very violence" of the past and its "superstitious nature" created monuments to dissolute empires, forged structures to withstand the danger of eradication (86).

If a cultivated landscape should epitomize the specific social and cultural values of its population, as Cooper believes, then is it tragic that the United States lacks monuments to monarchies and feudalism? European cities are burdened by buildings that were formed by the "prevalence" of a "warlike spirit," whereas America is relatively free from such unsightly hindrances (86). These feudal buildings "are likely" to "outlast modern works of the same nature," for those who built them imagined a future dedicated to the same principles that governed them: "They not only built for the future, in those days, but they expected posterity to work with them; as one generation lay down in their graves, they called another generation to their pious labor" (86–87). While Americans are "in some measure influenced by those days of chivalry and superstitious truth," they are not bound by them (87). Susan Cooper recognizes just how much materiality matters in shaping a coherent social philosophy. By affirming agency, Cooper extends her contention that European architecture is ill-suited for America. "Thus it is that there is not in those old countries," she observed, "a single natural feature of the earth upon which man has not set his seal" (88). Cooper finds a triumphant strength in "how different from all this" is the "fresh civilization of America" (88, 89). Much of the Republic's nature remains wild, and thus, for Cooper, Americans fashioning a modern nation are not burdened by the decisions of their ancestors. She predicates her vision of post-Revolutionary American settlement, as her father did before her, on the absence of such architectural monstrosities as Willoughby's Hutted Knoll, a feudal building that overdetermines present possibilities.

Critical of the current state of national life, Cooper complains that Americans are "the reverse of conservators," failing to preserve markers of their own history (89). Here Cooper's position reproduces contemporary class-based arguments against the depredations of laissez-faire capitalism and, chiefly, the cautions of her own father in such novels as *Home as Found, The Deerslayer,* and *Wyandotté.* Yet, for Cooper, there is freedom in Americans being "the borderers of civilization," for that position enables them to "act as pioneers" (89). Conscious of her verbal echo of the title of her father's novel, Cooper recalls her readers' attention to what it meant to be a pioneer in the immediate vicinity of Cooperstown. She extends her examination of American society by freighting the landscape with predictive power; Cooper observes that "the peculiar tendencies of the age are seen more clearly among us than in Europe" (89). The unfolding of the American scene, measured by its architecture, its landscape design, and its consequent social refinements, is more than a matter of local interest. It is a barometer of the age, a register of the future. The promise of America resides in the availability of a wilderness that can be settled as Cooperstown has been.

Inheritors of Western social tradition, yet free from the constraints of modern Europe's determining environment (for "many parts" of the Old World "have an old, worn-out, exhausted appearance"), Americans should fashion an architecture suited to the more "subtle" nineteenth century, the age in which frontier settlements like Cooperstown have taken root (90, 89). America's historic monuments are not to be found in man-made ruins but within nature itself. Paraphrasing Louis Agassiz, Cooper notes that "as the surface of the planet now exists, North America is, in reality, the oldest part of the earth," simultaneously more ancient and more vigorous than the natural environment of Europe (90). While Americans have failed as historic conservationists, they have not yet irrevocably denuded their landscape, and so can still alter their interaction with it.

Cooper continues by returning to Agassiz, who "tells us that in many particulars our vegetation, and our animal life, belong to an older period than those" of Europe (90). Agassiz believed that vegetation that existed only in fossil state in Europe continued to flourish in North America. By the 1850s Agassiz was the most prominent natural historian in the United States, and Cooper's citation of his work testifies to her familiarity with contemporary natural history.[68] Agassiz wanted to understand nature through, as Edward Lurie suggests, "the perceptions provided by direct experience."[69] While Agassiz straddled "the two worlds of empiricism and idealism," he also knew "that nature, if it meant anything at all, was to be understood as a whole, a historical and contemporary unit of experience."[70] Agassiz's conception of nature, which dominated natural history prior to Darwin's 1859 publication of *On the Origin of Species*, rested on the assumption that local environments were shaped by divine power for particular ends. Advancing this notion of separate creations, he argued in *Lake Superior* (1850) that "the geographical distribution of organized beings displays more fully the direct intervention of a Supreme Intelligence in the plan of Creation, than any other adaption in the physical world."[71] Agassiz's sense of the uniqueness of each region's natural history undergirds Cooper's promotion of a specific American architecture or interaction with the landscape. If, as Agassiz maintains, different parts of nature have been separately created for a particular, divine purpose, then Americans, who have not completely altered their environment, are positioned to interpret properly their physical world. And by accurately reading their landscape, they can build dwellings in harmony with their surroundings.

Cooper ends her essay with an enigmatic turn. Seizing a "sprig of wych-hazel," Cooper's narrator plays a "game of architectural consequences" in which she imagines the landscape as it might have appeared if the culture that had formed it had been driven by different forces (91). The inroads of civilization disappear, and with a wave of the wand the landscape is restored to wilderness. But "merely razing a village" and restoring the valley to its virginal state does not "satisfy the whim of the moment," and so the spell is cast again, until she beholds "a spectacle which wholly engrosse[s]" her attention (91–92). The conjuring wand has produced the valley as it would have appeared "had it lain in the track of European civilization during past ages; how, in such a case, would it have been fashioned by the hand of man?" (92). In the midst of this reverie, in which everything is "so strangely altered," the narrator requires "a second close scrutiny" to convince herself that this is "indeed the site of the village which . . . disappeared a moment earlier" (92). Only through an intense examination of "all the natural features of the landscape" is she assured that it is the valley, and not herself, that has been recast (92). Noting the geographically appropriate vegetation and recognizing the familiar contours of the lakeshore, she understands that her reimagined history of cultural production is what changed the landscape. Quickly "all resemblance ceased," for the hills are now "wholly shorn of wood," and the "position of the different farms and that of the buildings" has "entirely changed" (92). The little town has "dwindled to a mere hamlet" (92–93).

The valley is now dominated by two structures, the church and an "old country house," which give the surrounding habitations their meaning, or at least arrange them in "various grades of importance" (93). The church and manor house define the social structure of this European-style village; all its citizens share one religion, and just as clearly they are cast into a delineated social hierarchy facilitated by the architectural style. Cooperstown's bustling industry becomes, in the "European" hamlet, "two or three small, quiet-looking shops"; its wooden bridge is replaced by a "massive stone" one guarded by "the ruins of a tower" (93). By recomposing the scene in the form of a European village, Cooper underscores the differences between American and European society. While the denuded European landscape contains buried "ancient coins" and the ruins of "feudal castles," the relationship of its current occupants to their environment is entirely predetermined (93). Unlike the social roles in the less-ordered American scene, those of the Europeans in this view are already fixed. In sharp contrast, the current state of U.S. architecture and civic planning permits the natural proliferation and change of the social relations of Americans. Both William Cooper and James Fenimore Cooper argue for a reasonable progression of American development. Building on their arguments, Susan suggests that America has been liberated from constraining influences because no pre-Revolutionary patterns survive to overly complicate the prospect of forming a democratic community. In effect, the Coopers maintain that a blank slate is awaiting the arrival of an architect who will build for the future instead of the past.

The narrator's reverie is disrupted by "a roving bee, bent apparently on improving these last warm days, and harvesting the last drops of honey" (94). As Washington Irving reminds us, bees were widely perceived as "the heralds of civilization, steadfastly preceding it as it advanced from the Atlantic borders."[72] The bee, cast here as a symbol of an intrusive market economy, quite literally stings the narrator out of her Hudson River fancy and reminds her that the rural location from which she views the American scene might soon fall victim to the energies of regnant capitalism. Or perhaps, having imagined the appearance of the valley as if it had been shaped by European cultural advancement, readers of her essay will understand the danger of choosing foreign models as social guides. Informed and reminded of the real history of settlement of the region, they can recall, as they move forward, what created structural integrity and social stability within Cooperstown itself.

Prior to her wych-hazel fancy, Cooper contemplates the current state of American architecture, suggesting that "it is yet too unformed, too undecided to claim a character of its own, but the general air of comfort and thrift which shows itself in most of our dwellings, whether on a large or a small scale, gives satisfaction in its own way" (91). This critique is not melancholic; rather, it is framed as a recognition that America is a nation whose identity will be decided in the present, a borderland between a determining past and an unknown future. While American architecture may lack a character of its own, that absence will not obstruct the progress of future generations. She encourages a movement toward preservation, which would enable the development of an American aesthetic cognizant of the particular character of the nation's environment through the erection and perpetuation of stable, usable houses that would frame a proper identity for the entire human-shaped environment. By registering the vulnerability of older aesthetic perspectives that proceed from a reliance on

European cultural models, she argues for their rejection. Anything built on such foreign foundations is doomed to collapse; alien to New World soil, such buildings could never take root without damaging the natural environment. At the same time, she maintains that Americans need not heedlessly pursue forms of architectural and landscape design capable of reflecting a democratic cultural order. Only by considering her two texts in tandem can a reader fully appreciate Susan Cooper's conception of the linkage between cultural forms and nature as dependent on the imagination. Instead of further damaging their environment by constructing badly designed buildings, Americans, she argues, should imagine the consequences of their choices before plunging ahead, working with—rather than in opposition to—their natural environments. Since assembled aesthetic failures encumber the formation of a national culture by articulating inappropriate social codes, she promotes the imagination (and not the landscape) as the arena for testing the consequences of any new construction. She cautions her contemporaries to see the danger of the classically styled Greek Revival homes and the feudalistic Hutted Knoll on the printed page and to not be in a rush to duplicate these aesthetic failures in the uncharted regions of the western frontier. Moving beyond residual aesthetics, beyond requiems for an America that has suffered for importing European cultural models, Susan Cooper makes a case for preserving the wild as the locus of the imagination.

5

"In the Midst of an Uncertain Future"

Remodeling the Legacies of American Domesticity

Edgar Allan Poe's last (and unfinished) tale, "The Light-House" (1849), raises more questions than it answers. The fragmented narrative contains three brief journal entries, all presented as being written by an anxious writer who has secured, with some difficulty, the sinecure of lighthouse keeper. Exhausted by the faithlessness of "society," the narrator relishes the position because it allows him, "for once in my life," to be "*alone*."[1] A commercial cutter, bold enough to traverse the "190 or 200 miles" of rough seas separating the lighthouse from the mainland, deposits the narrator at his cloistered post so that he can make "way with my book" (924). Driven by a misanthropic impulse to find domestic seclusion, the narrator presumes that sequestering himself from social exchanges will spur him to write again. But just days into his new life, his obsession with the fragility of the lighthouse's foundation compromises his ability to focus on anything but the contours of his environment. As he explores his new residence, the narrator detects a structural flaw in the very building he imagined would insulate him from disruptions. He records, with exacting detail and increasing concern, his discovery that the "hollow" interior of "the shaft" stands "20 feet below the surface of the sea, even at low-tide" (925). With his confidence shattered, the narrator becomes paralyzed by the fact that "the interior at the bottom" is not "filled in with solid masonry" (925). The narrative culminates with the chilling observation that "the basis on which the structure rests seems to me to be chalk. . . . . ." (925). This evocative line—punctuated by the haunting reverberation of the ellipsis—ends Poe's final tale.

Given the narrator's fascination with the security and independence of his situation, the concluding line of the extant text raises the possibility that the lighthouse has been washed away by the turbulent tides. If such a reading maps Poe's ambitions, then, effectively, the tale dramatically stages the difficulty facing anyone searching for an unassailable footing. The discovery that the lighthouse has such an unsound foundation undermines the narrator's optimism concerning the possibilities attendant to domestic isolation. Traveling to the very edge of his community's borders in search of autonomy and surety, the narrator, in his search for domestic tranquillity, finds only a brittle structure surrounded by raging waters. The narrator's desperate figuration of a beacon of commerce as removed from the demands of exchange stands out as the most striking detail in the fragmented pages of "The Light-House." Like the burning pyres standing guard over the background of Cole's *Consummation of Empire*, the lighthouse illuminates the pathways of travel and trade. The realities of the economic role of the lighthouses creep into Poe's tale, and as such this final fragment insinuates that the illusion of a secure domestic remove—free from the impediments of society and the market—rings as hollow as the chalk underpinnings of the lighthouse itself. Even in this marginal location the narrator remains conjoined to the market revolution he fled.

The narrator aims to radically distance himself from everyone and everything, yet he ends up residing in a structure designed to guide global interactions. In effect, he occupies a space that orchestrates transposition on the macro level, even as he fancies himself distant from the clamorous demands of society. Maurice S. Lee has observed that "the point that" Poe's "writings make so well is that perversity is never far from reason."[2] While the narrator's reason ambitiously leads him to the lighthouse, he perversely inhabits a commercial beacon with a hollow substructure. Reason cannot plot him a course away from social entailments, as Poe stresses the difficulty facing a writer who attempts to segregate himself from circulation. Louis A. Renza argues that "The Light-House" symbolizes the ways in which Poe's "works at bottom said nothing, or more accurately that what they did express could never stand as beacons of truth for others."[3] Striving to liberate Poe from critics who pigeonhole his work, Renza asserts that Poe cannot be so easily confined, because his "semiotic faithlessness" had "little place in a U.S. culture where one might think to invent or at a minimum reconstruct a new identity from scratch."[4] Renza's argument recapitulates a timeworn critical tradition: historically, Poe's critical marginalization sprang from reading him as disengaged from American culture, as scholars repeatedly resubscribed to Vernon Parrington's claim that "the problem of Poe, fascinating as it is, lies quite outside the main current of American thought."[5] While Poe has enjoyed an unrivaled afterlife in popular culture, most traditional studies of American literature continue to figure him as an anomaly in national literary history.[6] Such practice miscalculates how Poe's works reflect and encode the variegated state of early-nineteenth-century culture. In short, to reiterate a question posed by Terence Whalen, "If Poe isn't in step with his time where is he?"[7]

The lingering perception of Poe as a solitary genius unconcerned with cultural contexts has been fruitfully challenged by a number of critics who have attempted to demonstrate Poe's engagement with political and social movements.[8] Yet, "not surprisingly," Terence Whalen observes, "these attempts to historicize Poe falter in the face of Poe's own ahistorical diatribes against democracy and human perfectibility."[9] Whalen argues that Poe actively cultivated a sense of himself as a "politically neutral author," a move that allowed Poe to reconcile his work to the demands of either a "Whig or a Democratic" readership.[10] Still, Poe's accommodations to the fluctuating tastes and demands of the decidedly partisan publishing industry should not be misconstrued as an innate aversion to commenting on political and social movements. Simply put, it would be a mistake to confuse anti-*Democratic* with antidemocratic. In their focus on the relationship between artistic production and domestic spaces, even the fragments of "The Light-House" reverberate with Poe's concerns with the uncertainties of the mid–nineteenth century. Far from dissociated from the mores of his contemporary moment, Poe is, at heart, a social critic.

The work of such scholars as Katrina E. Bachinger, Theron Britt, Joan Dayan, Monica Elbert, Jonathan Elmer, J. Gerald Kennedy, Maurice S. Lee, and Meredith McGill has advanced our understanding of Poe's complex relationship with the emerging market revolution and the social tensions of the Jacksonian Era.[11] The works of these critics have engendered new interpretations of Poe's career, and collectively they point toward the necessity of deeply considering how Poe's engagement with cultural concerns informs his presentation of the domestic. The precariousness of social position—often figured architecturally—under the sway of Jacksonian democracy is, arguably, the unacknowledged theme of many of Poe's tales. Throughout his tales, Poe's narrators express deep-seated concerns about the hollowness of their domestic situations, as he recursively destabilizes the prevalent notion that houses might ever provide refuge from social demands. The legitimate terror of "The Light-House" resides in its representation of the idea that even a domestic remove of two hundred barely navigable miles cannot disencumber the anxious writer from the swirls of circulation and exchange; if anything, the lighthouse roots him even deeper in economic webs of association. Even in the isolated confines of the lighthouse, the narrator still experiences the restlessness he tried so desperately to flee. Poe's construction of the narrator's continued anxiety erodes the popular conception of the house as a sanctuary impervious to the vicissitudes of an external social order.[12]

The Jacksonian period was one of unusual uncertainty for American society, characterized by rapid and unpredictable economic change, social mobility, racial violence, and underlying fears of mobocracy and rootlessness.[13] Andrew Jackson was continually lauded as the paradigmatic "self-made" man, and his ascendancy in 1828 seemingly opened up vistas of social mobility. Jacksonian democracy was, to its critics, synonymous with what James Fenimore Cooper called "goaheadism," a state of mind characterized by unexamined action and a wholesale rejection of the past. In the wake of Jacksonian enthusiasm, which lasted well into the 1840s, many Americans were adrift in the riptides of unending change. Edgar Allan Poe, in many of his works, traces the dark side of Jacksonian social mobility, the terror resulting from how an ardent faith in self-determination disrupts every aspect of society, by charting how domestic spaces are not free from the pressures of the public sphere. Jacksonian ideology offered no stable anchor for identity formation; instead it was predicated on the premise that each individual held sole responsibility for forging his own identity. When self-fashioning is grounded on such a precarious foundation, the possibility of being genuinely rootless—of having no place in the world—consistently surfaces as an ever present danger. Gillian Brown argues that "in the midst of change" to the presiding economic system "the domestic sphere provided an always identifiable place and refuge for the individual: it signified the private domain of individuality apart from the marketplace."[14] Even as Brown persuasively reconfigures the domestic as a circle inhabited by all Americans, her view of the home as a constant refuge from what the historian Charles Sellers calls "the market revolution" is overtly optimistic.[15] As Poe's "Light-House" intimates, domestic refuge was (at best) hard won, and, even when found, it provided unsound protection from the surging invasiveness of the marketplace.

From the beginning of the Jacksonian Era and through the middle decades of the of the nineteenth century, crippling economic fluctuations, rapid national expansion fueled by an improved infrastructure and mechanical developments in transportation, and a loosening of voting restrictions combined to create both a larger enfranchised population and a much more ungrounded electorate. Tapping into the cultural anxieties born from these social changes, Poe serially returns to destabilized domestic spaces to evince the unease of Jacksonian society. Disgruntled by his failure to inherit John Allan's fortune, diminished by endless financially driven relocations, embodying certain southern antebellum attitudes toward race and class, and disdainful of the tyranny of the majority, Poe personifies the underpinnings of Jacksonian life. Instead of presenting Poe's early tales as divested of political discourses, we need to recover how they survey the cultural uncertainties of the Jacksonian Era by representing the house, not as a sanctified space, but as barely capable of warding off public demands that impinged on the private sphere. American cultural development was not about gradual progressiveness; it is more accurately characterized by continual panic over disunion and dissolution. Poe's tales foreground these uncertainties by representing the domestic as continually beset and endangered by outside factors, and as such they provide unique windows into the chaos of antebellum American culture.[16]

For numerous writers of the late antebellum period, destabilizing market forces were cohabitants of their domestic lives. Popularly, the home was being refigured as a feminine space, while the marketplace was defined as the only masculine cultural space. In this climate of separate spheres, late-antebellum male writers felt dislocated and perhaps even emasculated. Working from home, and often not a home of their own, many of these writers worried about the effects of spatial location on personal identity. Poe's life and work are emblematic of both the fragility of the domestic as a refuge from the market and a simultaneous desire to realize that ideal. From the steadfast refusal of John Allan (Poe's foster father) to adopt him legally, through his break with Allan in 1830, Poe's life was a series of domestic disappointments. After his expulsion from West Point for conduct unbecoming a future officer, Poe's domestic unease only increased. Poe spent the last eighteen years of his life (1832–49) wandering from city to city and from house to house, residing at some point in almost every major urban center on the eastern seaboard of North America.[17] Distraught and disillusioned by his own failure to secure a stable domestic situation and by his wife Virginia's death, Poe spent 1849 in a futile search for financial backing for a new literary magazine. In the midst of this personal chaos he drafted "The Light-House." Uneasy about the solidity of his own fragile social position, Poe, whose life entailed a constant struggle to balance market pressure and domestic security, personifies the darker side of Gillian Brown's figuration of houses as harbors from social concerns.

Fragment or not, "The Light-House" details, albeit figuratively, the pressures facing a writer in his quest to find a stable position removed from the demands of society. In effect, "The Light-House" seizes on widespread cultural representations of houses to expose the hollowness of reverential conceptions of the domestic. "Ideologies like domesticity become popular," Lora Romero writes, "not because they provide the masses with a finite and orderly set of beliefs relieving them from the burden of thinking but instead because they give people an expansive logic, a meaningful vocabulary, and rich symbols through which to *think* about their world."[18] Attuned to the ways in which the Jacksonian social nexus symbolically deployed domestic spaces, Poe positions his lighthouse keeper to call into question ideological figurations of the house as an asylum. In her insightful study of political and economic dimensions of the American literary marketplace, Meredith L. McGill contends that "the strategic generality of time and space in many of Poe's tales" effectively "serves to locate them within a culture of literary dislocation."[19] McGill marks Poe's indecipherable settings as a purposeful method of locating his readers within "the 'gloomy, gray, hereditary halls,' of fiction itself."[20] Still, Poe's evisceration of the particulars of time and space does not render his tales void of contextual markers; rather, his tales evidence a particular precision in the descriptions of domestic spaces, and, indeed, this preoccupation with the design and furnishing of interiors reoccurs throughout Poe's fiction. Although he had enormous difficulty securing a permanent residence, Poe never relinquished the search for a suitable independent domestic space. His work continually displays this desire through an attention to interior design and architectural style. More than just a passing trope or an attempt to satisfy the demands of the magazine market, Poe consistently employs architecture as a determining factor in identity formation.

In particular, his sketch "The Philosophy of Furniture" (1840) argues for the crucial effect of domesticity on the national consciousness. "In the internal decoration, if not in the external architecture of their residences," Poe writes, the "Yankees alone are preposterous" (382). Conducting a hasty survey of international decorative practices, Poe condemns the current state of interior design in the Republic. The cause of the problem emanates from the deplorable fact that Americans have fashioned "an aristocracy of dollars," resulting in their merging "in simple *show* our notions of taste itself" (382 and 383). Terence Whalen describes Poe's complaints in "The Philosophy of Furniture" as emblematic of his rejection of "the very premise of the culture of surfaces."[21] The prevalence of judging an object's value by economic and not aesthetic means, for Poe, demonstrates the madness of a nation attuned only to shimmering superficiality. In the United States "the cost of an article of furniture has at length come to be" the "sole test of its merit in a decorative point of view" (383). Such folly reduces American houses to ornate display cases for the wealth of their inhabitants. "There could be nothing more directly offensive to the eye of an artist," Poe concludes, "than the interior of what is termed in" America "a well-furnished apartment" (384). Habitually confounding "the two entirely separate ideas of magnificence and beauty," Americans ceaselessly replicate bad habits; they replace aesthetic sensibilities with commercial ones. The prevalence of such indiscretions—even in a culture that reveres home and hearth—only magnifies the cost of interior design transgressions.

Unless the nation reforms its practice of interior decoration, Poe argues, the future growth of the Republic will be compromised. The "inartistical arrangement" of American rooms, with a prevalence of furniture arranged in "straight lines" or "clumsily interrupted at right angles," has a detrimental effect on the development of the nation (383). Like Andrew Jackson Downing, who railed against the artificiality of geometric landscape gardening, Poe champions irregularity and intricacy in domestic design. Interiors that rigidly adhere to preconceived layouts ignore the possibilities of the local, whereas designs predicated on more esoteric conceptions of spatial arrangement herald the uniqueness of a particular setting. Such an individualized style, Poe asserts, would be an aesthetic benefit to a house's occupants, a treasure not measured by cost but in its effects on shaping demeanor. The geometric sameness of interiors hampers personal expression and turns the sanctified space of the home into a site of mechanical reproduction. "As we grow rich," Poe prophesies, "our ideas grow rusty" (386). This corrosion of national sentiments will eventually transform houses into disposable objects, for, as the neglect of interior design spreads, it can only diminish the importance of the domestic. If all houses replicate the same patterns, then no one will have any particularized sense of his or her own domestic identity.

The ideal room Poe describes appears as a strange mélange of crimson and gold: a large, "oblong" space with one door, two windows on the opposite wall, two rosewood sofas and two similar chairs, a marble table, shelves that "sustain two or three hundred magnificently bound books," a pianoforte, one mirror (circular and small), some large "landscapes of the imaginative cast," an Argand lamp, and, in every "rounded" corner a "large and gorgeous" vase filled with "a profusion of sweet and vivid flowers" (387). Poe sketches a room of leisure, designed to heighten the aesthetic sensibilities of its occupants, a refuge from the chaos of the world. Sadly, this crimson and gold chamber exemplifies the type of room that Poe could never afford to occupy. Despite his own domestic dislocation, Poe advocates for interior design practices modeled on more than just mere economic factors. As even its very title makes clear, "The Philosophy of Furniture" asserts that domestic design matters and that the consequences of continual mispractice are national in scale.

Driven by circumstances to New York City in 1844, Edgar Allan Poe soon became, in the words of Kenneth Silverman, "wretchedly depressed in spirits."[22] Poe had moved to New York with the hope of "living for the future," but the chaotic streets of Manhattan depressed him.[23] Poe's distaste for New York may have been linked to the binding need he felt to be there: New York was the nation's publishing center, and by the mid-1840s Poe (having exhausted most other means of support) needed to be close to the heart of the magazine industry. Yet he felt imprisoned in the city, where he was continually confronted by others enjoying the luxuries and economic freedom he so desired. Like Cooper's Effinghams, Poe was a self-styled cultural aristocrat, but in Manhattan—where capital was king—it was hard to maintain social distinctions without resources. In the end, Poe wanted to flee Manhattan just as much as the Effinghams did. Hoping to find in the rustic Bronx the type of genteel domestic life he craved, Poe moved his family to a small cottage in Fordham.

Poe's joy over the removal to Fordham, expressed in several pieces he wrote while living there, mirrors the tendency of his characters to seek domestic refuge. Repeatedly, Poe employs the aesthetics of architecture and interior design as a means of calibrating a character's psychological situation. Poe's characters are defined, he suggests again and again, by their domestic situations. In effect, Poe draws a correlation between the interior of houses and an individual's well-being. In sketches such as "Landor's Cottage" and "The Domain of Arnheim" (written while Poe lived in Fordham), Poe argues that the proper construction of houses and landscapes allows for the enjoyment of a fuller aesthetic life. In particular, "Landor's Cottage" explores how the house serves as the center of identity formation.[24]

Snuggled in an unidentifiable byway in one of the "river counties of New York," amid a serpentine path of "superintended" greenery, and bordered by a rivulet and private lake, Landor's cottage is a "combination of novelty and propriety" (886, 887, and 893). With the visible absence of any machinery or crops, the cottage does not suggest a farmhouse but an urban fantasy of rural life, a snapshot of the ideal rustic retreat. An "unpretending" dwelling, "its marvelous *effect*" lies "altogether in its artistic arrangement *as a picture*" (893). Irregular in its design and layout, Landor's cottage embodies, for Poe, the paradigmatic possibilities of domestic architecture. Describing Poe's affinity for spasmodic as opposed to merely picturesque domestic scenes, Joel R. Kehler argues that "if there is one characteristic shared by the architecture of Poe's landscape fiction it is a bold eclecticism for which no apology is offered."[25] Landor's cottage avoids the impropriety of symmetry, for its unequal wings (with the "western wing" approximately "one third less" than the eastern wing) frame a rectangular section located "not exactly in the middle" of the structure (893). An elongated covering, built sturdily enough to avoid the unsightly necessity of an overabundance of supporting pillars, oversweeps the exterior of the cottage to form "the roofs of two piazzas" (893). With one main entranceway, "not exactly in the middle division" but a "little to the east," and "two windows" to "the west," the facade's irregularity highlights the picturesque effect of the cottage. For Poe, symmetrical designs represented an uncritical devotion to geometric planning, a practice that infested the nation with the delusory disease of an undeviating sameness instead of the more pleasing aesthetic possibility born of variations.

The interior of the cottage, or rather the public space that the narrator scrutinizes, appears decorated by a devotee of "The Philosophy of Furniture." The parlor, in particular, has an "excellent" carpet and curtains "tolerably full, and hung *decisively*," which compose the room with a proper reverence (897). Although the color scheme replaces the crimson and gold of the platonic parlor with a creamy white and green, the room's design contains only these two colors and intertwines them in all the minor ways in which "The Philosophy of Furniture" advocates. The suitable "astral lamp" is present, just as "each angle of the room" exhibits a "vase, varied only as to its lovely contents" of flowers (897). The walls have lithographs "fastened" to them and not hung on cords, as Poe cautions against in the earlier text (897). Landor's cottage would appear to be, given the argument of "Philosophy" about the restorative powers of such an environment, Poe's ideal domestic environment. Catherine Rainwater maintains that Poe deploys irony in "Landor's Cottage" to manifest how the narrator's "lack of sensitivity" blinds him to the prisonlike qualities of Landor's idiosyncratic construction.[26] Yet dismissing as mere irony Poe's depiction of this idealized space misses the point of the tale. Landor's landscape does not imprison simply because it reflects a unique and adapted vision of design; rather, as "The Philosophy of Furniture" suggests, the ready acceptance of mass-produced interiors is the real tragedy afflicting the nation. "Landor's Cottage" stands as the archetype of the rural residence, the perfect house, a space liberated from labor and commerce. At the opposite end of the ordered architectural spectrum resides the mansion at the core of one of Poe's most famous tales, "The Fall of the House of Usher." Landor's cottage radiates stability, the harmony of a well-articulated, personal vision. Conversely, Usher's ancestral mansion seems menaced by its surroundings. Only hereditary custom links Roderick Usher to his abode; none of its interior or exterior characteristics reverberate with his personal vision, and as such it replicates the critique of depersonalized interiors that "The Philosophy of Furniture" and "Landor's Cottage" map.

The mysterious cause of the collapse of the House of Usher has been a constant source of energetic speculation. As the "deep and dark tarn" engulfs "the fragments of the '*House of Usher*,'" the "time-honored"—yet branchless—Ushers fade from existence (336, 318). Poe's fascination with the blurring association of a family without "collateral issue" and an antiquated house suggests a context for "Usher" too often neglected (319). Instead of functioning as a site of cultural order, the pseudoaristocratic House of Usher fails to extend any issue beyond the boundaries of its own unstable foundation. The "legitimate" terror of "Usher," written during the wildfires of Jacksonian social mobility, stems from its depiction of how the Ushers are rendered obsolete by a society seeking to eradicate any markers of an artificial aristocracy, and any other way "in which some men sought to manufacture privilege for their own benefit."[27]

For the surrounding "peasantry," the "quaint and equivocal appellation of 'House of Usher'" has long "seemed to include" both "the family" and their "mansion" (318, 319). This traditional compounding of inhabitant and structure compromises Roderick's individuality. Oppressed by the structural and design decisions of his ancestors, Roderick Usher inhabits a baleful relationship with his own home. Denied, architecturally, the possibility of independence, he remains tethered to the "melancholy House of Usher" in ways that are difficult for the narrator to describe (317). Usher incarnates the danger of inhabiting a domestic residence that denies him the possibility of self-expression. Prohibited by circumstance from making the House of Usher into Usher's house, Roderick suffocates under the weight of his domestic inheritance.

The "vacant eye-like windows" of the mansion look blank because the original Ushers have long since ceased to dwell within its walls, and none of the family's descendants have remade the house in their own image. Stocked with "profuse, comfortless, antique, and tattered" furniture, the domestic furnishings of the house have simply "failed to give any vitality to the scene" (320–21). Roderick's "cadaverousness of complection" matches "the crumbling conditions of the individual stones" of the house's exterior (321). When the house collapses, when the fracture that continually threatens its stability implodes, the last two Ushers perish. The tale affirms the impossibility of separating the house and its inhabitants. The miasma that envelops the mansion, emanating "from the decayed trees, and the gray wall," prematurely antiquates both its inhabitants and their house (319). Bound by the architectural and design vision of corpses, the modern Ushers inhabit a materially poisonous atmosphere. Roderick, Poe informs us, believes in the "sentience of all vegetable things," and in particular senses that in "the gray stones of the home of his forefathers" resides a consciousness (327). This ghostly cognition haunts Roderick, even as it nails him fast to the house. Denied the opportunity to fashion a home that expresses his individuality, he is consumed and erased by the house. As the nation overindulged on the idea of regeneration through mobility, static pseudoaristocratic houses became untenable spaces. In effect, the listless Ushers exemplify the class eclipsed by Jackson's iconoclastic remaking of the social order.

When Roderick declares himself "the last of the ancient race of the Ushers," his prophecy conveys alarming reverberations for more than just Poe's tale (323).[28] Fears about a vanishing sense of privilege and position were a by-product of the rampant alterations occurring in the nation. By the mid-1830s, with Manhattan as the epicenter of the market revolution, speculation and credit had replaced production and cultivation as America's keywords. As homesteaders poured into previously "unsettled" spaces they altered political power in the country, so much so that by 1840 Ohio (admitted to the Union only in 1803) had surpassed Virginia in both total population and the size of its congressional delegation. The erosion of generational ties to local communities culminated in an undercutting of the geographically informed allegiances that had habitually shaped political practice. Considered against these contexts "Usher" might be more at home in the 1830s than readers typically imagine.[29]

Perhaps the most profound critique of 1830s America is Alexis de Tocqueville's *Democracy in America*, a text marked by a determination to discern, as the title of one of his chapters asks, "why the Americans show themselves so restive in the midst of their well-being."[30] Throughout *Democracy in America*, Tocqueville deploys the phrase "in the midst" to describe the instabilities he witnesses around him, wondering how "in the midst of an uncertain future" and how "in the midst of the universal movement of society" the nation has managed to keep from fracturing apart.[31] Poe's tales explore the ramifications of life "in the midst" of Jacksonianism, registering the dystopianism of Tocqueville's equivocations. Americans, much to Tocqueville's horror, are so consumed by a mania for speculation and mobility that they even figure domestic houses as disposable products. "In the United States, a man carefully builds a dwelling in which to pass his declining years," Tocqueville records, "and he sells it while the roof is being laid; he plants a garden and rents it out just as he was going to taste its fruits."[32] Tocqueville's observation vividly captures just how out of place the completely depersonalized, antiquated House of Usher, and its static inhabitants, are in the midst of such perpetual motion.

Poe's macabre tales overflow with insane narrators who, in part, blame their malaise on intolerable domestic situations. The house, in the world of Poe's fiction, offers no haven from the terror of the outside world. The gothic horrors that confront Poe's characters emerge from inside the very houses they occupy; they are not simply external complications. To some extent Poe's figurations of the house as a site for gothic disruptions replicates familiar formulas. Yet his attraction to the house and his specificity of language suggest his attention to the minute details of domestic architecture. Perhaps his desire to inhabit a house of his own, an oasis decorated and arranged according to his own domestic style, informed his depictions of houses. Those figures forced to dwell in a house designed or owned by others, as in the case of Roderick Usher, are driven insane (at least in part) by their domestic situations. Comparatively, those with the means to acquire houses that reflect their own aesthetic vision, like Landor, live in harmony with their surroundings.

Increasingly in the mid-nineteenth century, the separation between domestic and commercial spheres became a central tenet of American cultural life. For Poe, whose workplace was almost always some rented domestic space, this oversimplified division caused concern. Reductively, masculinity was grounded in the public marketplace while femininity was measured by domestic capability. If the domestic, if the home, was figured solely as feminine space, then Poe's characters, and by extension the writer who created them, were effeminate. Feeling guilty about his failure to provide for his family's welfare, Poe approached the perception of his work-place as feminine in an overdetermined fashion. Troubled by the notion that a retreat from the marketplace somehow constituted a recoiling from masculinity, Poe sought to disavow the prevalent conception, which postu-lated that potency was tied to an engagement with the marketplace. Haunted by his own inability to purchase a house for his family, Poe refig-ured the house as the center of American cultural production, as the source of identity formation, not just for the nation as a whole, but as the space from which aesthetic creation originated. As the market revolution expanded, Poe interrogated the currency of the illusion of the domestic as an arena freed from the tumult of the public sphere to belie the myriad ways in which modernization and the rush to change disrupted the entirety of national life.

II

"O that the multitude of chimneys" would "betray, in smoky whispers," Nathaniel Hawthorne dreams in "Sights from a Steeple" (1831), "the secrets of all who, since their first foundation, have assembled at the hearths within!"[33] Such a disclosure would afford a newfound familiarity with "the mystery of human bosoms" (192). If houses could speak, Hawthorne surmises, local and, by extension, national history would be readily available to him. Behind "the interior of brick walls," Hawthorne contends, resides the cultural life of the Republic (192). Frederick Crews aptly likens the narrator of "Sites from a Steeple" to a "self-indulgent peeper" who, situated in "his lofty perch, envisions an ecstasy of voyeurism."[34] Crews' description vividly captures the voice of the tale, for the narrator clearly longs to invade domestic interiors to better understand the social order he observes below him. Regretfully, since he cannot dis-cern any means to "uncover every chamber," these private interiors remain shielded from his vision (196). While he knows that dramas unfold "in some of the houses over which my eyes roam so coldly," he cannot break through the wall and witness hidden scenes (196). "The narrator's distance from others," Nancy Bunge writes, "robs him and his reflections of sub-stance."[35] As Bunge implies, "Sites from a Steeple" underscores Haw-thorne's desire to overcome physical separation and intrude into private spaces. More ominously, the tale also reifies the idea that domestic spaces are constantly under surveillance, endangered by external observers searching for ways to commodify the private realm for personal gain. Hawthorne yearns for houses to "betray" their secrets, so that he can transform them into marketable products. In short, the tale proposes invading domestic realms to expose private dramas to public view.

Critics have long imagined Hawthorne's short fiction as primarily concerned with probing the darkness of the human consciousness.[36] But the
oft-anthologized "My Kinsman, Major Molineux," "Young Goodman
Brown," and "The Birth-Mark" do not fairly represent the entire range of
themes contained in Hawthorne's short fiction. In his discerning study of
Hawthorne's early tales, Michael J. Colacurcio indexes how "roughly two-
thirds of the seventy-odd tales and sketches Hawthorne succeeded in publishing between 1830 and 1838 have not been taken into significant in-
terpretative account."[37] Little has changed in the two decades since
Colacurcio made his observations. While Colacurcio does not propose
reducing Hawthorne's career to a statistical analysis, he demonstrates the
importance of thinking through the implications embedded in the following question: "What if it should turn out that for every Goodman Brown
there were two Old Maids in a Winding Sheet?"[38]

Meredith L. McGill maintains that "the occlusion of much of Hawthorne's early work has been the presumption of a consensus as to the aesthetic value of individual tales and sketches."[39] Even as he points toward
the range of Hawthorne's writing, Colacurcio still privileges certain tales
based on their "literary" merit.[40] Yet many of the very tales that critics
have dismissed on aesthetic grounds, as McGill demonstrates, "circulated
more widely in Hawthorne's day than the historical tales that critics have
justly come to value."[41] The very popularity of what critics have termed
Hawthorne's minor fiction evinces the necessity of considering how these
tales reflect and encode operant structures of thought and feeling. The
quest to uncover the hidden interiors of social life is the central preoccupation of the majority of Hawthorne's short fiction. Analogous to this concern is his firm belief that such an investigation would be best undertaken
by an examination of contemporary domestic spaces.

Much critical ink has been spilled trying to unpack the meanings of
Hawthorne's concerns about the "mobs of scribbling women" who dominated the mid-nineteenth-century literary marketplace. Milette Shamir
argues that Hawthorne attempts to distinguish his own desire "to pene-
trate the privacy of the home" from the actions of other writers by "claiming" a "supremacy of the imagination."[42] Shamir continues by suggesting
that Hawthorne labors to position the "Romance" as capable of seeing into
"the middle-class home without infringing on its privacy and endangering
its very existence."[43] But as Teresa A. Goddu maintains, Hawthorne's
efforts to "veil his position," by asserting "his own status as male author
with a cultural capital exempt from commodification," is really only an
attempt to "hide his entrance into the marketplace."[44] Critics who mark
Hawthorne's work as significantly different from that of popular sentimental writers by focusing on "Young Goodman Brown" and ignoring tales
like "Sites from a Steeple" reprise this false teleology. As Joel Pfister

argues, "the Hawthorne who was fired as Surveyor of Customs knew his mid nineteenth-century New England not so much as the Puritans' 'howling wilderness' that Young Goodman Brown allegorized as ruled by devils, but as the howling marketplace."[45] Hawthorne's intimate awareness of the influence of the market on national identity informed his short fiction. Many of his tales manifest this recognition by exploring the vexed relationship between the private and public realms. Observing how the engines of the market revolution were striving to remodel every aspect of national life, Hawthorne focused on the one corner of the national scene supposedly apart from the marketplace to consider just how dramatically Jacksonian goaheadism was affecting domestic identity. Hawthorne questioned the validity of representations of houses as asylums by considering the ways in which the market revolution engulfed the domestic sphere, impairing the house's capacity to provide refuge from the encroachments of a restless hunger for change.

By grounding his interest in national identity in questions about domestic design, Hawthorne moved to understand the effects of renovation and modernization on historic patterns of development. Within any number of his tales, Hawthorne employed houses as registers of national history and cultural identity. Like Poe, Hawthorne questioned the cultural ramifications of positing the domestic as the only refuge from the marketplace. In so doing, Hawthorne moved to differentiate his own invasions of the domestic as distinct from other incursions, laboring to privilege his own productions as unsullied by commercial concerns. But as "Sites from a Steeple" registers, Hawthorne also understood that if the house was a refuge from socially driven market investments, the solace it offered was no better than a fragile reprieve. Focusing on domestic exchanges, the narrators of many of Hawthorne's tales consider the relationship of the public to the private, and continually, like the narrator of "Sites from a Steeple," privilege what happens inside houses above the concerns of any external social order. "Hawthorne's sketches," Kristie Hamilton writes, "offer clear, explicit illustration that leisure and a life imbued with momentum, time off and time on, are part and parcel of the same system."[46] For Hamilton, Hawthorne proffers the domestic as a reprieve from the marketplace. Yet Hamilton also registers Hawthorne's deep-seated knowledge of the ligaments that connect the public and private realms. Even as Hawthorne maintains that household secrets are the tales that should be retold, he also realizes that such an endeavor hastens the commercialization of the domestic realm, even if he attempts to veil his own role in such a transformation. "Sites from a Steeple" is not an aberration, nor simply an attempt to meet market demand; rather, the tale records an earnest desire to access the Republic's interior life by reading domestic scenes. In "Sites from a Steeple," Hawthorne displays his method for finding suitable subjects;

hidden behind the walls of houses, the sketch argues, the material from which he wants to craft his fictions resides, and his aim as a writer is to locate some way of bridging that distance.

Cramped in the garret of his grandparents' Salem house, in an "atmosphere without any oxygen of sympathy," Hawthorne lived with his mother and sisters for over seven years after his graduation from Bowdoin.[47] In this house he first attempted to become a professional writer; it was here where he drafted "Sites from a Steeple" and his other early tales. Hawthorne resided at 12 Herbert Street in Salem until his marriage in 1842 to Sophia Peabody—after a three-year engagement, prolonged because of economic uncertainty—when he rented the Old Manse in Concord. Forced, after a blissful three-year period, to leave the Old Manse, Hawthorne relocated to his mother's house until his appointment at the Salem Custom-House enabled him to rent his own quarters. His tenure as a surveyor of Customs lasted another three years, and again, in 1849, he was obligated to dwell under another's roof. After almost two decades of domestic dependency, his prosperity rose at midcentury with the publication of *The Scarlet Letter, The House of Seven Gables, A Wonder-Book for Boys and Girls*, and *The Blithedale Romance*. The financial windfall from these texts allowed Hawthorne to buy in 1852, at the age of forty-eight, the Wayside, in Concord, the first house that he ever owned.[48] Terence Martin has called the 1850s Hawthorne's "public decade" because of his productivity, suggesting, as well, that during this period he began to imagine "home" in a broader and more national way that he had previously.[49] Prior to his publication outburst and before he ventured to Europe to work in England and travel in Italy, Hawthorne's vision of the meaning of home was deeply informed by his own inability to achieve domestic independence. Perhaps in response to his own domestic uncertainty, Hawthorne's short fiction of the 1830s and 1840s interrogates the cultural reification of the domestic as a stabilizing and pacifying influence on both personal and national identity. These questions spill into "The Custom-House" sketch and *The Scarlet Letter* as well, two texts that narrate his own exile from the domestic isolation of the Old Manse and his forced entry into the public sphere. While the recurrence of this theme may have been an attempt to match market expectations, to provide the balance between leisure and work that Hamilton suggests readers were looking for, it also betrays Hawthorne's concerns about dislocation and stability. In particular, three of Hawthorne's tales, "The Ambitious Guest," "Fire-Worship," and "The Old Manse," epitomize how Hawthorne explored the social meaning of architecture as a means of considering the current state of the Republic's social nexus. The themes contained within these tales reappear throughout *The Scarlet Letter*, the first novel Hawthorne wrote after his Old Manse period, and by tracing the evolution of

Hawthorne's treatment of the domestic from his short fiction into *The Scarlet Letter*, a deeper sense of his absorption with the idea of the house as removed from the public sphere emerges.

The disaster that befell Samuel Willey of Crawford Notch, New Hampshire, provided Hawthorne with a prime opportunity to examine the cultural phenomenon of the beatified house. Willey was the proprietor of a small inn located in an isolated pass of the White Mountains. On 28 August 1826, the rumblings of an oncoming avalanche drove the Willeys from their home. The cascading rocks and thundering earth bypassed the house, miraculously leaving it unscarred, and yet buried the family, which was now outside the house, in its wake. The irony of the event, which soon after achieved national attention in the popular press, was predicated on the fact that if the Willeys had remained inside their home they would have been spared. For inexplicable reasons, the landslide circumnavigated the house and decimated everything else—including the family seeking to outrun it—in its path.[50] The next morning, rescuers arrived on the scene to find unmade beds and strewn clothing as the only "residents" of the empty house. By leaving the security of their hearth, the Willeys had fled pell-mell into the avalanche. The nation's imagination was captivated by this instance of the house as a safeguard against the fury of nature, for it fueled representations of the domestic as a sanctified space. "Before the Willey disaster," Eric Purchase writes, "popular opinion rarely questioned the fundamental compatibility of Man and Nature, but the slide pointed up the disparity between America's agrarian philosophy and the lived experience of ordinary people such as the Willeys."[51] As Americans struggled to interpret the import of the slide, the miraculously unscathed Willey house became a monument to the ideal that in the domestic sphere Americans could find harbor from the chaos surrounding them. Moreover, as John F. Sears notes, the incident "supplied Americans with ruins on a grand scale," an "American version of the destruction" embodied in such foreign locales as Pompeii and Egypt.[52] The Willey house soon gained national attention as a tourist site after the disaster, for as Eric Purchase advances, "people marveled at the sheer perversity of nature in destroying a whole family at a stroke while leaving its house untouched."[53] Hawthorne, who traveled through Crawford Notch and vacationed in the White Mountains during the summer of 1832, made the Willey tragedy the subject of his 1835 sketch "The Ambitious Guest."

In his tale, Hawthorne focuses not on the aftermath of the calamity but on the family's activities immediately preceding their fatal evacuation. Through most of the narrative, Hawthorne depicts the Willeys as comfortably gathered around their hearth, hoping to ward off the chill of a storm with the consolation of their communal interactions. Their security, he writes near the end of his story, was shattered when "a sound, abroad in the night, rising like the roar of a blast," led them to "simultaneously" cry "The Slide! The Slide!" (332–33). Quickly the "victims rushed from their cottage, and sought refuge in what they deemed a safer spot" (333). Playing with his readers' awareness of the fate of the unnamed Willeys, Hawthorne delays depicting the tragedy to build up suspense in the tale. When he finally turns to the shocking event, the weight of his observation that "Alas! they had quitted their security and fled into the pathway of destruction" carries more narrative force than if he had started with the well-known facts of the case (333). Hawthorne chillingly notes how the avalanche broke into "two branches" and skirted the house—shuddering "not a window there," yet burying the retreating family under masses of earth and debris (333).

Hawthorne's concluding turn focuses on the discoveries of the rescue party who arrived on the scene to witness the aftermath of the slide. As they approached the area, they spied a "light smoke" trailing out of "the cottage chimney," produced by the embers still "smouldering" in the Willeys' convivial "hearth" (333). With the artifacts of an interrupted domestic life vividly on display, the ghostly house appeared as if "the inhabitants had but gone forth to view the devastation of the Slide, and would shortly return" (333). Even in its abandoned state, the house seemingly exuded peace and comfort. Yet Hawthorne's tale, written about a decade after the actual catastrophe, is not a conventional retelling of the Willey tragedy. The events of the landslide became for Hawthorne an occasion to reflect on the cultural preoccupation of the sanctity of the home. By imagining a domestic history for the family and having them meditate on issues of fate and memory just prior to their destruction, Hawthorne turned a singular event into a tale with far-reaching resonance.

In Hawthorne's imagined scene on the eve of destruction, almost every member of the family fantasizes about leaving the house; even the familial patriarch finds himself "wishing we had a good farm, in Bartlett, or Bethlehem, or Littleton, or some other township round the White Mountains; but not where they could tumble on our heads" (329).[54] Perhaps his spurt of melancholy springs from the unsettling weather swirling around the house, but more seems to be at stake. Hawthorne opens his tale by noting how this family dwells in "solitude" to service the needs of "a great artery, through which the life-blood of internal commerce is continually throbbing" (325). The "primitive tavern" that the family operates feeds and shelters travelers, teamsters, stagecoach drivers, and traders traversing the White Mountains; in effect, the family, unnamed by Hawthorne throughout the tale, dwells in a dangerous location to serve commercial exchanges. The patriarch's dream of different life, his ambition to be a yeoman farmer, coterminously expresses a desire to be economically independent. The horror of the house-untouched-by-the-avalanche is that it stands ready to accept any other set of nameless occupants willing to serve the needs of the market economy. While the current unnamed occupants might have been safe had they remained in the house, they would also then have gone on dwelling in constant danger of having the mountain rain down on them. If they had survived the slide, this family would have, at best, been able to continue in their tenuous refuge from the calamities of a hostile world. Instead of memorializing the family, Hawthorne ends his tale with a portrait of an empty house awaiting the return of anyone willing to dwell in the pass to ensure the continued flow of this artery of commerce. By the end of the tale, it is not entirely clear if the house provides shelter from external forces or serves to imprison its occupants into serving a particular economic role. In figuring the house as prisonlike, Hawthorne complicates the popular conception that the survival of the Willey house was evidence that the domestic was an asylum, for he implies that the family would have been safe only if they never ventured outside their front door. If the house was a refuge, its capacity to protect and shelter offered no consolation outside its limited frame.

Hawthorne's "Fire-Worship" echoes the blurred figuration of the house that Hawthorne lays out in "The Ambitious Guest." Within the sketch, the narrator expresses a concern with how mechanical developments are remodeling traditional patterns of domestic life. The adoption of modern conveniences that Hawthorne examines in "Fire-Worship" (1843) suggests the uncertainty brought about by innovations and modernizations. Part of the domestic comfort of the house, Hawthorne observes in "Fire-Worship," resides in its ability to foster contact with elemental forces. The "great revolution in social and domestic life" that the "ungenial stove," airtight and forged of cast iron, was creating in American homes was "fast blotting the picturesque, the poetic, and the beautiful out of human life."[55] Traditional fireplaces are much more evocative than their modern replacements, and Hawthorne fears the shift from the older form to the new invention carries with it a loss of aesthetic value. By placing in an "iron prison" that "quick and subtle spirit whom Prometheus lured from heaven to civilize mankind, and cheer them in their wintry desolation," Americans are in danger of losing their connections with the natural world as well as hastening a breakdown of domestic intimacy (138). A traditional fireplace embodies a connection to the past, placing current inhabitants in line with experiences of their predecessors. The widespread adoption of these new, impersonal heat sources would serve to disassociate the present from time-honored domestic habits. Enclosed stoves will eventually transform the house, Hawthorne suggests, into a diorama representing a revolution in the arrangements of daily life. The propensity of Americans to so quickly seize on industrialized gadgets is detrimental to national development. The mass-produced parlor stove, as Joel Pfister writes, "facilitates and symbolizes industrial America's colonization of the home."[56] Fearful of the ways in which familial interaction would be endangered by the commercialization of the domestic, Hawthorne's "Fire-Worship" offers a jeremiad aimed at warning Americans away from the dangers of novelties.

The substitution of stoves for fireplaces was expediting the incursion of the marketplace into the interiors of domestic life, because, in Hawthorne's figuration, the design shift served to weaken the intellect and the social imagination. Elevating fire to the status of prime mover, Hawthorne declares that fire "is the great artizan and laborer by whose aid men are enabled to build a world within a world," to erect a secure habitation amid "the rough creation which Nature flung to us" (139). In effect, Hawthorne ties the flickering flame of an open hearth to larger concerns of settlement and domestication, going so far as to posit that traditional fireplaces anchor social and cultural development. "While a man was true to the fireside," Hawthorne asserts, "so long would he be true to country and law" (140). If that connection is severed by industrialization, Hawthorne intimates, no such social harmony can be guaranteed.

An open fire reminds man that the fire, which Hawthorne personifies, might "run riot through the peaceful house," yet "this possibility of mad destruction" only makes "his domestic kindness the more beautiful" (141). By agreeing "to dwell" in close proximity and only occasionally "thrusting his red tongue out of the chimney-top," fire warms families but also warns them of its power to destroy (141). In effect, fireplaces demand vigilant attention, while cast-iron stoves hubristically allow home owners to imagine that they have tamed nature. The open fireplace is an "invaluable moral influence" on mankind, and locking it away curtails its power to promote a constant, humble appreciation of the power of nature (145). In the end "all moral intercourse," Hawthorne fears, will "be chilled with a fatal frost," as individuals seek "separate corners, and never gather" communally because the gifts of modernization allow them to be warmed separately (146). The importance of continuing to inhabit and preserve storied houses informs the construction of Hawthorne's "Old Manse," a sketch that echoes the orthodoxy of "Fire-Worship" in its celebration of how domestic sites house the current generation in the social energies of the past.

"Houses of any antiquity, in New England, are so invariably possessed with spirits," Hawthorne writes in "The Old Manse," that "the matter seems hardly worth alluding to" (17). Still, the intimations of former residents, and of the complexity of America's settlement history, dominate Hawthorne's account of his domestic life at the Old Manse, the first house he inhabited apart from his extended family. Fresh from his disheartening experiences at Brook Farm in 1841, Hawthorne found a dreamy utopian life when, after his marriage to Sophia Peabody in July 1842, he rented the

Old Manse and occupied it for the next three and a half years. The solitude and stability of the Old Manse, Hawthorne felt, would allow him to attain finally the long-sought "treasure of intellectual gold" (34). Hawthorne's "writing style in the sketch—the apparently meandering structure, the slow-paced sentences, the images of peace and quiet—also serves," Larry J. Reynolds observes, "to convey a political conservatism antithetical to the political activism at the other end of town."[57] Dismayed by the unending celebration of change and originality that he felt the transcendentalists promoted, Hawthorne crafted (even on the sentence level, as Reynolds suggests) "The Old Manse" as a rejoinder to Emersonian calls for an unfettered relationship with the world. Instead of carving "whim" into the lintels of his front door as he abandons it, Hawthorne solemnizes how houses of antiquity protect their occupants from the uncertainties of a culture overindulging on the idea that constant change and motion unquestionably produce progress.

The Old Manse was conceived of as a retreat from public exchanges, and Hawthorne celebrates it as a structural embodiment of the possibilities of a remove from circulation. Situated "between two tall gate-posts of rough-hewn stone," the Old Manse is offset from the "road" where "ordinary abodes" are normally situated (3). "In its near retirement, and accessible seclusion," the Old Manse is the perfect "spot" for the residence of a clergyman or a writer (4). Sheltered from the outside material world, which the house has "not quite the aspect of belonging to," Hawthorne is for the first time unconnected from the cacophony of the marketplace (4). Situated to remove and protect the occupant from daily exchanges, the Old Manse that Hawthorne portrays is a hermitage from the swirls of ceaseless change. The house revives the spirit and sharpens the ability to get "rid of old delusions" and avoid "new ones" (29). While he was there, Hawthorne confesses, "It seemed to me that all the artifice and conventionalism of life was but an impalpable thinness upon its surface" (1142). As a shelter from modernity, the Old Manse allowed Hawthorne contact with the practices of the past, creating a domestic situation that, he argues, provides a more regenerative way of life. Leland S. Person Jr. argues that the difficulties of Hawthorne's personal life during this period, the pressures of being an almost destitute new husband and father, led him to use the sketch as a means of exploring "the possibility of non-relational, autogenetic creative power."[58] By extending the line of Person's argument, and connecting it to Hawthorne's consistent privileging of the independent peacefulness of his domestic remove, what becomes apparent is how the sketch carefully positions Hawthorne as perfectly situated to imbibe the domestic history of the nation.

Within the Old Manse, Hawthorne is swaddled in the folds of national history. In his "garret," he rummages through "heirlooms," ancient books, and papers "from the days of the mighty Puritan divines" (17). From the "northward" window of his "study" he gazes at the spot where "the outbreak of a long and deadly struggle between two nations" began, and contemplates the local folktale concerning the youth who ceased "chopping wood" at the Old Manse to enter the fray at nearby Concord (6). A short walk from the house brings him to the ruins of an Indian village, where Thoreau teaches him to search for arrowheads. America's various pre-Revolutionary pasts are readily available in a short circuit around the house. By simply walking the grounds of the Old Manse Hawthorne can read multiple delineations of America's prenational history, and then return to his hearth to consider his connection to them.

Looking at the roof of the Old Manse causes Hawthorne to reaffirm its historic position in the landscape. "The beams and rafters, roughly hewn, and with strips of bark still on them," along with the "rude masonry of the chimneys," endow the upper stories with a "wild and uncivilized" look (16–17). The interior of the parsonage recalls the rough-hewn exteriors of a wilderness hut, yet this disorder is private and thus domesticated. As such, the house never announces anything short of permanent, reasoned settlement, serving as a tangible register of the length of the cultivation of land. Crammed with artifacts and shrouded by a veil of history, the house removes Hawthorne from the tumult of the market revolution and affirms his sense of the domestic as a historic screen from such chaos. In many ways Hawthorne's depiction of the Old Manse reflects how he was, as Robert Milder argues, "wary of his response to the wildness and proffered bounties of external nature" and how "against the thrust of his aesthetic, intellectual, and psychosexual attraction to freedom he upheld a domestically centered conservatism."[59] The garret tactually allows Hawthorne to experience a sedentary version of wild nature, reinforcing—rather than unsettling—him. Composed of "lumber that each generation has left behind it, from a period before the Revolution," the exposed beams and rafters also allow Hawthorne to dwell with and in the past (16).

The shade of the riverbank provides him with a sanctuary "only less sacred in my remembrance than the hearth of a household-fire" (25). Within the narrative Hawthorne casts himself as nestled away from the public sphere. This narrative strategy, coupled with his silence about his own personal difficulties, results in the projection of the Old Manse as providing the perfect blend of tangible history and domestic seclusion. Yet his isolation cannot sustain itself, because he only rents and does not own the house. The arrival of workmen "making a tremendous racket" startles Hawthorne, and his domestic reverie comes to a rapid end, overwhelmed by "horrible whispers" (33). These intruding voices talk of "brushing up the external walls with a coat of paint," an idea that disturbs Hawthorne so much that he compares the act to "rouging up the venerable cheeks of one's grandmother" (33). This infringement signals that he will have to leave the Old Manse, a "spot so sheltered from the tumult of life's ocean" (33). Observing that "the hand that renovates is always more sacrilegious than that which destroys," Hawthorne grudgingly resigns himself to moving on (33). His melancholy over the damage done to the house unnerves him, a condition exasperated by his observation that the damage is irreparable. The workmen and their client do not hold the proper reverence for the Old Manse. Instead of appreciating the house as a reservoir of American domestic practices, they seek to remodel it so drastically that it will lose, for Hawthorne, all its historic associations. Even a storied home like the Old Manse is a tenuous sanctuary, providing only a brief reprieve that quickly becomes undone by the cultural appetite for restless renovation and change. Driven from the house, Hawthorne ventures, as the "newspapers announce," from the shelter of "the Old Manse to a Custom-House" (33–34). This forced relocation ends Hawthorne's isolation from the market and compels him to reside in a dilapidated monument to commercialism. As Hawthorne moves from the Old Manse to the Salem Custom-House, he reenters the marketplace, a move that renders him no longer capable of veiling his involvement in commercial exchanges.

III

Hawthorne continually reminisces about his more peaceful life at the Old Manse throughout the "Custom-House" sketch, his introductory frame for *The Scarlet Letter* (1850). By contrasting his former convivial existence with the mind-numbing circumstances into which he finds himself displaced, Hawthorne accentuates the severity of his dislocation. The dreariness of Salem weighs on him, and his recollections of the Old Manse highlight just how deadening he finds his new environment. While Hawthorne is "invariably happiest elsewhere," Salem has an almost strangling "hold" on his "affections" that seems to always draw him back to the town.[60] On these "streets" his progenitors have "mingled their earthy substance with the soil" for "nearly two centuries and a quarter," and throughout Salem he confronts his family's history (8–9). Salem's old timber houses are "planted" as "deep" in the soil as his family's own roots, a local geographical connection rare for anyone living in the midst of the rampant social mobility of the period (8). Yet, in his move from the fecundity of the Manse to the stagnation of the Custom-House, Hawthorne simultaneously suffers a sea change in his relationship with the past. At the Old Manse history was vividly alive, and he happily found himself a cotenant of a variety of national traditions and domestic customs. In the Custom-House, cobwebs cover the dusty boxes in which the past has been packed

away even as the present appears dead and stagnant. The change in location, in effect, forces Hawthorne, as Michael Davitt Bell notes, to dwell in
a "community of ruins and near-corpses."[61]

Hawthorne depicts Salem as a graveyard, portraying his coworkers as
superannuated agents who function, as Dan McCall argues, as "human
embodiments of Salem itself: dilapidated vestiges of vitality, shells, which
can only suggest, as rotting houses do, that once there was life inside
them."[62] Amid this forlorn squalor, Hawthorne labored for three years as
a surveyor of customs. Unfortunately, there was hardly anything for
Hawthorne to inspect, as the burgeoning success of the ports of New York
and Boston had left Salem's waterfront, with its "decayed wooden warehouses," bereft of activity" (4). Whereas the isolation of the Old Manse
revived Hawthorne, the very same remove from social exchanges at the
Custom-House only marks his precarious dependency. Hawthorne cannot
enjoy the solitude that his position provides him, because he understands
himself to be a mere tributary of the fluctuating currents of party politics.
Hawthorne secures the sinecure of an unnecessary position as payment for
his loyalty, but his appointment also stigmatizes his need for assistance in a
cultural order predicated on individual self-fashioning. It is this "sensitivity about dependency," Gloria C. Erlich notes, that "fuels the animus
against civil service permeating" Hawthorne's preface.[63] Far from comfortable in his new surroundings, Hawthorne fears that if he continues in
his position he will quickly become just another rusty cog in the patronage
machine.

The daily lives of his fellow civil servants haunt Hawthorne's imagination, a damaging condition considering how, in the words of Bryce
Traister, "the permanent employees of the Custom House represent a de-
masculinization of the independent male, as the 'go-forward' movement of
Jacksonian social mobility and autonomy collapses into the inertia of
record-keeping and tellingly, storytelling."[64] In comparison to his rustic
ease at the Old Manse, Hawthorne feels prematurely buried in the Salem
Custom-House. Harbored in such close proximity to the sterility of the
Salem port, he understands that his pointless position effectively emascu-
lates him as well. While the Federal-style Custom-House testifies to a
Jacksonian faith in the future, its location in the midst of abandonment and
decay complicates the optimism projected by its facade. Massively fabricated of solid brick, the Custom-House is a fish out of water amid a sea of
rotting wooden warehouses. Ornamented with a "half dozen wooden pillars," and guarded by "an enormous specimen of the American eagle"
emblazoned "over the entrance," the Salem Custom-House is a monument of unrealized possibility (5). The retainers who staff its unvisited
offices are forced to confront this duality every time they cross the threshold of the Custom-House, and Hawthorne sketches this visual dissonance

to draw attention to his reading of the town's built environment and, by extension, to the project of interpreting Salem's social history.

Salem has "few" buildings "which pretend to architectural beauty," and in Hawthorne's estimation the Custom-House is no exception (8). Built with an "idea of subsequent prosperity destined never to be realized," the "airy hall" above "the Collector's apartments, remains unfinished to this day, and, in spite of the aged cobwebs that festoon its dusky beams, appears still to await the labor of the carpenter and mason" (28). The second floor of the Salem Custom-House remains rudely unfinished, with its "brick-work and naked rafters" untouched by "panelling and plaster" (28). The reality of the economic depression of the Salem shipyards causes Hawthorne to doubt, rightly, that the second story will ever be completed. Since the building "contains far more space than its occupants know what to do with," the unfinished upper rooms have become a disheveled repository for "rubbish" and "musty papers" (28). Here, in this dustbin of history, Hawthorne stumbles upon the manuscript of Surveyor Pue and the moth-eaten rag of Hester Prynne's scarlet letter. At the rustically finished garret of the Old Manse, Hawthorne rapturously observed how the very timber of its roof testified to the layered settlement history of the United States; comparatively the bare, ruined choir of the Custom-House symbolizes only the futility of attempting to project the future course of the Jacksonian market revolution.

Embedded within the preface, and indeed in Hawthorne's categorization of the building itself, abides a meditation on the relationship between architecture and social order. The Custom-House stands as an unfinished monument to the past's assumptions about the future. Built to regulate the very trade that has retreated from its wharfs, the Custom-House is transformed, in Hawthorne's preface, into the epitome of the tangible burdens of history. Since Salem was a port city, whose stature would rise and fall based on the tides of commerce, the Custom-House was conceived of as its symbolic heart. Imaging that Salem would prosper, the framers of the Custom-House had envisioned it as a monument to the town's future possibilities; they built the exterior larger than necessary, assuming that the town would one day require a two-story customhouse. That day never came. The wooden buildings neighboring the brick Custom-House stand in visible decay, and the Custom-House's stately facade masks the abandoned distress of its interiors. By so thoroughly reading the emptiness of this structural center of Salem, Hawthorne reveals the totality of its miasmas of depression. The burden of the building oppresses Hawthorne's spirits so totally that he frames his only exit as springing from a beheading: a metaphoric guillotine of political change forces Hawthorne out of the Custom-House and back into the literary marketplace. "The force of the Hawthornian romance lies in the insinuation that every house has a corpse in the cellar, that even the most domesticated of scenes," Milette Shamir notes, "harbors the strange and uncanny."[65] In his preface to *The Scarlet Letter*, Hawthorne reveals that the Custom-House has betrayed its secrets to him, enabling him to transform them into the source of inspiration for his novel. In still another attempt to veil his own reentry into the market-place, he also positions himself as a "Decapitated Surveyor," yet one more cadaver littering the Custom-House. In this setting Hawthorne is unable to dwell with the past, as he did at the Old Manse; the instabilities engendered by political change force him to leave the Custom-House and commodify history.

In a recent consideration of the metapolitics of Hawthorne's preface, and of the ways in which those politics inform the novel that follows, Donald E. Pease observes that "traditions of Hawthorne scholarship can be distinguished by the different significance each has attributed to the change in Hawthorne's symbolic identity following his ejection from the Custom-House."[66] For much of its reception history Hawthorne's preface was dismissed as unconnected to the novel it introduces, reduced to the status of a biographical account of the conditions under which Hawthorne left civil service to become a professional author.[67] Since the publication of Jonathan Arac's important essay, "The Politics of *The Scarlet Letter*," which sought "to read a relation between the fiction of the 1640s and the history of around 1850" by considering "the relation of 'The Custom-House' to 'The Scarlet Letter,'" critics have increasingly interpreted the preface as a register of the romance's connection to the political and cultural life of Hawthorne's Republic.[68] Building upon the foundations of both of these traditions, an even more recent critical turn has sought to unpack how the preface informs the novel by virtue of its focus on the difficulties of artistic production under the sway of the gendered market revolution. Robert K. Martin, in the aptly titled "Hester Prynne, C'est Moi: Nathaniel Hawthorne and the Anxieties of Gender," for instance, suggests "'The Custom-House' is above all an essay in sexual politics."[69] For Michael Gilmore, "the fictive world portrayed in *The Scarlet Letter* is only nominally the world of Puritan Boston," since Hawthorne's "pervasive emphasis on visual processes" within the text "effectively reproduced the texture of inter-change in a society where observation and appearance had become all-important: the market society of Jacksonian America."[70]

Sandra Tomc synthesizes these various critical strands by noting how the preface reflects "the more general cultural relocation of authorship from the public to the private sphere," in its depiction of how "Hawthorne's dismissal from the Custom-House at once severed his connection to public life and forced him into a new reliance on the very market against which he had so strenuously defended himself."[71] Similarly, T. Walter Herbert notes that "the 'classic' male writers of this period negotiated the paradox of the public and private, not because it was considered unsuitable for a man to have a public role but because their sense of the writer's true identity featured the stewardship of an inward flame of inspiration, antithetical to the sordid traffic of the marketplace."[72] Both Herbert and Tomc trace the links between "The Custom-House" and *The Scarlet Letter* to explore how Hester's marginalized position as an artist reflects Hawthorne's detachment from the marketplace after his own dismissal from the public sphere. Considered in this light both Hester and the narrator of the "Custom-House" sketch emerge from their respective confinements faced with the challenge of inaugurating new social roles for themselves. Moreover, each can depend only on artistic talent, one as seamstress and the other as writer, to forge a new identity. "The possibility of radical new beginnings," as Brook Thomas maintains, "is a preoccupation of *The Scarlet Letter*."[73] Both the decapitated surveyor and the paroled seamstress, as Thomas' precisely phrased summation records, struggle to reestablish themselves. They also find themselves released from buildings that mark the hypocrisy of the social orders they inhabit; thus Hawthorne's figuration of the importance of architecture in both texts binds the "Custom-House" sketch to *The Scarlet Letter*. Without question Hawthorne's life was irrevocably altered by his ejection from the patronage system; and, as Tomc and Herbert observe, this eviction caused him to confront questions about authorial identity and spatial location. Yet, arguably, what has consistently been neglected in readings that seek to bridge the narrative distance between preface and *The Scarlet Letter* is how the concerns of the "Custom-House" sketch wed themselves to the novel by performing readings of architectural spaces. Both texts register how the built environment reflects the structures of thought and feeling that dominate a social order, and reading the connections between Salem's Custom-House and the houses of Hawthorne's Boston as such allows a deeper insight into the design of his romance.

The Scarlet Letter opens with a focused attention on a door "heavily timbered with oak, and studded with iron spikes" (47). A crowd stands before this door, waiting for its rusty hinges to swing open and allow the hidden to become visible. Yet neither the chapter "The Prison-Door" nor the actual door it describes reveals any secrets. First, Hawthorne dwells on the necessary steps undertaken by a community hoping to found a new society. "Whatever Utopia of human virtue and happiness they might project," the "founders of a new colony" unfailingly recognize the exigency of building both a "cemetery" and a "prison" (47). The Puritans' transatlantic migration, which they undertook to remove themselves from sin and corruption, cannot distance them from needing to build physical embodiments of the very things they had hoped to leave behind. What the opening frame of the novel underscores, as David Leverenz notes, is that "inwardness has been shut up and spiked, along with youthful hopes and the virgin land."[74] Indeed, as the opening chapter makes explicitly clear, the only untarnished thing on the scene is the "wild-rose bush, covered, in this month of June, with its delicate gems," that brightens the door of the jailhouse (48).

That Hawthorne "pays almost as much attention to a rose bush as he does to the appearance and moral significance of Puritan America's first prison" strikes Michael J. Colacurcio as a curious opening for the novel, and prompts him to try to unravel the associations Hawthorne establishes between Hester and Ann Hutchinson.[75] As Colacurcio advances, the importance of this "sweet moral blossom" should be underscored, as should the connection that Hawthorne establishes between it and Ann Hutchinson. Still, the wild rosebush has often drawn readers away from the initial symbols that the novel offers: the door and the prison. Architecture and material structures play decisive roles in *The Scarlet Letter*. While, as Michael T. Gilmore writes, "*The Scarlet Letter* is a book preoccupied with speaking and writing," it is also a text fixated with the relationship between spatial location and identity formation.[76] Just as the dilapidated wharves of Salem mirrored the state of the residents of the Custom-House, in the text of the novel itself Hawthorne continually uses architectural surfaces to map the interiors of his characters.

"The setting of *The Scarlet Letter*," Nina Baym contends, "is in part a series of symbolic contrasts around a constellation of images."[77] By untangling the ways in which Hawthorne deploys contending images of light and dark and town and wilderness, many readers have reconstructed the text as establishing dual social worlds. Hawthorne's close attention to the description of the structural productions of the Puritans complicates any reading that simply divides the novel's concerns into the separate spheres of wilderness and civilization; as Baym asserts, these "two symbolic systems do not simplify; they add rich ambiguity."[78] While the wilderness does contrast with the public sector, the ethical geography of the novel is not so easily mapped. Simply put, the wilderness does not function as the only location for rebelliousness in *The Scarlet Letter*. For all the possible connections between the wilderness and unruliness, only in Boston do challenges to the Puritan order actually arise. Native Americans, whom Hawthorne narratively associates with savagery, are seen only within the confines of the town. Similarly, it is in the marketplace that the drunken Spanish sailors congregate. The supposed witch, Mistress Hibbins, also "appears" only inside the boundaries of the sanctified settlement. Indeed, she inhabits the same house as the overseer of civic law, Governor Bellingham, further subverting the valence of any attempts to dualistically divide the novel. In his nuanced *Office of The Scarlet Letter*, Sacvan Bercovitch observes that "the polarity of the self and society remained central through the successive discourses of libertarianism, federalism, and Jacksonian individualism," and that the continuing cultural capital of this duality caused Hawthorne to explore how "its negative pressures" and "its positive form" fundamentally conjoined in "the symbolic structures of the American ideology."[79] Hawthorne locates these polarities within the very frame of the Governor's Hall, and as such he emphasizes, just as he does with the Custom-House in the novel's opening gambit, the importance of interpreting the design of architectural sites to fully understand the state of a cultural order.

Situated at the opposite end of town from the prison, the Governor's Hall dominates the domestic landscape of *The Scarlet Letter*. Described as a private "mansion," Bellingham's house contrasts, starkly, with the fledgling community's other rudimentary architectural productions (100). Both the governor's residence and the seat of political authority for the community, the building serves two purposes, and Hawthorne explores the tensions operant in these differing functions in his depiction of the house. Fearing that the leaders of her theocratic society contemplate removing Pearl from her care, Hester goes to Bellingham's house to appeal her case under the pretext of delivering a pair of gloves. After she confirms her worst fears, she pleads with Dimmesdale to intercede on her behalf and let Pearl remain with her. While the scene at the governor's house serves an important plot function, it also reinforces Hawthorne's preoccupation with considering houses as registers of cultural life. By prying open this house's secrets and exposing them to view, Hawthorne can focus on the heart of his narrative subject: the relationship of an individual to society and how that exchange is informed by history and architectural location.

Hawthorne describes Bellingham's "large wooden house" as "built in a fashion of which there are specimens still extant in the streets of our elder towns" (103). Like the old wooden houses of Salem, these artifacts are now often "moss-grown, crumbling to decay, and melancholy at heart with the many sorrowful or joyful occurrences, remembered or forgotten, that have happened, and passed away, within their dusky chambers" (103). Having unpacked in his preface the tensions between the stately exterior of the Custom-House's brick facades and its decaying interiors, Hawthorne has already demonstrated the urgency of not confusing exterior design with inner security. The governor's house "had indeed a very cheery aspect" with "walls being overspread with a kind of stucco, in which fragments of broken glass were plentifully intermixed" (103). Whenever the sunlight fell "aslant-wise over the front of the edifice, it glittered and sparkled as if diamonds had been flung against it by the double handful" (103). The wooden frame is plastered with stucco to create the illusion that the house has been fashioned out of carved stone instead of timber; the inclusion of the broken glass adds a shimmering surface to the governor's house out of step with the austere environment of seventeenth-century Boston. Indeed, the "brilliancy might have befitted Aladdin's palace, rather than the mansion of a grave old Puritan ruler" (103). To further the effect of the house as an antiquated stone mansion, the facade has also been "decorated with strange and seemingly cabalistic figures and diagrams, suitable to the quaint taste of the age, which had been drawn in the stucco when newly laid on, and had now grown hard and durable, for the admiration of after times" (103). These decidedly European practices indicate that Bellingham has imported European designs seemingly at odds with the Puritans' distaste for adornment. In short, the house built to shelter the governor of a colony dedicated to shunning artifice has, instead, transplanted glittering aristocratic pretensions.

When Hester enters the governor's house, she not only crosses a threshold but seemingly undergoes a transatlantic crossing as well. This change in setting is signaled by the presence of a "serf" wearing a "blue coat, which was the customary garb of serving men at that period, and long before, in the hereditary halls of England," who greets her at the door of Bellingham's mansion (104). The furnishings and decor suggest that Bellingham has "planned his new habitation after the residences of gentlemen of fair estate in his native land" (104). While he has admitted the necessity of "many variations, suggested by the nature of his building materials, diversity of climate, and a different mode of social life," what form those modifications have taken remains unclear (104). Perhaps in using stucco instead of carved stone, and planning a garden of vegetables instead of ornate flowers, Bellingham has incorporated native materials and practical necessities. Still, as far as possible, Bellingham has rebuilt England in Boston's green and pleasant land. With his "ponderous chairs," imposing table of "Elizabethan" taste, the "row of portraits, representing the forebears of the Bellingham line," and the "suit of mail" so "highly burnished as to glow with white radiance," Bellingham has furnished his house as an English hereditary estate (105). The material argument framed by the house troubles any semblance of surety the Puritans might have concerning what it was that they think they left behind.

At the heart of the community live both the armored leader of its civic affairs and his sister, who attempts to seduce those on society's margins to follow a malevolent path. Mistress Hibbins, like the decorative features and the design of the house itself, recalls the divisive influences that the transatlantic migration was meant to leave behind. Hibbins' "ill-omened physiognomy" casts "a shadow over the cheerful newness of the house" (116). Much critical attention has focused on how Dimmesdale, the person entrusted with the community's salvation, jeopardizes social stability. But even if Dimmesdale had not been a secret sinner, the health of this "new" community would be undermined by its structural center being so emblematic of European practices and structures of thought. The governor's neo-European mansion suggests that the members of this community have transplanted all the circumstances they fled, implying that they will never attain the separation they so passionately seek. When leaving the house, Hester replies to an invitation from Mistress Hibbins to join her in the forest that evening by proclaiming that if she had lost Pearl she would have "willingly gone with thee into the forest, and signed my name in the Black Man's book too, and that with mine own blood" (117). Hibbins' solicitation originates from "a chamber-window" of the Governor's Hall (116). From a private room within the public structure, she tries to entice Hester to sin. Only the possibility of the state intruding on her private, domestic life moves Hester to consider Hibbins' proposal, and then only as a hypothetical reaction to a problem she never faced. More than exposing anything about Hester, the episode at Bellingham's house revels it as a structural container of both law and licentiousness. This last spectacle at the governor's house accentuates that this building shelters two social narratives, one of civil law and the other of recalcitrant passions. Just as the Custom-House displays the complicated hold of the past on the present, the governor's house contains two divergent forces that operate simultaneously and compete to form the basis for the social order entrusted to his care. Shelter to both Bellingham and Hibbins, the Governor's Hall accommodates the duality of the two worlds of the romance; within its walls dwell both light and darkness, wildness and order. As such, the governor's house mirrors the house that lodges two other figures more central to Hawthorne's plot.

Dimmesdale and Chillingworth reside in a house owned by "a pious widow, of good social rank" (126). Since the two are "lodged in the same house," the "ebb and flow of the minister's life tide" passes "under the eye of his anxious and attached physician" and self-appointed judge and jury (125). Dimmesdale's bachelorhood has "doomed" him to "eat his unsavory morsel always at another's board, and endure the life-long chill which must be his lot who seeks to warm himself only at another's fireside" (125). This domestic dependency, ungenial and frigid, reveals Hawthorne's deep conviction of the solace of an independent domestic life. Lora Romero proposes that "home is such a powerful symbol" in Hawthorne's work "because he associates it with that which is most familiar: the self."[80] Yet, far from providing Dimmesdale with a homosocial idyll, his domestic setting forces him to dwell in a state of constant surveillance. Dimmesdale's domestic situation seems designed to deny him the possibility of any privacy, pressuring him to always retain a public facade. That performativity belies the troubles of his interiority, never allowing him the reprieve that privacy might afford him. T. Walter Herbert labels Hester's plight as stemming from her involvement in a "double-marriage," suggesting that "Hester's two husbands are inseparable opposites; they are figures of the split manhood that sustained the domestic ideal, and Hester cannot have one without the other."[81] Dimmesdale becomes a decaying shell of his former self because of his own involvement in the complexities born from these double marriages. Driven to dwell apart from the source of his possible domestic comfort, he cohabits with Chillingworth, a coercive situation that forces him to constantly reside in a dependent state of torment and conflict.

Conversely, Hester dwells in isolation "on the outskirts of the town." Although "not in close vicinity to any other habitation," in an "abandoned" tiny "thatched cottage," she lives in a healthier environment than Dimmesdale (81). Hester's removal from society simultaneously liberates her from the constraints of its panoptic gaze, and her privacy furnishes her the opportunity to confront the queries of her spirit in a way that constantly alludes Dimmesdale. "In this little, lonesome dwelling, with some slender means" that she possesses," Hester "establishe[s] herself, with her infant child" (81). In some ways Hester still lives under "the inquisitorial watch" of Boston's elect, but her isolation also marks self-sufficiency. Unlike Dimmesdale in his domestic dependency, Hester moves away from the ever present judgment of society, to occupy a house that provides her some seclusion. She does not, and indeed cannot, mask her sin, but finds a way to inhabit a space that does not consistently prove detrimental to her health. This is not to say that she suffers less than Dimmesdale but that, within the architectural logic of "The Custom-House Sketch" and of Hawthorne's romance, her domestic autonomy (her capacity to be by her own fireside) disentangles her from the demands of the public sphere. In other words, unlike the domestic arrangements of the decapitated surveyor and the troubled minister, Hester's domestic situation offers her respite from the pressures and demands of social exchange.

At the conclusion of the novel Hester returns to repossess the cottage, which since her flight to Europe has "never once been opened" (261). At the "threshold" of the cottage Hester pauses, for, "perchance, the idea of entering, all alone, and all so changed, the home of so intense a former life," is "more dreary and desolate than even she could bear" (261–62). The narrator declares that Hester has returned of her own "free will" and seems comforted by the fact that she appears driven to adopt the scarlet letter anew (263). Upon her reappearance in Boston, Hester's cottage becomes a haven for women who "in the continually recurring trials of wounded, wasted, wronged, misplaced, or erring and sinful passion" suffer from "the dreary burden of a heart unyielded" (263). They seek out Hester to find consolation and reassurance, and in effect her cottage serves to provide a private space for whoever needs to borrow its comforts. Assuring her visitors that "when the world [shall] have grown ripe for it, in Heaven's own time, a new truth [will] be revealed, in order to establish the whole relation between man and women on a surer ground of mutual happiness," Hester acts as a physician for the spiritual ills of the community (263). Her isolated cottage becomes a site of architectural importance for her society, a harbor for those who have no private hearth of their own, a space free to some degree from surveillance. Visitors leave Hester's cottage armed with the knowledge that cultural change will happen, not instantaneously, but through gradual social reform. Brook Thomas argues that "*The Scarlet Letter* implies that the nascent formation of an independent civil society precedes and helps to generate a democratic state."[82] By establishing her own house as an independent site that stabilizes her social order, Hester sanctions the cottage as contributing to the formation of a democratic state. She becomes a guardian of other wayward souls and counsels them on how to bear the tribulations of slow cultural change. Hester's cottage, like the Old Manse, does not contain unresolvable, competing narratives; it does not shelter, or represent, fundamental tensions that cause social disquietude. Rather it is a place of domestic authority, and therefore it becomes a social model. Removed from the marketplace, the cottage offers individuals shelter and respite, extending to the future, through Hester's preservation of its domestic independence, a semblance of hope. Unlike the argument framed by the architects of the Custom-House, Hester's cottage defines progress as procedural. The cottage does not require the future to dwell within a fixed context; instead, it grounds the past's hold on the present by suggesting that growth unfolds at a measured pace. Thus, *The Scarlet Letter* ends by positing a different kind of architectural relationship between citizens and the state than the preface articulates. Unlike the Custom-House, Hester's cottage harbors those adrift in the public sphere, not by imprisoning them into a delusory relationship with the past's unrealized expectations, but by sheltering them from the prying eyes of the marketplace. In Hester's cottage, they are allowed to pause before having to return to the public sphere.

IV

"A papered chamber in a fine old farm house—a mile from any other dwelling, and dipped to the eaves in foliage," Herman Melville writes in "Hawthorne and His Mosses" (1850), "is the place to write of Hawthorne."[83] Generations of critics have interpreted Melville's lavish review of *Mosses from an Old Manse* as a declaration of Melville's realization that, as F. O. Matthiessen suggests, he was "living at a moment of ripeness for American life and art."[84] Melville biographers have typically focused on the essay as a turning point in Melville's writing career, consistently pointing toward it as a "cardinal moment, emotionally and intellectually," in

Melville's development.[85] Andrew Delbanco describes the review as "Melville's announcement to the world of his own genius."[86] For Richard Brodhead, Melville's "critical masterpiece" is a "sustained rhapsody," which displays the "new levels of expressive energy" that charged Melville after he first encountered Hawthorne.[87] In the last few decades, critics have more directly explored how Melville's "frankly erotic language" informs our views of the intimate relationship between the two writers during the period when they resided in close proximity in the Berkshires.[88] Such readings often regard the review as the opening note in Melville's courtship (sometimes imagined metaphorically and sometimes figured as literal) of Hawthorne.

While the exact nature of Melville's feelings toward Hawthorne remain elusive, the charged familiarity of "Hawthorne and His Mosses" reveals how Hawthorne's *Mosses from an Old Manse* struck a chord with Melville. In prose that can only be described as overripe, Melville's review attempts to establish a kinship between reader and writer, between an imagined national culture (from Vermont to Virginia) and individual citizens, and most importantly between fiction and reality. Without question, Melville sustains his deepest affection for those tales which mark contemporary domestic moments. Noting how one of the "most remarkable features" of the essay is its "presumptive intimacy," Clark Davis regards the review as an exercise in self-fashioning, wherein Melville indulges in "a self-fulfilling form of inquiry: by imagining a truth in others, the individual is creating his own dream of union, an erasure of difference."[89] Melville extends that blurring of boundaries between subject and object into the material realm by consistently privileging the relationship between author and house as crucially decisive. Again and again, Melville celebrates Hawthorne's work as architecturally informed. Hawthorne and the Old Manse blend into one another, an admixture that Melville declares the source of Hawthorne's inspiration. In the much remarked passage in which Melville compares Hawthorne with Shakespeare, Melville argues that the nation's authors will not "come in the costume of Queen Elizabeth's day" but shall "smell" of America's "beeches and hemlocks" and have the "broad prairies" in their souls (246, 249). America's writers will not dwell in stone castles or foreign palaces; instead, Melville boldly proclaims, they will dwell in storied old houses like the Old Manse or the Vermont farmhouse that Melville's "Virginian" finds himself in when he first discovers Hawthorne.

From its opening line, "Hawthorne and His Mosses" moves to establish the connections between writers and houses and the ways in which spatial location informs reading and writing. Throughout the review, Melville asserts that Hawthorne's genius springs from his domestic and natural environments; he does not seek to imitate foreign models but represents the bounty of his own local culture. Situated in a rustic homestead,

Hawthorne provides a model for American cultural development. Gillian Brown describes Melville's elevation of Hawthorne as the first stage in a complex process of identity formation wherein the author becomes an object of veneration only to be consumed by the reviewer through an act of literary cannibalism. "The cannibalistic logic of Melville's aesthetics," Brown suggests, "works to highlight an autonomy of self."[90] The self gains autonomy, in other words, by actively co-opting the practices of another. During the onrush of the market revolution, as Ellen Weinauer suggests, "the relationship between possession, self-possession, and authorship was under constant and often anxious negotiation."[91] In "Hawthorne and His Mosses," Melville collapses the identities of house and author, as his title foreshadows. Melville's preoccupation with domestic identity reveals itself through how Melville methodically reads Hawthorne architecturally. In so doing, Melville reads Hawthorne as deploying the domestic as a counterbalance to the anxious negotiations Weinauer suggests unsettled self-fashioning.

In the "exquisite" tale "Fire-Worship," Melville observes, Hawthorne argues for the preservation of the Republic's identity-defining domestic traditions (241). Melville applauds Hawthorne's preservationist aesthetic. For Melville, "Fire-Worship" reifies the role of nature in the nation's development. Building on the implications of this reification, Melville posits that by virtue of the fact that both he and Hawthorne occupy rural houses, they both are able to disconnect from the trauma of the Jacksonian market revolution. Refusing the implications of the separate-spheres argument, which suggests the division of the home from the marketplace, Melville argues that Hawthorne is the paradigmatic American writer because his work is domestically centered. Melville's review effectively announces his belief that American cultural history is attached to the Republic's domestic architecture. Yet, like Hawthorne and Poe before him, Melville also underscores how figuring the house as the only space capable of providing a reprieve from restlessness belies the pervasive ways in which goaheadism is altering national mores.

Although Melville had achieved significant public attention with *Typee* and *Omoo*, he began to shift his authorial ambitions and interests at the middle of the nineteenth century. During the summer of 1850, Melville not only met Hawthorne and published "Hawthorne and His Mosses" but also began to contemplate moving his family to Pittsfield, Massachusetts. Enlivened by a vacation in the Berkshires, Melville decided that he could no longer live in Manhattan. Borrowing three thousand dollars from his father-in-law, he put a down payment on a 160-acre farmhouse he called "Arrowhead."[92] The purchase of the property was but the first step in Melville's unaffordable designs; he also planned, as the Pittsfield *Sun* reported in October 1850, "the erection, at no distant day, as we under-

Figure 15. House at Arrowhead, drawing by Herman Melville, from
***Herman Melville: Mariner and Mystic* by Raymond Weaver.** Collection of
The New-York Historical Society (negative number 79716d).

stand, of 'a house to suit him' in a beautiful grove on the premises."[93] Like
Hawthorne, Melville imagined his ideal workplace as located in the upper
portion of a house. When he purchased Arrowhead, he dreamed of renovating the house to build such a room. Melville hoped that this writing
tower would afford him commanding views of "the mountain ranges from
the Catskills to Saddleback (and beyond, to Vermont)" and provide him
the privacy he needed to write.[94] The tower was only one aspect of
Melville's building schemes; he also envisioned a house large enough to
accommodate his entire extended family (see fig. 15). While he never
broke ground on his planned "estate," the home he did inhabit had a profound effect on his writing. Arrowhead was a rambling Georgian farmhouse originally built in 1780. The exterior of the house, notably the roof,
had been modified in 1840 in the Federalist style. Melville planned and
undertook numerous modifications himself, most notably the addition of a
porch on the house's north side. Melville and his extended family (his wife,
their five children, his mother, and his three sisters) resided at Arrowhead
for thirteen years before he was forced, like Hawthorne, to leave his rustic
retreat for a custom-house. But prior to his return to New York and his

reluctant acceptance of an assayer's job, Melville enjoyed the liberation that a farmhouse afforded.

While in residence at Arrowhead, Melville was enormously productive, even as he was losing his audience. At Arrowhead, Melville wrote *Moby-Dick, Pierre, Israel Potter,* and *The Confidence-Man,* novels for which he had enormous hopes, but whose metaphysical speculations fell on deaf ears. Still, the move to Arrowhead allowed him for the first time the kind of domestic seclusion that Hawthorne championed and that Melville so admired in "The Old Manse." During his residence at Arrowhead the house became, in Melville's work, a refuge from the terror of the marketplace. While the domestic figures as central in a range of Melville's works—from his depictions of the domestic in *Typee,* to the ship as house in *Moby-Dick,* to his architectural obsession with both Saddle Meadows and the Church of the Apostles in *Pierre,* to his questions about home and market in "Bartleby"—Melville literalized these questions in "I and My Chimney." His use of the materiality of Arrowhead in "I and My Chimney" made it a vivid embodiment of his concerns about the widespread cultural belief in the regenerative powers of the home. Melville had dreamed that the remove to Arrowhead, named by him after the numerous relics of Native Americans he discovered on the property, would sequester him from the disruptions of the commercial sphere. That separation was not so easily achieved. The possibility of disruptive domestic innovations suggested, for Melville, the encroachment of the market revolution into the one area popularly imagined as outside the public sphere. If that penetration was allowed, then home owners would be in danger of losing their self-sufficiency. Like Hawthorne in "Fire-Worship," Melville was arguing for the necessity of preserving the traditional domestic practices that had been the hallmarks of American culture. If the house was remodeled in favor of technological innovations, Melville feared, then Americans would be in danger of separating themselves from their own cultural inheritance.

In "I and My Chimney," originally published in *Putnam's Monthly Magazine* in March 1856, Melville makes specific use of the architectural design of Arrowhead as inspiration. The tale takes up the cause of Hawthorne's "Fire-Worship," as Melville introduces a threat to the domestic as a means of architecturally measuring how the present inhabits the legacies of the past. "I and My Chimney" advances that the supposed benefits of progress actually endanger the nation. In so doing, the tale positions the house as a sanctuary but also records how the preservation of this space as free from market-driven interventions comes at a significant cost. Building on the themes of Hawthorne's tale, Melville investigates how houses link the present to the past, serving as, in effect, avatars of cultural memory and history. Edward Rosenberry was the first critic to note how "I and My Chimney" is informed very particularly by Hawthorne. Rosenberry argues that Melville seizes on Hawthorne's hearth imagery as "emblematic of domestic and patriotic loyalties" to advance his own considerations of these questions.[95] Building on Rosenberry's observations, John Allison suggests that Melville incorporates "heavy allusions" to Hawthorne's "sketches of domestic architecture and life" into "I and My Chimney" as a means of endorsing "Hawthorne's special brand of conservatism and to maintain a role as Hawthorne's cultural ally."[96] Objecting to interpretations that cement their readings of "I and My Chimney" solely in the biographical, Stuart C. Woodruff maintains that the chimney symbolically represents historical reality.[97]

The house described in "I and My Chimney" mirrors the house in which it was written. Melville's sister Augusta described Arrowhead as having been "built after that peculiarly quaint style of architecture which places the chimney—the hugest in proportions—immediately in the center, & the rooms around it."[98] The massive chimney at the heart of Melville's tale replicates Arrowhead's chimney so faithfully that Melville's brother Allan had lines from the tale inscribed on the Arrowhead chimney after he purchased the house from Herman. The idea that Melville depicts an actual fireplace in his fiction does not reduce the tale to a mere a biographical portrait; rather, he uses existent material resources to critique, just as Hawthorne does in "The Old Manse," the current rush to remodel every aspect of domestic life. As Laurie Robertson-Lorant observes, "Melville's complex symbolism is never merely self-referential."[99] Melville depicts the narrator's struggle to preserve his chimney in order to speak to larger cultural concerns. In effect, the tale records the larger national conflict between conservatism and progressivism, between preservation and goaheadism. "The narrator's house, with its double flues and warring factions," Robertson-Lorant writes, "suggests a 'house divided,' a common metaphor for sectional conflict even before Abraham Lincoln made the phrase memorable."[100] Melville, like Lincoln after him, understood that the crisis born from national sectionalism was rampant as well in domestic design, and that its expression in either the public or the private sphere had national ramifications.

At the opening of the tale, the narrator confesses that "I and My Chimney" are both "two grey-headed old smokers" who "reside in the country" (352). The massive chimney at the center of the narrative, the house, and the marital problems of the narrator of "I and My Chimney" is so expansive that it disrupts domestic life. "Though I always say, *I and my chimney*, as Cardinal Wolsey used to say, *I and my King*, yet this egotistical way of speaking," the narrator confesses, "wherein I take precedence of my chimney, is hardly borne out by the facts; in everything, except the above phrase, my chimney taking precedence of me" (352). The question of who

has precedence over whom is at the heart of this tale. The narrator catalogs his family's objections to the centrality of the chimney only to dismiss
them. Refusing to heed their complaints, the narrator counters that in all
likelihood the house was built around the chimney for its shelter—and not
theirs—and to violate this design would be heretical. The chimney "has
the centre of the house to himself, leaving but the odd holes and corners"
for the human inhabitants (353).

   While the narrator appears bemused by this architectural arrangement,
his wife and daughters are perplexed by his reverence for the chimney. In
the narrator's view, his kinswomen are captivated by modern fashion, failing to appreciate what history has framed for them. "Nothing but newness," the narrator fears, seems to please his wife (362). Instead of celebrating the chimney for its solidity, his wife commissions plans to cut a
passageway through its center to create a more modern interior layout.
Even speculating about the cost of such a misguided remodeling rankles
the narrator, for "if you demolish the foundation," he wonders, "what is to
support the superstructure?" (360). To tinker with one part of the chimney
would, in the narrator's estimation, result simply in its destruction. Refusing to abide by his wife's desire to have him "domestically" "abdicate," the
narrator sets himself up as the conservator of the architectural legacies of
the past (362). The battle between the old and the new takes place on
two fronts within the tale, as Melville suggests that the beloved "old-
fashioned" chimney, and the house it presides over, are simultaneously
endangered by the poor state of current practice and a widespread lack of
respect for previous productions (353). In demonstrating how previous
modifications of the house weakened its solidity, Melville's narrator lays
the ground on which he steadfastly refuses to allow further alterations to
diminish the house.

   Prior to his occupancy of the house, "a temporary proprietor" fixed a
leaky roof by hiring workmen to saw "the old gable roof clean off" (356).
The "modern roof" designed to replace the original appears "more fit for a
railway wood-house than an old country gentleman's abode" (356) The
loss of usable space pales in comparison to how the renovations have disrupted the house's relation with its environment. The modifications have
driven nature from the house. Birds that resided in the old roof's crevices
have been forced to build anew elsewhere. Further, the ill-conceived
remodeling exposes to the elements fifteen feet of the chimney's upper
portion previously sheltered within the interior frame. These newly
uncovered bricks are not, like the chimney's uppermost masonry, weather-
proofed, and they almost immediately begin to decay. Thus, the initial
"improvement" of the house caused it to deteriorate, as if these adjustments to the original design betrayed the significance of the home. This
botched "surgical operation" had transformed the house from unique a

vernacular site into a prosaic, boxlike structure (356). Moreover, the hack-
work necessitates further remodeling, as the narrator's "mortgagor" com-
mands him to tear down a portion of his chimney or have his "policy of
insurance" voided (357). The house thus becomes the victim of temporary
occupancy, a signal of the damning costs of geographical restlessness. For
the narrator all these violations are too much to bear, as he laments that
"all the world over, the picturesque yields to the pocketesque" (357).

The account of the damage done to the narrator's house and chimney is
foreshadowed by his opening salvos against contemporary architectural
practices. In current design schemes, builders locate hallways in the middle of buildings, a practice that ends up creating "houses which are strictly
double houses" (353). Building fireplaces on exterior walls, instead of
locating them in the center of houses, creates a situation wherein "one
member of the household is warming himself at a fire built into a recess of
the north wall" while "another member, the former's own brother, perhaps, may be holding his feet to the blaze before a hearth in the south
wall—the two thus sitting back to back" (353). Unlike houses with "one
federal stock in the middle of the house," these new double-hearth houses
fail to create "a proper fraternal feeling" because they draw individuals
away from one another (353). In short, as Allen Moore Emery writes, "the
narrator is apparently engaged in a form of political allegory in which
styles of chimney-building can be taken to stand for various forms of government."[101] Certainly, Melville's alienated north- and south-facing
brothers reflect the divisiveness (by the mid-1850s) of the regional and
sectarian differences plaguing the country. But Melville carefully refuses to
oversimplify the issue facing this "quarrelsome family," as he underscores
that both brothers have lost their fraternal feelings by remodeling their
federal chimney (353).

The narrator condemns urbanization and modernization for spreading
the disease of multiple chimneys, a design schema that undermines the
solidity of new construction. These multiple fireplaces depend on separate
flues that are "surreptitiously honeycombed into walls; so that these last
are here and there, or indeed almost anywhere, treacherously hollow, and,
in consequence, more or less weak" (353–54). In "these degenerate days,"
when every aspect of design and construction suffers in comparison to the
productions of the past, no one builds anything with an eye toward future
stability (355). In urban spaces, the narrator observes, "there is a large
rivalry in building tall houses," creating an unending cycle of building and
remodeling as home owners competitively "send" for an "architect" to
needlessly clap "a fifth and sixth story on top of his previous four" (354).
Getting and spending, these urban builders lay waste to their houses. By
commodifying the domestic, they reduce their houses into staging
grounds for competition. The narrator aligns his wife's goaheadism with

these cultural mispractices, and sets his own conservationist aesthetic against her desire to remodel the chimney. But his wife becomes a stand-in for any other "meddlesome architectural reformer" more generally, a group that the narrator rails against because of the reformers' destructive appetite for change (377). These new draftsmen, the narrator announces, have "no gift for putting up anything" and thus are always "intent upon pulling down" (377). As "labyrinthine an abode" as his house is, the narrator does not want to see it dismantled, but rather he wants to preserve the domestic order framed for him by his singular "federal stock" (364 and 353). Those critics who read "I and My Chimney" as an extended phallic joke reflective of Melville's own dissatisfaction with his marriage, as, in Robert Milder's words, an attempt to write "seriocomically" about his "melancholia," miss the larger thrust of Melville's argument.[102] As folklorist and architectural historian Henry H. Glassie has observed, "Freudian interpretations notwithstanding," Melville's tale reflects a New England remodeling trend during which many homeowners sought to alter their interior design from a "central chimney to a central hall plan."[103] Rather than trying to root his own marital discord in a contemporary architectural practice, Melville more likely wanted to ground questions about the current state of the Republic in contemporary attitudes toward residual architecture. It was Melville's desire to sound out the relationship between the past and the present through the image of a traditional fireplace that led him to Hawthorne.

The narrator of "I and My Chimney" refuses to waver in his political stance—if the debate about chimney types and the kinds of fraternal bonds they either create or sever is indeed a political allegory—effectively refusing to leave his guard post to ensure that the chimney remains intact. Stubbornly he directs a cease and desist letter to his wife's contractor, telling him to abandon plans for the removal of the chimney, dated "Chimney Side, April 2" and signed "I and my Chimney" (371). To ensure the continual preservation of the house, the narrator resorts to bribing his wife's builder. Yet she remains restless, and her continual plans to assault the chimney force him to remain in his house for "seven years," since he fears his absence would provide her the opportunity to remodel the house without his consent (377). Steadfast in his refusal to allow the house to be further violated by modernizations, the narrator stands guard against anyone championing architectural innovations. Melville, again, frames the problem nationally, as the narrator decries the fact that "in various parts of the country" domestic "reformers" have been "prevailing upon half-witted old folks to destroy their old-fashioned houses" (377). The narrator wants to conserve the domestic legacies of the past because they stabilize the social order more firmly than whims of the moment ever could. Within the logic of the tale, renovations only engender further alterations. By resisting the call for needless change, the narrator hopes to forestall entering the riptide of endless renovations.

In a final act of defiance, the narrator scoffs at those who label him "a sort of mossy old misanthrope" for "standing guard over my mossy old chimney" (377). In this last paragraph, which ends empathically with the statement that "I and my chimney will never surrender," Melville signals the connection between this tale of domestic conservation and Hawthorne and his mossy Old Manse (377). Whereas Hawthorne is forced to remove himself from the sanctity of the Old Manse because of the arrival of workmen, Melville's chimney guardian refuses to allow the destruction of his historic house.

In his clarion call to preserve the structural legacies of the past, Melville does more than echo Hawthorne's concerns about the future direction of the nation. Cautioning against contemporary breakdowns in historic patterns of social organization, Melville urges his fellow citizens to recapture their fraternal feelings and recognize the traditions that have framed the nation. Through the frame of domestic disruptions Melville, like Poe and Hawthorne, recapitulates post-Revolutionary anxieties about the ambiguity and complexity of national histories to advance his questions about the state of cultural praxis. By detailing the ways in which contemporary designs were predicated on a destructive fervor for unexamined remodeling, Melville anticipates Abraham Lincoln's concerns about how political renovations were endangering national stability. Constant renovations were pushing the nation to the brink of fracture; and as Lincoln, Poe, Hawthorne, and Melville all demonstrate, Americans were deluding themselves if they imagined that these alterations had no effect on social order. By calling for Americans to draw their attention back to the palimpsest of the nation's architectural landscape, they each demonstrate how the empty promise of progress through unending change was predicated on imagining the social order as constructed on a tabula rasa, as completely unaffected by anything that the past had framed. By looking back toward the tangled banks of the nation's multivalent domestic histories, Lincoln and Melville deploy the image of a divided house as a warning about the consequences of electing for change instead of preservation.

Notes

1. "When Buildings Are of Durable Materials": The American Home and the Structural Legacies of History (pages 1–36)

1. Abraham Lincoln, *The Collected Works of Abraham Lincoln*, ed. Roy B. Basler (New Brunswick: Rutgers University Press, 1953), 2:461. All further references to Lincoln's prose are from this volume unless otherwise noted, and page numbers will be cited parenthetically in the chapter.
2. Eric Foner and Olivia Mahoney, *A House Divided: America in the Age of Lincoln* (New York: W. W. Norton, 1990), 66.
3. The sheer number of texts that deploy Lincoln's phrase in their very title displays the ways in which "the house divided" metaphor has been consistently deployed to mark the crisis that resulted in the Civil War.
4. Richard Sewell, *A House Divided: Sectionalism and Civil War, 1848–1865* (Baltimore: The Johns Hopkins University Press, 1988), xi.
5. In addition to serving as the title for Foner and Mahoney's and Sewell's volumes, Harry V. Jaffe titles his study of the Lincoln-Douglas debates with a similar echo; see Harry V. Jaffe, *Crisis of the House Divided: An Interpretation of the Issues in the Lincoln-Douglas Debates* (Chicago: University of Chicago Press, 1959).
6. Jaffe, 30.
7. David Herbert Donald, *Lincoln* (New York: Simon & Schuster, 1996), 206.
8. Julia A. Stern, *The Plight of Feeling: Sympathy and Dissent in the Early American Novel* (Chicago: University of Chicago Press, 1997), 239 n3.
9. Grantland S. Rice, *The Transformation of Authorship in America* (Chicago: University of Chicago Press, 1993), 3.
10. Michael E. Gardiner, "Wild Publics and Grotesque Symposiums: Habermas and Bakhtin on Dialogue, Everyday Life, and the Public Sphere," in *After Habermas: New Perspectives on the Public Sphere*, ed. Nick Crossley and John Michael Roberts (Oxford: Blackwell Publishing, 2004), 29.
11. Gardiner, 29.
12. Michael Warner, *Publics and Counterpublics* (Brooklyn: Zone Books, 2002), 68.
13. Warner, 68.
14. Amy Kaplan, *The Anarchy of Empire in the Making of U.S. Culture* (Cambridge, Mass.: Harvard University Press, 2002), 25.
15. From its advent, American Studies has paid scant attention to the intersection of cultural order and domestic architecture. While classic studies, such as those undertaken by Annette Kolodny, R. W. B. Lewis, Leo Marx, Richard Slotkin, and Henry Nash Smith, have discussed the mythic status of American nature, few have addressed the practical implications of a culture quite lit-

erally constructing itself. Figuring the project of nation building as a narrative act, we have consistently overlooked the actual labor undertaken by the citizens of the early Republic. More contemporary critics such as Nina Baym, Gillian Brown, Ann Douglas, Amy Kaplan, Lora Romero, and Jane Tompkins have centered their work on the American domestic, but they have accorded little attention to homebuilding. Indeed, their writing is focused primarily on textual production. This project addresses that absence by providing a thick description of the formation of national identity as that process is registered in the building and furnishing of homes.

16. Recently scholars such as Douglas Anderson, Lori Merish, Susan Ryan, Shelby Streeby, Adam Sweeting, and Priscilla Wald have explored the intersections of sociopolitical enfranchisement with domestic writing, popular journalism, and the emergence of a consumer culture. However, their studies have not addressed how domestic architecture itself impacts definitions of the body politic or informs conceptions of national identity. Critics such as Michael Branch, Lawrence Buell, Kris Fresonke, Christopher Irmscher, Christopher Looby, Pamela Regis, and Thomas Slaughter have offered a countervailing reading of antebellum culture by rekindling interest in the importance of natural history writing. While they have reestablished how studies of the American environment informed cultural production, they have neglected to articulate how conceptions of indigenous nature affected the construction of domestic residences. By underscoring the interdependence of domestic design and social praxis, I refocus attention on how antebellum Americans understood that it was within the walls of houses that these two issues were synthesized.

17. See James Gilreath and Douglas Wilson, eds., *Thomas Jefferson's Library: A Catalog with the Entries in His Own Order* (Washington, D.C.: Library of Congress, 1989).

18. See Benedict Anderson, *Imagined Communities* (New York: Verso, 1983), and Eric Hobsbawm, "Inventing Traditions," in *The Invention of Tradition*, ed. Eric Hobsbawm and Terence Ranger (Cambridge: Cambridge University Press, 1983), 1–14.

19. Donald, 197.

20. Abraham Lincoln, *The Collected Works of Abraham Lincoln*, ed. Roy B. Basler (New Brunswick: Rutgers University Press, 1953), 3:19. All further references to Lincoln's first reply to Douglas are from this volume, and page numbers will be cited parenthetically in the chapter.

21. See Lisa West Norwood, "Domesticating Revolutionary Sentiment in Susan Fenimore Cooper's *Mount Vernon: A Letter to the Children of America*," in *James Fenimore Cooper: His Country and His Art*, vol. 12 (Oneonta: SUNY Oneonta Press, 1999), 62.

22. Patricia West, *Domesticating History: The Political Origins of America's House Museums* (Washington, D.C.: Smithsonian Institution Press, 1999), 4.

23. West, 5.

24. Susan Fenimore Cooper, *Mount Vernon: A Letter to the Children of America* (New York: D. Appleton and Company, 1859), 9.

25. West, 26.

26. See Elswyth Thane, *Mount Vernon Is Ours: The Story of Its Preservation* (New York: Duell, Sloan, and Pearce, 1966), 10.

27. Thane, 11.

28. See W. Barksdale Maynard, "'Best, Lowliest Style!' The Early-Nineteenth-Century Rediscovery of American Colonial Architecture," *Journal of the Society of Architectural Historians* 59.3 (2000), 344; and Robert J. Allison, "First in the Hearts of His Countrymen," *Reviews in American History* 27.3 (1999), 358.

29. Robert F. Dalzell Jr. and Lee Baldwin Dalzell, *George Washington's Mount Vernon: At Home in Revolutionary America* (New York: Oxford University Press, 1998), 226.

30. For more information on Ann Pamela Cunningham, the Mount Vernon Ladies' Association, and the purchase of Mount Vernon see Steven Conn, "Rescuing the Homestead of the Nation: The Mount Vernon Ladies' Association and the Preservation of Mount Vernon," *Nineteenth Century Studies* 11 (1997), 71–93.

31. The success of the this endeavor can, perhaps, best be understood by the fact that Mount Vernon was the only spot of neutral ground recognized by both sides during the Civil War, so much so that both armies allowed supplies and workmen to pass through their lines to Mount Vernon unmolested.

32. Efforts to finish the Washington Monument, just a few miles from Mount Vernon in Washington, D.C., were completely stalled by the 1850s; it had remained little more than a marble stump since construction had briefly begun on it in 1848.

33. Henry Wiencek, *An Imperfect God: George Washington, His Slaves, and the Creation of America* (New York: Farrar, Straus, and Giroux, 2003), 10. My aim here is not to resolve current critical debates about the founders' complex relationships to the institution of slavery but rather to explore how, in the design and construction of Mount Vernon, Washington choose to represent his connections to and dependence on the nefarious system of slavery.

34. Robert F. Dalzell, "Constructing Independence: Monticello, Mount Vernon, and the Men Who Built Them," *Eighteenth-Century Studies* 26.4 (1993), 545.

35. Jean B. Lee, "Mount Vernon Plantation: A Model for the Republic," in *Slavery at the Home of George Washington*, ed. Philip J. Schwarz (Mount Vernon: Mount Vernon Ladies' Association, 2001), 18.

36. Norwood, 63.

37. Maynard, 344.

38. Dalzell, "Constructing Independence," 577.

39. Dalzell and Dalzell, *George Washington's Mount Vernon*, 34.

40. Joseph J. Ellis, *His Excellency: George Washington* (New York: Knopf, 2004), 52.

41. See Dalzell and Dalzell, *George Washington's Mount Vernon*, and Ellis for a detailed analysis of Washington's financial dealings and the revenues he generated from Mount Vernon as opposed to his other landholdings.

42. Dalzell and Dalzell, *George Washington's Mount Vernon*, 47.

43. Dalzell, "Constructing Independence," 564.

44. Thomas Tileston Waterman, *The Mansions of Virginia, 1706–1776* (Chapel Hill: University of North Carolina Press, 1946), 272.

45. Waterman, 272.

46. Possibly, the recently married Washington did not want to inflict a construction project on his new spouse, but since he disrupted much of their married
life with domestic renovations, this contention is not entirely plausible.
Martha Washington was finally so displeased with the continual redecoration
of the house that she declared that her private chamber should be plainly
finished, and proclaimed it off-limits to her husband's further purview. See
Dalzell and Dalzell, *George Washington's Mount Vernon*, 203.

47. Dalzell, "Constructing Independence," 564.

48. See Richard Brookhiser, *Founding Father: Rediscovering George Washington*
(New York: Free Press, 1996), for a suggestive, if also very pointedly partisan,
reading of the ways in which Mount Vernon appeared like a "plain English
country gentleman's home of five or six hundred pounds a year" (80).

49. George Washington to Samuel Vaughan, 14 January 1784, in *The Papers of
George Washington: Confederation Series Vol. 1*, ed. W. W. Abbot (Charlottesville:
University of Virginia Press, 1992).

50. Dalzell and Dalzell, *George Washington's Mount Vernon*, 12.

51. Washington produced a hand-copied conduct guide, "Rules of Civility," by
which he attempted to govern his behavior. See, among others, Richard L.
Bushman, *The Refinement of America: Persons, Houses, Cities* (New York: Vintage,
1993), 31–32.

52. See Thane, 11.

53. George Washington to George William Fairfax, 26 June 1786, in *The Papers
of George Washington: Confederation Series Vol. 4*, ed. W. W. Abbot (Charlottesville: University of Virginia Press, 1995).

54. George Washington to George William Fairfax, 26 June 1786, in *The Papers of
George Washington: Confederation Series Vol. 4*, ed. W.W. Abbot (Charlottesville:
University of Virginia Press, 1995).

55. The demands of the ceaseless tide of visitors finally became so bad that Washington attempted to find a surrogate to supervise and receive the visitors.
"With this view" in mind, Washington Irving writes in his biography of
Washington, "he bethought him of his nephew, Lawrence Lewis." For the
sake of his own health as well as Martha's, Washington implored Lewis to
relieve him of the encumbrance of hospitality; Lewis did relocate, intermit-
tently, to Mount Vernon, but Washington never found the full-time relief
that he sought. Still, he never spurned his guests. Although he had a strong
desire to pursue other endeavors, he felt accountable to those who called on
him. See Washington Irving, *Life of George Washington*, vol. 5 in *The Complete
Works of Washington Irving* (Boston: Twayne Publishers, 1982), 450.

56. Dalzell, "Constructing Independence," 574.

57. George Washington to Sarah Cary Fairfax, 16 May 1798, in *The Papers of
George Washington: Retirement Series Vol. 3*, ed. W. W. Abbot (Charlottesville:
University of Virginia Press, 1999).

58. George Washington to Sarah Cary Fairfax, 16 May 1798, in *The Papers of
George Washington: Retirement Series Vol. 3*, ed. W. W. Abbot (Charlottesville:
University of Virginia Press, 1999).

59. See, for more information on the shifts in where the slaves were quartered, Dennis J. Pogue's insightful essay on the recent archeological diggings undertaken at Mount Vernon aimed at developing a better understanding of the life of Washington's enslaved labor force. Dennis J. Pogue, "Slave Lifeways at Mount Vernon: An Archaeological Perspective," in *Slavery at the Home of George Washington*, ed. Philip J. Schwarz (Mount Vernon: Mount Vernon Ladies' Association, 2001), 111–35.

60. Wiencek, 11.

61. Dalzell and Dalzell, *George Washington's Mount Vernon*, 17.

62. Dalzell and Dalzell, *George Washington's Mount Vernon*, 17.

63. See Fiske Kimball, *Domestic Architecture of the American Colonies and the Early Republic* (New York: Scribner's, 1922), 98–99 and 222–23.

64. Dalzell and Dalzell, *George Washington's Mount Vernon*, 92 and 93.

65. Wiencek, 10.

66. Lorena S. Walsh, "Slavery and Agriculture at Mount Vernon," in *Slavery at the Home of George Washington*, ed. Philip J. Schwarz (Mount Vernon: Mount Vernon Ladies' Association, 2001), 73.

67. Thomas Jefferson, *Writings* (New York: Library of America: 1984), 278–79. All references to *Notes on the State of Virginia* are from this volume, and page numbers will be referred to parenthetically within the chapter.

68. The practice was even odder when builders, like George Washington, strove to make their wooden houses appear to be fashioned out of stone. Clearly the aesthetic of masonry was preferred, but the practice of wooden construction continued.

69. Timothy Sweet, *American Georgics: Economy and Environment in Early American Literature* (Philadelphia: University of Pennsylvania Press, 2002), 98 and 99.

70. See Sweet, 97–100.

71. Peter S. Onuf, *Jefferson's Empire: The Language of American Nationhood* (Charlottesville: University of Virginia Press, 2000), 69.

72. Onuf, *Jefferson's Empire*, 162.

73. Rhys Isaac, "The First Monticello," in *Jeffersonian Legacies*, ed. Peter S. Onuf (Charlottesville: University of Virginia Press, 1993), 97.

74. Considered in this light, Jefferson's recurrent calls for emancipation and enforced colonization in *Notes* are consistent extensions of his desire to imagine a republican empire. Slavery enabled agricultural practices that fostered mobility and ran counter to Jefferson's hopes for a landscape of yeoman farmers. Onuf, *Jefferson's Empire*, 147–88, and also Lewis P. Simpson, "The Ferocity of Self: History and Consciousness in Southern Literature," *South Central Review* 1 (1984), 67–84.

75. Thomas Hallock, *From the Fallen Tree: Frontier Narratives, Environmental Politics, and the Roots of a National Pastoral, 1749–1826* (Chapel Hill: University of North Carolina Press, 2003), 99.

76. See Thomas Jefferson to Abigail Adams, 22 February 1787, Thomas Jefferson to Stiles, 24 December 1786, Thomas Jefferson to Madison, 30 January 1787, and Thomas Jefferson to William Stephens Smith, 13 November 1787,

in *The Papers of Thomas Jefferson*, vol. 11, ed. Julian P. Boyd (Princeton: Princeton University Press, 1955).

77. Thomas Jefferson to William Stephens Smith, 13 November 1787, in *The Papers of Thomas Jefferson*, vol. 12, ed. Julian P. Boyd (Princeton: Princeton University Press, 1955).

78. Joseph J. Ellis, *American Sphinx: The Character of Thomas Jefferson* (New York: Alfred A. Knopf, 1998), 100.

79. Gordon S. Wood, "The Trials and Tribulations of Thomas Jefferson," in *Jeffersonian Legacies*, ed. Peter S. Onuf (Charlottesville: University of Virginia Press, 1993), 409.

80. Ellis, 101.

81. Jan Lewis, "'The Blessings of Domestic Society': Thomas Jefferson's Family and the Transformation of American Politics," in *Jeffersonian Legacies*, ed. Peter S. Onuf (Charlottesville: University of Virginia Press, 1993), 117. Lewis' argument builds on the work of Jack N. Rakove, so in addition to Lewis' essay see also Jack N. Rakove, "The Structure of Politics at the Accession of George Washington," in *Beyond Confederation: Origins of the Constitution and American National Identity*, ed. Richard Beeman, Stephen Botein, and Edwin C. Carter II (Chapel Hill: University of North Carolina Press, 1987), 261–94.

82. Christopher Looby, *Voicing America: Language, Literary Form, and the Origins of the United States* (Chicago: University of Chicago Press, 1996), 104.

83. Jay Fliegelman, *Declaring Independence: Jefferson, Natural Language, and the Culture of Performance* (Stanford: Stanford University Press, 1993), 167.

84. Joyce Appleby, "Jefferson and His Complex Legacy," in *Jeffersonian Legacies*, ed. Peter S. Onuf (Charlottesville: University of Virginia Press, 1993), 14.

85. Jack McLaughlin, *Jefferson and Monticello: The Biography of a Builder* (New York: Owl Books, 1988), 93.

86. Jefferson's desire to control every aspect of Monticello's construction stands in stark contrast to the practices of both Lincoln and Washington, who also remodeled existing houses but did not attempt to exercise the same level of control.

87. As quoted by McLaughlin, 3. McLaughlin's source is the manuscript "Journal of Anna Maria Brodeau, wife of Dr. William Thornton of Washington, D.C." located in the Library of Congress.

88. William Howard Adams, *Jefferson's Monticello* (New York: Abbeville Press, 1983), 46.

89. Isaac, 96–97.

90. Dalzell, "Constructing Independence," 577.

91. Thomas Jefferson, *The Garden and Farm Books* (reprint, Golden, Colo.: Fulcrum, 1987), 53.

92. Thomas Jefferson to Benjamin H. Latrobe, 10 October 1809, in *The Papers of Thomas Jefferson, Retirement Series Vol. 1*, ed. J. Jefferson Looney (Princeton: Princeton University Press, 2005).

93. Jefferson, as Lucia Stanton explores, was obsessed with the profits and possibilities of his nail manufactory, often rising at dawn to weigh the amount of nail rod given to his enslaved craftsmen and returning at dusk to weigh the

nails they had produced to determine how much material each had "wasted" in production. See Lucia Stanton, "'Those Who Labor for My Happiness': Thomas Jefferson and His Slaves," in *Jeffersonian Legacies*, ed. Peter S. Onuf (Charlottesville: University of Virginia Press, 1993), 153–55.

94. As quoted in McLaughlin, 5.

95. For examples of such readings see Susan R. Stein, *The Worlds of Thomas Jefferson at Monticello* (New York: Harry N. Abrams, 1993); William Howard Adams, *Jefferson's Monticello* (New York: Abbeville Press, 1983); and Jack McLaughlin, *Jefferson and Monticello: The Biography of a Builder* (New York: Owl Books, 1988).

96. See Lewis, "'The Blessings of Domestic Society,'" for an extended account of how these three factors were for Jefferson intertwined.

97. Dalzell and Dalzell, *George Washington's Mount Vernon*, 192.

98. Henry S. Randall, *The Life of Thomas Jefferson* (New York: Derby and Jackson, 1858), 3:330.

99. Hospitality was a social code by which the tenuous bonds of the social fabric were maintained, and to ignore one's obligation toward visitors would be regarded as vulgar. Within an American context, this was complicated by the supposed erasure of a hierarchical class system; in the aftermath of the Revolution, the cult of republican brotherhood promulgated social equality, meaning that every man should feel at ease asking another for hospitality. Thus, in a sense, all Americans capable of making the trip to Washington's and/or Jefferson's houses felt it their fellow countryman's responsibility to offer care.

100. See Lewis, "'The Blessings of Domestic Society,'" for a deeper sense of Jefferson's desire for and concern about fame and its demands.

101. Plaster decorations in the entrance hall include an eagle surrounded by clouds and eighteen stars, suggesting its completion date to be after Louisiana was admitted as a state in 1812 and before Indiana became the nineteenth state in 1816.

102. Thomas Jefferson to James Dinsmore, 8 June 1805, as quoted by Stein, 63.

103. Stein, 61.

104. Stein, 61.

105. Jay Fliegelman writes that the Windsor chair, "because its rounded back accommodated the body's form (rather than imposing a 'rectitude' on it) not only offered comfort without luxury" but was emblematic of "republican simplicity without a sacrifice of style." See Fliegelman, 72.

106. Lewis, 137.

107. Moreover, the aesthetic of a boundary of omission reveals the ways in which Jefferson sought to spatially mask the presence of slavery, to reduce its visual impact by submerging the slave quarters on the exterior and devising ways to render the work of slaves on the interior invisible. By walling off the public and private spheres, Jefferson sought to carve out a space of privacy that was liberated both from intrusion and from overt evidence of enslaved labor; both of these disruptions are moved as far offstage as possible in Jefferson's design.

108. See Susan Stewart, *On Longing: Narratives of the Miniature, the Gigantic, the*

Souvenir, the Collection (Baltimore: The Johns Hopkins University Press, 1984), 157.

109. Stein, 63.

110. Thomas Jefferson to James Dinsmore, 28 January 1804, as quoted by Stein, 377.

111. See chapter 4 of Hallock's *From the Fallen Tree* for an insightful discussion of Jefferson's vision of natural history as embodied in *Notes on the State of Virginia*.

112. In addition to Fliegelman, Looby, Hallock, and Sweet, see Douglas Anderson, "Subterraneous Virginia: The Ethical Politics of Thomas Jefferson," *Eighteenth-Century Studies* 33.2 (2000), 233–49; Mitchell Robert Breitwieser, "Jefferson's Prospect," *Prospects: An Annual Journal of American Cultural Studies* 10 (1985), 315–52; Wayne Franklin, *Discoverers, Explorers, Settlers: The Diligent Writers of Early America* (Chicago: University of Chicago Press, 1979); and Christopher Looby, "The Constitution of Nature: Taxonomy as Politics in Jefferson, Peale, and Bartram," *Early American Literature* 22.3 (1987), 252–73. For an in-depth analysis of the lingering importance of Jefferson after his death, and the ways in which *Notes* was read in service of those refigurations of Jefferson, see Merrill D. Peterson, *The Jefferson Image in the American Mind* (New York: Oxford University Press, 1960).

2. "No Longer Assigned Its Ancient Use": Biloquial Architecture and the Problems of Remodeling (pages 37–79)

1. Henry Laurens to John Bartram, 9 August 1766, in *The Correspondence of John Bartram, 1734–1777*, ed. Edmund Berkeley and Dorothy Smith Berkeley (Gainesville: University Press of Florida, 1992), 672.

2. Thomas P. Slaughter, *The Natures of John and William Bartram* (New York: Alfred A. Knopf, 1996), 158.

3. Henry Laurens to John Bartram, 9 August 1766, *Correspondence*, 671.

4. Henry Laurens to John Bartram, 9 August 1766, *Correspondence*, 671.

5. Henry Laurens to John Bartram, 9 August 1766, *Correspondence*, 672.

6. John Bartram to William Bartram, 15 July 1772, *Correspondence*, 749.

7. See Gordon Sayre, "The Mound Builders and the Imagination of American Antiquity in Jefferson, Bartram, and Chateaubriand," *Early American Literature* 33.3 (1998), 225–49, for an in-depth reading the of the cultural preoccupation with ruins during the late eighteenth century in the United States.

8. Thomas Hallock, *From the Fallen Tree: Frontier Narratives, Environmental Politics, and the Roots of a National Pastoral, 1740–1826* (Chapel Hill: University of North Carolina Press, 2003), 165.

9. Myra Jehlen, "The Literature of Colonization," in *The Cambridge History of American Literature*, ed. Sacvan Bercovitch (New York: Cambridge University Press, 1997), 1:133.

10. Anderson continues by suggesting that even as Bartram marks the "civil crisis within which his *Travels* takes place" by including (and in some cases reimagining) a few key dates, he deeply camouflages this chronology so as to render

it almost inconsequential. See Douglas Anderson, "Bartram's Travels and the Politics of Nature," *Early American Literature* 25.1 (1990), 4.

11. Kris Fresonke, *West of Emerson: The Design of Manifest Destiny* (Berkeley: University of California Press, 2003), 30.

12. Christopher Iannini, "The Vertigo of Circum-Caribbean Empire: William Bartram's Florida," *Mississippi Quarterly* 57.1 (Winter 2003/2004), 148.

13. Iannini, 148.

14. Michael Warner, "What's Colonial about Colonial America?" in *Possible Pasts: Becoming Colonial in Early America*, ed. Robert Blair St. George (Ithaca, N.Y.: Cornell University Press, 2000), 62.

15. Christopher Looby, "The Constitution of Nature: Taxonomy as Politics in Jefferson, Peale, and Bartram," *Early American Literature* 22.3 (1987), 254.

16. Looby, 252.

17. In her compelling reading of Crèvecoeur, Greeson demonstrates how many early American travelogs deploy a narrator native to the mid-Atlantic region southward as a means of figuring the southern districts as an "internal Other for the new nation—as simultaneously *a part and apart* from the United States," thereby becoming a means by which "early U.S. writers both acknowledged the persistence of their recent colonial past and disavowed it." These travelogs, of which *Travels* is arguably a part, employ the South as a counterpoint to the construction of a post-Revolutionary national U.S. identity. Bartram's return to his southern botanical expedition a decade and a half after completing it, reflects this pattern of deploying the South as a register of the post-colonial challenges facing the stability of the emerging nation. See Jennifer Rae Greeson, "Colonial Planter to American Farmer: South, Nation, and Decolonization in Crèvecoeur," in *Messy Beginnings: Postcoloniality and Early American Studies*, ed. Malini Johar Schueller and Edward Watts (New Brunswick: Rutgers University Press, 2003), 105.

18. See Francis Harper's introduction to *The Travels of William Bartram* (Athens: University of Georgia Press, 1998), xxix. All references to *Travels* are from this volume, and page numbers will be cited parenthetically hereafter in the chapter.

19. Edward Cashin, *William Bartram and the American Revolution on the Southern Frontier* (Columbia: University of South Carolina Press, 2000), 248.

20. Anderson, 9.

21. While many critics have remarked on the rhetorical function of Bartram's version of his early encounter with the Seminole who menaces him in chapter 3 of *Travels*, the episode has a counterpoint toward the end of Bartram's venture when he comes across what he perceives, at first, to be "a predatory band of Negroes" (298). In each instance, Bartram assumes that he will fall victim to violence at the hands of a racial other he encounters in the wild; while in both cases he is never harmed, the episodes effectively function as bookends to his account, underscoring the mobility and presence of Native Americans and enslaved Africans in the area he hopes to "clear" by virtue of his taxonomic imagination.

22. Pamela Regis, *Describing Early America: Bartram, Jefferson, Crèvecoeur, and the*

Influence of Natural History (Philadelphia: University of Pennsylvania Press, 1999), 78.

23. Regis, 78.

24. The immense popularity, both in Europe and North America, of Constantin Francois Volney's *Les Ruins; ou, Méditation sur les Révolutions des Empires* (1791), published the same year as Bartram's *Travels*, is perhaps the most famous example of this sensibility.

25. A few days after leaving this relic of Spanish colonialism, Bartram paddles to the relinquished patent of Dennis Rolle in East Florida. Having "obtained from the [English] crown a grant of forty thousand acres of land," Rolle attempted to establish an estate and surrounding town (96). "It seems, from an ill concerted plan in its infant establishment, negligence, or extreme parsimony in sending proper recruits and other necessassaries [*sic*], together with a bad choice of citizens," Bartram concludes, "the settlement by degrees grew weaker, and at length totally fell to the ground" (96–97). A once promising estate of forty thousand acres was now "mouldering to earth" (97). Rolle's failure, Bartram reminds us, is only another turn of the cyclical colonization pattern of the area, for it appears that "the aborigines of America had a very great town in this place" (97). By noting the ruins of a Native American town underneath the wreckage of Rolle's patent, Bartram underscores the complex history of the area while simultaneously highlighting just how difficult it is to establish an enduring settlement. Two groups had tried to build large towns in this area, and all that remained of both attempts was being reclaimed by resurgent vegetation. For Bartram, the idea that Rolle's work could be as impermanent as that of the vanishing Native Americans was disturbing, for it demonstrated the failure of well-funded European settlements in an area that Bartram hoped might become part of the southeastern United States.

26. See Slaughter's textual note in Bartram, *Travels and Other Writings* (New York: Library of America, 1996), 626.

27. Cashin, 257.

28. John Bartram to Jared Eliot, 24 January 1757, *Correspondence*, 415.

29. Slaughter, *The Natures of John and William Bartram*, 78.

30. See Slaughter, *The Natures of John and William Bartram*, 40.

31. See Russell Reising's compelling reading of the ways in which *Wieland* inculcates recurrent themes of domestic violence in the United States. Russell Reising, *Loose Ends: Closure and Crisis in the American Social Text* (Durham: Duke University Press, 1996), 25–73.

32. Both Donald Berthold and Janie Hinds draw some connections between Brown and Bartram. Berthold links *Edgar Huntly* and Bartram via their interests in the picturesque, while Hinds links Brown's figuration of Old Deb and her dogs to a variety of natural historians. See Dennis Berthold, "Charles Brockden Brown, *Edgar Huntly*, and the Origins of the American Picturesque," *William and Mary Quarterly* 41.1 (1984), 62–84, and Janie Hinds, "Deb's Dogs: Animals, Indians, and Postcolonial Desire in Charles Brockden Brown's *Edgar Huntly*," *Early American Literature* 39.2 (2004), 323–54.

33. Charles Brockden Brown, *Wieland & Memoirs of Carwin*, ed. Sydney J. Krause and S. W. Reid (Kent, Ohio: Kent State University Press, 1977), 11. All references to *Wieland* are from this volume, and page numbers will be cited parenthetically hereafter in the chapter.

34. Alan Axelrod, *Charles Brockden Brown: An American Tale* (Austin: University of Texas Press, 1983), 66.

35. Robert Lawson-Peebles, *Landscape and Written Expression in Revolutionary America* (New York: Cambridge University Press, 1988), 236.

36. In an interesting reconfiguration of Brown's lack of early financial success as a novelist, Nina Baym points out that Brown "entered American literary history, via William Dunlap's two volume eulogizing biography, *The Life of Charles Brockden Brown* (Philadelphia: James P. Parke, 1815)." Baym's essay examines Dunlap's biography in terms of how it seeks to apologize for Brown's lack of early financial success because of the "cultural immaturity" of the emerging Republic. Counter to many critics who suggest that Brown's inability to support himself through his work as a novelist was because of a "failure of seriousness" among readers in the young Republic, Baym argues that the "failure of seriousness" lay with Brown's text rather than the state of cultural development in the nation. See Nina Baym, "A Minority Reading of *Wieland*," in *Critical Essays on Charles Brockden Brown*, ed. Bernard Rosentahl (Boston: G. K. Hall & Co, 1981), 87–103.

37. William Dunlap, *The Life of Charles Brockden Brown* (Philadelphia: James P. Parke, 1815), 2:89.

38. *North American Review* 9 (June 1819), 74.

39. See Gordon S. Wood, *The Creation of the American Republic, 1776–1787* (New York: W. W. Norton, 1969), and Steven Watts, *The Romance of Real Life: Charles Brockden Brown and the Origins of American Culture* (Baltimore: The Johns Hopkins University Press, 1994), for more detailed accounts of the uneasiness of the post-Revolutionary period.

40. Julia A. Stern, *The Plight of Felling: Sympathy and Dissent on the Early American Novel* (Chicago: University of Chicago Press, 1997), 28.

41. Christopher Looby, *Voicing America: Language, Literary Form, and the Origins of the United States* (Chicago: University of Chicago Press, 1996), 177.

42. Elizabeth Jane Wall Hinds, *Private Property: Charles Brockden Brown's Gendered Economics of Virtue* (Newark: University of Delaware Press, 1997), 100. In her examination of *Wieland*, Hinds provocatively links the story to Poe's "Fall of the House of Usher," pointing out how in both instances the family and the house become interchangeable signifiers. Like Poe's mysterious Ushers, "the fate of the Wielands is inextricably bound together with their various properties" (112).

43. Peter Kafer, *Charles Brockden Brown's Revolution and the Birth of the American Gothic* (Philadelphia: University of Pennsylvania Press, 2004), 124. Kafer's account of Brown tends very heavily toward a biographical accounting of the novels, but he also maps the ways in which *Wieland* may be rooted in the particular settlement histories of Pennsylvania, including a suggestive observation that Wieland Sr.'s temple may have its roots in a tabernacle built on the

Wissahiccon by Johannes Kelpius and his fellow millenarians who settled in Chicester, Pennsylvania, in 1695–96 (see Kafer, 117).

44. Brown supplements, for example, his main narrative with the subplot of Louisa Conway—a destitute "orphan" also undone by strange circumstances— to underscore that the dissolution of Theodore Wieland's senses is not an isolated incident. Louisa Conway is a minor figure in *Wieland* whose purpose as a dispossessed child is to prove that the precariousness of the Wielands' lives is mirrored in many individuals around them. Further, Brown offers the inexplicable precedent of the spontaneous combustion of Theodore's father as another example of the consistent presence of the unknowable.

45. Christopher Looby, *Voicing America*, 162.

46. Edward Sill Fussell, "*Wieland:* A Literary and Historical Reading," *Early American Literature* 18.2 (1983), 173.

47. Jane Tompkins, *Sensational Designs: The Cultural Work of American Fiction, 1790–1860* (New York: Oxford University Press, 1985), 50. While Tompkins' reading of Brown's politics in the chapter titled "What happens in *Wieland?*" is provocative, I share Christopher Looby's sense that she overestimates the ways in which we can connect Brown's famous sending of a copy of the novel to Thomas Jefferson as a clear signal of Brown's political intentions in the novel.

48. Bill Christophersen, *The Apparition in the Glass: Charles Brockden Brown's American Gothic* (Athens: University of Georgia Press, 1993), 37.

49. Shirley Samuels, "*Wieland:* Alien and Infidel," *Early American Literature* 25.1 (1990), 50.

50. David Kazanjian, *The Colonizing Trick: National Culture and Imperial Citizenship in Early America* (Minneapolis: University of Minnesota Press, 2003), 161.

51. His frequent visits prompt him to form a relationship with Clara's "servant Judith," whom Carwin declares as coming from "a family where hypocrisy, as well as licentiousness, was wrought into her system" (201). Carwin's aside about Judith's "flexible" morals does more than simply explain how he was able to dupe Theodore and Pleyel about Clara's chastity (they *hear* Clara and see Judith during one of Carwin's escapades); it also reifies the theme that the past informs the character of individuals. Judith is promiscuous and deceitful because of how her domestic past has modeled her development.

52. See Charles C. Cole Jr., "Brockden Brown and the Jefferson Administration," *Pennsylvania Magazine of History and Biography* 72 (1948), 253–63.

53. Many of the political elite of the emerging Republic, including Washington and Jefferson, were subscribers to Bartram's text, which means that Jefferson at least had in his library (whether he choose to imagine them as connected or not) copies of both *Travels* and *Wieland*. In an even more ironic twist of fate, Jefferson was also during this period yet one more gentleman farmer living on the banks of the Schuylkill. As Francis Harper notes, "for a time, in the 1790s, Thomas Jefferson lived on the opposite bank of the Schuylkill" from Bartram, and "in the next decade, during his presidency, he and Bartram exchanged a number of very cordial letters, chiefly on natural history subjects" See Harper, xxix.

54. Charles Brockden Brown, *Edgar Huntly; or, Memoirs of a Sleep-Walker*, ed. Sydney J. Krause and S. W. Reid (Kent, Ohio: Kent State University Press, 1984), 3. All references to *Edgar Huntly* are from this volume, and page numbers will be cited parenthetically hereafter in the chapter.

55. Caroll Smith-Rosenberg, "Subject Female: Authorizing American Identity," *American Literary History* 5.3 (1993), 495.

56. Luke Gibbons, "Ireland, America, and Gothic Memory: Transatlantic Terror in the Early Republic," *boundary 2* 31.1 (2004), 26.

57. Peter Kafer estimates that at a normal pace a "walker" would have been able to cover "twenty" miles, but the runners "paced by horses carrying their provisions" were able to traverse "sixty-four miles" before they collapsed in exhaustion. See Kafer, 173.

58. Kafer, 176.

59. Stephen Shapiro, "'Man to Man I Needed Not to Dread His Encounter': Edgar Huntly's End of Erotic Pessimism," in *Revising Charles Brockden Brown: Culture, Politics, and Sexuality in the Early Republic*, ed. Philip Barnard, Mark L. Kamrath, and Stephen Shapiro (Knoxville: University of Tennessee Press, 2004), 238.

60. See Joyce Appleby's *Inheriting the Revolution: The First Generation of Americans* (Cambridge, Mass.: Harvard University Press, 2000) for her fluid and far-reaching reading account of the formation of post-Revolutionary national identity. Appleby is particularly strong in her mapping of how "America's revolutionary ideology got refracted through economic initiatives, social mores, and personal relations" (24).

61. In this regard Brown's efforts in *Edgar Huntly* are a precursor to James Fenimore Cooper's unraveling of his own father's claims to the territory of Cooperstown in *The Pioneers*. Both Brown and Cooper choose these moments of postcolonial history to record their own unease with the possessive claims that American settlers have made on the "wilderness." See chapter 4 for an in-depth discussion of Cooper's use of the house metaphor.

62. Paul Downes, "Sleep-Walking Out of the Revolution: Brown's *Edgar Huntly*," *Eighteenth-Century Studies* 29.4 (1996), 424.

63. Arguably, Brown includes the convolutions of Weymouth's mysterious depositing of his fortune in Waldegrave's bank account (which allows Huntly to briefly imagine that he can marry Waldegrave's sister and inherit this sizable dowry) to underscore the ways in which Huntly imagines that his future happiness is dependent on securing an inheritance.

64. Hinds, *Private Property*, 135.

65. Sydney J. Krause, "Penn's Elm and *Edgar Huntly*: Dark 'Instruction to the Heart,'" *American Literature* 66.3 (1994), 476.

66. Timothy Sweet, *American Georgics: Economy and Environment in Early American Literature* (Philadelphia: University of Pennsylvania Press, 2002), 117. Norman Grabo also convincingly reads Huntly's journey as one from "wilderness" to "civilization." See Grabo, *The Coincidental Art of Charles Brockden Brown* (Chapel Hill: University of North Carolina Press, 1981).

67. Christophersen, 164.

68. See Robert S. Levin, *Conspiracy and Romance: Studies in Brockden Brown, Cooper, Hawthorne, and Melville* (New York: Cambridge University Press, 1972) 15–57, for an indispensable reading of how Brown's novels inculcate the latent fears over foreign influences that the Alien and Sedition Acts were meant to address. See also Frank Suffelton, "Juries of the Common Reader," in *Revising Charles Brockden Brown*, 88–114.

69. The exactness of this description is prefigured by the lengthy and minute description of Clithero's box, which Huntly breaks open in his ham-handed attempt to discover Clithero's secrets, but the attention to the box and its material construction is the lone other example, which only reaffirms Gardner's point. See Jared Gardner, *Master Plots: Race and the Founding of an American Literature, 1787–1845* (Baltimore: The Johns Hopkins University Press, 1998), 71.

70. By comparison, Brown's description of the Selby house, the much praised second house he "discovers," stresses its sophistication and architectural accomplishment (even as he also stresses how odd it is that these exteriors do not harmonize with the interior domestic disharmony), noting that its "materials had undergone the plane, as well as the axe and saw . . . the windows not only had sashes, but these sashes were supplied, contrary to custom, with glass . . . I gathered from these tokens that this was an abode not only of rural competence and innocence, but some beings, raised by education and fortune, above the intellectual mediocrity of clowns" (837–38).

71. In his attempt to return to Norwalk, Huntly is shot at (because they mistake him for a "native") by the posse, which has set out to avenge the death of a "farmer [who] was shot in the fields" (250). When this farmer's house is burned, a "troop of rustics" sets out to avenge this incursion (250).

72. Hinds, *Private Property*, 138.

73. Gary E. Moulton, ed., *The Journals of the Lewis and Clark Expedition*, 13 vols. (Lincoln: University of Nebraska Press, 1983–2001), 10:182. In the remaining text of this chapter, subsequent parenthetical citations of volume and page numbers refer to this Moulton edition of the *Journals*.

74. See almost any of Clark's entries from this period (December 1805), as they contain a litany of unending health complaints. The overall well-being of the Corps was being dramatically undermined by their inability to either stay dry or properly sleep, and Clark's dogged focus on directing the party to rapidly construct winter quarters was in part a response to his concern about the men's overall failing health and depressed spirits.

75. Stephen Ambrose's popular *Undaunted Courage* (New York: Simon & Schuster,1996) exemplifies this type of reading. Similarly, Frank Bergon compares the Lewis and Clark expedition to "the Epic of Gilgamesh and the Odyssey" in his essay "Wilderness Aesthetics," in *Lewis & Clark: Legacies, Memories, and New Perspectives*, ed. Kris Fresonke and Mark Spence (Berkeley: University of California Press, 2004), 37.

76. Thomas Hallock, *From the Fallen Tree: Frontier Narratives, Environmental Politics, and the Roots of a National Pastoral, 1740–1826* (Chapel Hill: University of North Carolina Press, 2003), 122.

77. Thomas P. Slaughter, *Exploring Lewis and Clark: Reflections on Men and Wilderness* (New York: Alfred A. Knopf, 2003), 64.

78. See Slaughter, 64, and Fresonke, 21.

79. Lewis' focus on returning east, an undercurrent that resurfaces throughout his entries in the *Journals* as early as mid-November 1805, is perhaps best reflected in his entry for 1 January 1806, where he writes that "our repast of this day tho' better than that of Christmas, consisted principally in the anticipation of the 1st day of January 1807, when in the bosom of our fiends we hope to participate in the mirth and hilarity of the day, and when with the zest given by the recollection of the present, we shall completely, both mentally and corporally, enjoy the repast which the hand of civilization has prepared for us" (6:151–52). The implicit counterpoint to Lewis' anticipation of the civilization of 1807 is the savagery he projects onto his present circumstances. Lewis writes no entry for 1 January 1805 while garrisoned at Fort Mandan, but Clark's entries for the holiday are quite cheerful when compared with the somber tones of both Clark and Lewis in 1806.

80. See for instance Clark's entry for 7 December 1804, which describes the joint hunt and especially his ethnographic observations about Mandan conceptions of the ownership of slain animals, and Clark's 1 January 1805 entry for an account of the New Year's celebration (3:253–54 and 3:266–67). The consistent interaction of the Corps and the Mandans is exemplified by Clark's entry for 31 December 1804, wherein he writes, "a Number of indians here every day our blck Smitth mending their axes hoes &c. for which the Squars bring Corn for payment" (3:264).

81. James P. Ronda, *Lewis and Clark among the Indians* (Lincoln: University of Nebraska Press, 1984), 206.

82. Ronda, 206.

83. Hallock, 132.

84. Fresonke, 34.

85. Ronda, 189.

86. Ronda, 183.

87. Although certainly familiar with both *Notes on the State of Virginia* and Jefferson's interest in architecture as a measure of cultural practice, Lewis does not echo Jefferson's contempt for wooden structures. Jefferson expresses his concerns about the failures of American architecture in *Notes* as a more generalized anxiety about the viability of the American experiment. Fearing that wooden houses do not serve to sufficiently root individuals in communities, Jefferson proclaims that "a country whose buildings are of wood can never increase its improvements to any degree," for each succeeding generation must devote time and labor to maintain poorly designed buildings. Within *Notes*, Jefferson chastises Virginians for their devotion to wooden structures and laments that this destabilizes their social order. The Clatsops, whose own dwellings were superior to those of the Corps, were seemingly in as much danger of vanishing from the landscape because of the impermanency of their dwellings as Jefferson imagined the citizens of Virginia to be. In essence, the Corps of Discovery had traveled across the continent only to find that houses in the West were in one sense mirror images of those of Virginia.

88. Clark goes so far as to suggest that the proposition to steal the canoe originated with "our interpt and Sever[al] of the party" and not from the captains

themselves, which is quite different from Lewis' use of "we" (6:428). For additional reflections on this episode see Ronda, 211–12.

89. On 7 December 1804, Clark observes that although Lewis and his party of hunters had killed fourteen buffalo, the Corps was only able to secure five of them, and "those we did not get in was taken by the indians under a Custom which is established amongst them, 'i'e. [*sic*] Any person Seeing a buffalow lying without an arrow Sticking in him, or Some purticular mark takes possession, many times (as I am told) a hunter who Kills maney Buffalow in a chase only Gets a part of one" (3:254). Clark's notation of this custom does not include any negative judgment concerning the conduct of the Mandans.

90. William Cronon, "The Trouble with Wilderness; or, Getting Back to the Wrong Nature," in *Uncommon Ground: Rethinking the Human Place in Nature*, ed. William Cronon (New York: W. W. Norton, 1996), 80.

91. Cronon is certainly not the first to employ the phrase "middle ground," which Leo Marx, in *The Machine in the Garden*, persuasively argues is the term that best defines the American experience of the mid–nineteenth century. Prior to Marx, Raymond Williams compellingly articulated the importance of this term, although in an English context, in *The Country and the City*. Cronon, 81 and 80.

3. "Home Bred Virtues and Local Attachments": New York and the Evolution of the American Home (pages 80–121)

1. Washington Irving to Henry Brevoort, 23 August 1815, in Irving, *Letters*, 4 vols., ed. Ralph M. Aderman, Herbert L. Kleinfield, and Jennifer S. Banks (Boston: Twayne, 1978–82), 1: 417.

2. Bad weather also contributed to the failure of P. & E. Irving and Company, as adverse winds prohibited the company's ships from leaving England. With their merchandise moored to Liverpool's docks, Washington and Peter felt their optimism drain away. While they might not have been able to overcome Peter's rash purchasing, the fact that they could not even ship their wares hastened the collapse of the firm.

3. Washington Irving, *A Tour of the Prairies*, in Irving, *The Crayon Miscellany*, ed. Dahlia Terrell (Boston: Twayne, 1979), 5. Details of this biographical sketch are drawn from Stanley T. Williams, *The Life of Washington Irving*, 2 vols. (New York: Oxford University Press, 1935). Williams' indispensable text remains the authoritative biography of Irving.

4. Williams, 151.

5. Washington Irving to Amelia Foster, April–May 1823, *Letters*, 1:743.

6. Jeffrey Rubin-Dorsky, *Adrift in the Old World: The Psychological Pilgrimage of Washington Irving* (Chicago: University of Chicago Press, 1988), 33.

7. See Rubin-Dorsky, chapter 1.

8. Rubin-Dorsky, 32.

9. For a more detailed sense of the cultural capital of Jackson's victory in New Orleans, see John William War, *Andrew Jackson–Symbol for an Age* (New York: Oxford University Press, 1953) especially chapter 1.

10. Indeed, histories and traditions were consistently being invented in Britain during Irving's residence as Walter Scott novels actively invent a particular vision of Scottish history. See Hugh Trevor-Roper, "The Invention of Tradition: The Highland Tradition of Scotland," in *The Invention of Tradition*, ed. Hobsbawm and Ranger (Cambridge: Cambridge University Press, 1983), 15–43, for a more detailed account of the invention of Scottish history during the early nineteenth century. See also Benedict Anderson, *Imagined Communities* (New York: Verso, 1983).

11. David Anthony, "'Gone Distracted': 'Sleepy Hollow,' Gothic Masculinity, and the Panic of 1819," *Early American Literature* 40.1 (2005), 111 and 112.

12. Alice Hiller, "'An Avenue to Some Degree of Profit and Reputation': *The Sketch Book* as Washington Irving's *entrée* and undoing," *Journal of American Studies* 31.2 (1997), 282.

13. Richard V. McLamore, "The Dutchman in the Attic: Claiming an Inheritance in *The Sketch Book of Geoffrey Crayon*," in *American Literature* 72.1 (2000), 34.

14. Bryce Traister, "The Wandering Bachelor: Irving, Masculinity, and Authorship," *American Literature* 74.1 (2002), 112.

15. This residual critical tradition is exemplified by Leslie Fiedler's suggestion that "the figure of Rip Van Winkle presides over the birth of the American imagination." See Leslie Fiedler, *Love and Death in the American Novel* (New York: Criterion, 1969), xx.

16. Michael Warner, "Irving's Posterity," *ELH* 67.3 (2000), 776.

17. Hazlitt continues by lambasting Irving for his inability to look "round to see what *we are*," instead of describing "us as *we were*." Focusing on England's rustic past, Hazlitt observes, "is a very flattering mode of turning fiction into history, or history into fiction." See William Hazlitt, *The Spirit of the Age* (London: Henry Colburn, 1825), 421–22.

18. Irving imitates Addison, Sterne, Goldsmith, and Fielding precisely because they were a generation of writers who never experienced the Revolutionary War. Moreover, they preceded the delusory and constricting debates about literary nationalism, which were hallmarks of the early nineteenth century (Addison died in 1719, Sterne 1768, Goldsmith 1774, and Fielding in 1754).

19. Washington Irving, *The Sketch Book of Geoffrey Crayon, Gent.*, ed. Haskell Springer (Boston: Twayne Publishers, 1978), 8 and 9. All references to *The Sketch Book* are from this volume, and page numbers will be cited hereafter in the chapter.

20. Disembarking in Liverpool, itself a modern commercial city, Crayon notes its similarities to New York. The reaction of most American travelers to Liverpool was, according to Christopher Mulvey, that "it looked so much like what they had left behind that a transatlantic crossing was a hard journey to make for so little in return." More concerned with the marketplace than with the legacies of antiquity, Liverpudlians occupied a very *American* social and structural environment. Irving cements this notion of commonality in his portrait of one of the "great men of Europe," from which "all animals" in America had "degenerated" (9). Crayon's "Roscoe" describes an English "celebrity" who, like any number of Americans, was a venture capitalist, philanthropist, and amateur historian, not a nobleman but an individual whose

"talents" and not his pedigree were responsible for his success (17). As John Whale argues, Crayon's portrait of Roscoe defines him "as the product of his surroundings" even as it articulates "the importance of his example in specifically transatlantic terms." By locating "Roscoe" at the threshold of his collection, Crayon offers the biography of an individual who could be at home on either side of the Atlantic. Irving portrays Roscoe as a model citizen of a modern and developing port city, a symbol of what Americans can strive for and attain. See Christopher Mulvey, *Anglo-American Landscapes: A Study of Anglo-American Travel Literature* (Cambridge: Cambridge University Press, 1983), 38; and John Whale, "The Making of a City Culture: William Roscoe's Liverpool," *Eighteenth-Century Life* 29.2 (2005), 92.

21. Jennifer Rae Greeson offers an insightful analysis of the how the trope of exploring American identity by venturing into the "wild" was tied to colonialism, in "Colonial Planter to American Farmer: South, Nation, and Decolonization in Crèvecoeur," in *Messy Beginnings: Postcoloniality and Early American Studies*, ed. Malini Johar Schueller and Edward Watts (New Brunswick: Rutgers University Press, 2003), 103–20.

22. See Penne L. Restad, *Christmas in America: A History* (New York: Oxford University Press, 1995), 20–21.

23. Restad, 27.

24. For examples of these types of readings see Peter Antelyes, *Tales of Adventurous Enterprise: Washington Irving and the Poetics of Western Expansion* (New York: Columbia University Press, 1990), and Rubin-Dorsky, *Adrift in the Old World*.

25. Both "Rip Van Winkle" and "The Legend of Sleepy Hollow" are complex narratives, and my intention in focusing on Irving's presentation of domestic architecture in each tale is not to deny the possibilities raised by other readings but rather to consider how Irving's treatment of domestic houses throughout *The Sketch Book* informs his intent in these two tales, which are all too often separated from their original publication context.

26. Jay Fliegelman, *Prodigals and Pilgrims: The American Revolution against Patriarchal Authority, 1750–1800* (New York: Cambridge University Press, 1982, 293.

27. McLamore, 48.

28. Steven Blakemore, "Family Resemblances: The Texts and Contexts of 'Rip Van Winkle,'" *Early American Literature* 35.2 (2000), 194.

29. Robert A. Ferguson, "Rip Van Winkle and the Generational Divide in American Culture," *Early American Literature* 40.3 (2005), 536.

30. Beginning with the second British edition of 1820, Crayon's "L'Envoy" became the volume's concluding sketch.

31. See Michael Warner, "Irving's Posterity," David Anthony, "'Gone Distracted,'" and David Greven, "Troubling Our Heads about Ichabod: 'The Legend of Sleepy Hollow,' Classic American Literature, and the Sexual Politics of Homosocial Brotherhood," *American Quarterly* 56.1 (2004), 83–110.

32. Greven, 91.

33. Anthony, 133.

34. Philip Hone, 26 May 1832, in *The Diary of Philip Hone*, 2 vols., ed. Bayard Tuckerman and Allan Nevins (New York: Dodd, Mead & Co., 1889), 1:54.

35. Irving, *A Tour of the Prairies*, in *Crayon Miscellany*, ed. Dahlia Kirby Terrell (Boston: Twayne Publishers, 1978), 7.
36. Mulvey, 8.
37. Mulvey, 9. See Mulvey's chapters 1 and 8–13 for an extended account of British reactions to life within the United States.
38. Fanny Kemble, for instance, arrived in New York just five months after the publication of *Domestic Manners of the Americans* and landed in the middle of a transatlantic debate about the virtues of American culture. In the aftermath of Trollope's biting critique, New Yorkers were anxious to demonstrate Manhattan's refinement to distinguished foreigners. Kemble's "hosts" tripped over themselves to convince her of America's sophistication. Driving around the southern tip of the island, Kemble was shocked at the pride New Yorkers exhibited in their built environment. One of her guides, she records, wanted to show her the architectural splendor of a noteworthy "old mansion." The description prepared Kemble for a building on a par with "Warwick Castle"; instead she saw a house that looked "like one of [England's] yesterday grown boxes." Kemble was stunned that a recently erected house could pass as a historic monument in America. "New York will surely, if the world holds together long enough," Kemble imagined, "become a lordly city, such as we know of beyond the sea." But at present, upper-class American homes were no match for English residences. "The works of men" in the Republic, Kemble advanced, were "in the very greenness and unmellowed imperfection of youth." While Americans should be proud of what they had accomplished, they should forgo constant comparisons of "their saplings to the giant oaks of the old world." By constantly comparing their city to European capitals, she concluded, New Yorkers only underscored the disparity between the two cultures. Frances Anne Butler Kemble, *Journal* (London: Murray, 1835), 1:67. Given her own desire to maintain a written record—with an eye toward publication—of her travels in America, the proclamation that she had not read Trollope may be disingenuous. For an in-depth biographical account of Kemble's time in Manhattan, see chapter 2 of Catherine Clinton, *Fanny Kemble's Civil Wars* (New York: Simon & Schuster, 2000).
39. Hiller, 289.
40. Washington Irving, *Abbotsford*, in *The Crayon Miscellany*, ed. Dahlia Kirby Terrell (Boston: Twayne Publishers, 1979), 125. All further references to *Abbotsford* are from this volume, and page numbers will be marked parenthetically in the chapter. For extended discussions of the relationship between Irving and Scott, see J. G. Lockhart, *Memoirs of the Life of Sir Walter Scott, Bart.* (Edinburgh, 1837), chapter 4; Pierre M. Irving, *The Life and Letters of Washington Irving* (New York: G. P. Putnam, 1863), 368–87, 438–44, 456, 457; and Williams, chapter 7.
41. Sir Walter Scott to Charles Carpenter, 4 August 1812, in *The Letters of Sir Walter Scott, 1811–1814*, ed. H. J. C. Grierson (London: Constable & Co., 1932), 151. All references to Scott's correspondence are from this volume, hereafter referred to as *Letters*.
42. Sir Walter Scott to Charles Carpenter, 4 August 1812, *Letters*, 151.

43. For an example of Scott's acceptance of acorns, see Walter Scott to Matthew Weld Hartstonge, 20 April 1812, *Letters*, 103–7.
44. Walter Scott to Lady Abercorn, 3 May 1812, *Letters*, 111.
45. Scott as quoted in Una Pope-Hennessy, *The Laird of Abbotsford* (New York: Putnam, 1932), 181.
46. Pope-Hennessy, 182.
47. Among other modern conveniences, Abbotsford had gas lighting and indoor plumbing.
48. See Pope-Hennessy, 234.
49. Scott as quoted by Pope-Hennessy, 234.
50. See Pope-Hennessy, 180.
51. Pope-Hennessy, 236.
52. Irving did indeed place spots of local knowledge into his American tales, such as drawing on the popular Tarrytown regional name of Van Tassel to authenticate his fictions.
53. Indeed it was Irving's moderate views concerning English culture that disrupted his friendship with James Kirke Paulding, his former collaborator on *Salmagundi*. Paulding accused Irving of being too pro–John Bull and chastised him for not promoting a new "American" literature but, instead, mediating cultural connections.
54. Washington Irving to Peter Irving, 8 July 1835, *Letters*, 2:835.
55. Washington Irving to Catherine Paris, 16 November 1832, *Letters*, 2:731–32.
56. Andrew Jackson Downing, *Landscape Gardening and Rural Architecture* (1852; reprint, New York: Dover, 1991), 353.
57. Downing, 35.
58. Downing, 354.
59. Washington Irving to Peter Irving, 8 July 1835, *Letters*, 2:835.
60. Kathleen Eagen Johnson, *Washington Irving's Sunnyside* (Tarrytown, N.Y.: Historic Hudson Valley Press, 1995), 3. For examples of how Sunnyside was used as a reproducible illustration of American domesticity, see Kathleen Eagen Johnson and Timothy Steinhoff, *Art of the Landscape: Sunnyside, Montgomery Place and Romanticism* (Tarrytown, N.Y.: Historic Hudson Valley Press, 1997), and Joseph T. Butler, *Visions of Washington Irving* (Tarrytown, N.Y.: Historic Hudson Valley Press, 1991).
61. See Johnson, 16.
62. Butler, 110.
63. Washington Irving to Peter Irving, 8 July 1835, *Letters*, 2:835.
64. Washington Irving to Peter Irving, 8 July 1835, *Letters*, 2:835.
65. Washington Irving to Peter Irving, 26 September 1835, *Letters*, 2:842. With Irving at Hell Gate were the widowed John Jacob Astor, Fitzgreen Hallack, Charles Astor Bristed (Astor's grandson), and Pierre Munro Irving (Washington's nephew).
66. Washington Irving to Peter Irving, 26 September 1835, *Letters*, 2:842.
67. Washington Irving to Peter Irving, 26 September 1835, *Letters*, 2:842.
68. Washington Irving to Peter Irving, 8 October 1835, *Letters*, 2:843–44.
69. Washington Irving to Peter Irving, 8 October 1835, *Letters*, 2:843–44.
70. Washington Irving to Peter Irving, 8 October 1835, *Letters*, 2:843–44.

71. Washington Irving to Peter Irving, 16 October 1835, *Letters*, 2:844.
72. Irving's promotion of Harvey as his architect can best be understood as a gift to his friend for his hard work as Irving's draftsman and foreman; Harvey, a painter with a smattering of architectural training, oversaw the reconstruction of Sunnyside mainly by implementing the changes Irving dictated, which in several instances Irving sketched out for Harvey's perusal.
73. See Johnson, 8.
74. See "Letter of Geoffrey Crayon to the Editor of the *Knickerbocker Magazine*," March 1839, in *Washington Irving Miscellaneous Writings, 1805–1859*, 2 vols., ed. Wayne R. Kyme (Boston: Twayne Publishers, 1981), 2:103. Hereafter abbreviated as *Writings*.
75. While evidence suggests that Irving conceived of this room as his bedroom, he rarely slept in it: after his brother Ebenezer and his daughters moved to Sunnyside, the house was so crowded that the room became a guest room, while Irving refitted his study so that he could sleep in that room. Later in his life, when Irving was in ill health, he moved upstairs but found this room (on the house's river front) too drafty and noisy as a result of the passing railroad cars, causing him to move across the hall.
76. Washington Irving to George Harvey, 23 November 1835, *Letters*, 2:844–46.
77. Irving, *Writings*, 2:101.
78. Irving, *Writings*, 2:103.
79. For an example of the initial critical reception of Irving's *Sketch Book* see Richard Henry Dana Sr.'s review in *North American Review*, September 1819. Dana accuses Irving, as Bryce Traister notes, of being "somehow un-American because of his protracted expatriatism." See Traister, 111.
80. The sketch was first published in the *Knickerbocker Magazine* in April 1839 and later revised and included in the volume sharing its name, *Wolfert's Roost* (1855). Among his revisions to the original magazine piece is the dropping of the Crayon persona as a narrative device in framing the sketch. See Washington Irving, "Wolfert's Roost," in *Wolfert's Roost*, ed. Roberta Rosenberg (Boston: Twayne Publishers, 1979), 3, 6, and 11.
81. Irving, *Wolfert's Roost*, 12.
82. Washing Irving to Sarah Van Wart, early December 1840, *Letters*, 3:64.
83. Washing Irving to Sarah Van Wart, early December 1840, *Letters*, 3:64.
84. T. Addison Richards, "Sunnyside: The Home of Washington Irving," *Harper's New Monthly Magazine* (December 1856), 12.
85. Richards, 12.
86. David R. Anderson, "A Quaint, Picturesque Little Pile: Architecture and the Past in Washington Irving," in *The Old and New World Romanticism of Washington Irving*, ed. Stanley Brown (Westport, Conn.: Greenwood Press, 1986), 139.
87. Richards, 2.
88. Richards, 2.
89. Richards, 2.
90. See Louis Legrand Noble, *The Life and Works of Thomas Cole* (1853; reprint, Hensonville, N.Y.: Blackdome Press, 1997), 145.
91. Cole's letter to Irving has not survived. See WI to Thomas Cole, 15 September

1835, *Letters*, 2:840. In the letter Irving apologizes for not having written back sooner to Cole, suggesting that Cole's letter was written some time earlier.

92. Irving, of course, moved to Sunnyside, and Cole settled farther north in Catskill, N.Y.

93. Ellwood C. Parry III, "Thomas Cole's 'The Course of Empire': A Study in Serial Imagery" (Ph.D. dissertation, Yale University, 1970), 135.

94. Angela Miller, *The Empire of the Eye* (Ithaca, N.Y.: Cornell University Press, 1993), 34.

95. Miller, *The Empire of the Eye*, 33.

96. Alan Wallach, "Thomas Cole: Landscape and the Course of American Empire," in *Thomas Cole: Landscape into History*, ed. Truettner and Wallach (New Haven: Yale University Press, 1994), 95.

97. For a fuller account of the "far-reaching implications" for American history that this trend contained, see William Kelly, *Plotting America's Past* (Carbondale: Southern Illinois University Press: 1983), 63–68 and 118–21.

98. Jackson's own popularity resulted, in part, from promoting the view that his policies offered the nation a return to the mores of the founding fathers, as he continually positioned himself as an opponent of cultural and political declension. Jackson's combat against the monster bank and his fervor to dramatically increase the electorate were part and parcel of his plans to stem the tide of corruption he understood to be threatening the integrity of the Republic. Figuring himself as the guardian of Jefferson's hopes for an "empire of liberty," Jackson sought to ensure that the United States would not collapse under the influence of an elite class that, he felt, was operating to undermine national expansion and democratization. The best works on the cultural impact of Jacksonian politics remain John William Ward, *Andrew Jackson: Symbol for an Age* (New York: Oxford University Press, 1953). and Charles Sellers, *The Market Revolution: Jacksonian America, 1815–1846* (New York: Oxford University Press, 1994). See also Marvin Meyers, *The Jacksonian Persuasion: Politics and Belief* (Stanford: Stanford University Press, 1957); Louis Masur, *1831: Year of Eclipse* (New York: Hill & Wang, 2001); and Ted Widmer, *Martin Van Buren* (New York: Henry Holt, 2005).

99. Meyers, 235.

100. For an in-depth account of the 1836 mayoral election see Edwin G. Burrows and Mike Wallace, *Gotham: A History of New York City to 1898* (New York: Oxford University Press, 1999), 608–10.

101. For in-depth analyses of the national consequences of this election, see Donald Cole, *Martin Van Buren and the American Political System* (Princeton: Princeton University Press, 1984), and John Niven, *Martin Van Buren: The Romantic Age of American Politics* (New York: Oxford University Press, 1983).

102. Sean Wilentz, *Chants Democratic: New York City and the Rise of the American Working Class, 1788–1850* (New York: Oxford University Press, 1984), 287.

103. Burrows and Wallace, 603.

104. Sellers, 43.

105. Sellers, 43.

106. Burrows and Wallace, 430.

107. Burrows and Wallace, 601.

108. This dominance of commercial interests in the city eventually drove the seat of federal government from Manhattan. Many southerners and New Englanders feared that New York's unchecked capitalism was detrimental to the growth of a republic. The abundance of foreign attitudes and practices fueled by commerce would, they feared, corrupt the government. See Burrows and Wallace, 299–306.

109. The first census recorded New York's population as 32,328 in 1790, with Philadelphia a close second with a population of 28,522.

110. Census data record the population of New York as 60,515 in 1800 and 123,706 in 1820.

111. Edward K. Spann, "The Greatest Grid: The New York Plan of 1811," in *Two Centuries of American Planning*, ed. Daniel Schaffer (Baltimore: The Johns Hopkins University Press, 1988), 11– 39.

112. Burrows and Wallace, 596.

113. Hone, 1:180.

114. Talbot Hamlin, *Greek Revival Architecture: Being an Account of Important Trends in American Architecture and American Life Prior to the War between the States* (New York: Oxford University Press, 1944), 145.

115. See Gary Wills, *Inventing America* (New York: Vintage, 1978).

116. Miller, *The Empire of the Eye*, 25.

117. Thomas Cole, *The Collected Essays and Prose Sketches*, ed. Marshall Tymn (n.p.: The John Colet Press, 1980), 135.

118. Frances Trollope, who toured most of the nation during her extended stay, found New York the only American city worthy of notice. "I think New York one of the finest cities I ever saw," she wrote, "and as much superior to every other in the Union (Philadelphia not excepted,) as London to Liverpool, or Paris to Rouen" (336; see volume citation below). "Its advantages of position are, perhaps, unequaled any where. . . . Situated on an island, which I think it will one day cover, it rises, like Venice, from the sea, and like the fairest of cities in the days of her glory, receives into its lap tribute of all the riches of the earth" (337). See Frances Trollope, *Domestic Manners of the Americans* (New York: Vintage Books, 1949).

119. Noble, 160.

120. Noble, 151.

121. See Raymond Williams, *The English Novel from Dickens to Lawrence* (New York: Oxford University Press, 1970).

122. See Angela Miller, "Thomas Cole and Jacksonian America: The Course of Empire as Political Allegory," *Prospects* 14 (1989): 65–92.

123. Thomas Cole, *Collected Essays*, 124.

4. "The Wants of Posterity": Community Construction and the Composing Order of American Architecture (pages 122–61)

1. James Fenimore Cooper, *Home as Found*, intro. Lewis Leary (New York: Capricorn Books, 1961), 113. All further references to this volume will be page numbers only, cited parenthetically in the chapter.

2. James A. Hamilton III named his house after his father's (Alexander Hamilton) birthplace in the West Indies. Hamilton's house was far from the only Greek Revival mansion constructed in the lower Hudson Valley, but the prominence of its owner and the fact that it was constructed during 1835, when Cooper was traveling back and forth between Cooperstown and Manhattan, makes it at least likely that Cooper was aware of its existence. My aim in using Nevis as an example of the type of construction that Cooper railed against stems from my sense that Hamilton's construction of the house would have doubly infuriated Cooper. Since Hamilton was a member of an established American family, Cooper's elitism would have maintained that Hamilton had a duty to offer a better architectural model. As George Dekker notes: "Confronted, so he believed, with a society abandoned to speculation and change, [Cooper] became more than ever convinced that the old country families, like the Jays, the Rensselaers, and the Coopers themselves, were the only hope for a civilized and dignified America—one in which the obsession with space would not entirely destroy the awareness of time." While Dekker does not mention the Hamiltons, they were exactly the type of landed family that Cooper hoped could counter the Jacksonian rush for unbridled change. See George Dekker, *James Fenimore Cooper: The American Scott* (New York: Barnes & Noble, 1967), 156.

3. The Effinghams' consternation over the sight of these Greek Revival houses was echoed by Andrew Jackson Downing in *Landscape Gardening and Rural Architecture* (1841), wherein Downing writes that "it has been well observed by modern critics, that there is no reason to believe the temple form was ever, even by the Greeks, used for private dwellings, which easily accounts for our comparative failure in constructing well arranged, small residences in this style." See Downing, *Landscape Gardening and Rural Architecture* (reprint, New York: Dover, 1991), 332.

4. John P. McWilliams Jr., *Political Justice in the Republic: James Fenimore Cooper's America* (Berkeley: University of California Press, 1972), 222.

5. Eric Sundquist, *Home as Found: Authority and Genealogy in Nineteenth Century American Literature* (Baltimore: The Johns Hopkins University Press, 1979), 6.

6. William P. Kelly, *Plotting America's Past: Fenimore Cooper and the Leatherstocking Tales* (Carbondale: Southern Illinois University Press, 1983), 171.

7. Signe O. Wegener, *James Fenimore Cooper versus the Cult of Domesticity: Progressive Themes of Femininity and Family in the Novels* (Jefferson, N.C.: McFarland & Company, 2005), 42.

8. Russell T. Newman, *The Gentleman in the Garden: The Influential Landscape in the Works of James Fenimore Cooper* (Lanham: Lexington Books, 2003), 2.

9. James Fenimore Cooper and his family resided in Europe for seven years, from June 1826 to November 1833. Upon his return he feared that the nation had become "a vast expansion of mediocrity."

10. Readings of *Home as Found* positing that the Effinghams represent Cooper's own opinions are as old as the novel itself. Shortly after its appearance, an anonymous novel, *The Effinghams; or, Home as I Found It*, ridiculed Cooper as an Effingham. For a more modern rendering, see Eric Sundquist's *Home as Found:*

Authority and Genealogy in Nineteenth Century American Literature, a reading that is predicated on a direct association of Cooper with the Effinghams.

11. Stephen Railton, *Fenimore Cooper: A Study of His Life and Imagination* (Princeton: Princeton University Press, 1978), 183.

12. Donald A. Ringe, *James Fenimore Cooper* (New York: Twayne Publishers, 1962), 78.

13. I am using "dis-ease" here in the sense that T. J. Jackson Lears articulates in *No Place of Grace: Antimodernism and the Transformation of American Culture, 1880–1920*. In his nausea over the "modernization" of American architecture, Cooper undertakes a retreat into the past not dissimilar to what Lears traces as happening later in the century. See T. J. Jackson Lears, *No Place of Grace: Antimodernism and the Transformation of American Culture, 1880–1920* (Chicago: University of Chicago Press, 1981).

14. McWilliams, 216. McWilliams goes so far as to suggest that *Home as Found* is America's first novel of manners, a claim perhaps no longer justifiable given the rediscovery of earlier texts that are equally concerned with mapping post-Revolutionary American cultural mores.

15. Donald Darnell, *James Fenimore Cooper: Novelist of Manners* (Newark: University of Delaware Press, 1993), 77.

16. Dekker, 155.

17. The idea that the trends along the Hudson would spread across the nation is more than just an instance of Cooper's New York–centric vision of America; since the Erie Canal was the nation's main commercial highway, the houses on the shores of the Hudson River were the first American billboards, advertising style to all who passed by them.

18. Even the hue of the house's exterior paint is made to match its environs, as it is painted a "yellowish drab" so that it will appear to blend in with the lower clouds of the valley and stand in opposition to many of the village's other homes, painted, in Cooper's eyes, a villainous white.

19. After some damage to "private" Cooper land, James Fenimore Cooper tried to prevent the citizens of Cooperstown from using a picnic ground that they had habitually enjoyed. Cooper's claims were refuted on the grounds that his father had allowed public access to the land, and a series of lawsuits ensued. Cooper contended that such custom was possible only by the choice of the landowner, who had the right to revoke the privilege. The affair of the point proved ruinous to Cooper, as he was popularly attacked for being undemocratic in trying to deny public access to the land. In defending himself against the claim to public access and then the libelous attacks, Cooper vindicated himself legally even as he brought more public scorn upon himself.

20. William Cooper, *A Guide in the Wilderness; or, the History of the First Settlements in the Western Counties of New York with Useful Instructions to Future Settlers* (1810; reprint, Cooperstown: Paul F. Cooper Jr., 1986). Further references to this volume will cite page numbers parenthetically in the chapter. Any study of William Cooper is indebted to Alan Taylor's insightful *William Cooper's Town: Power and Persuasion on the Frontier of the Early American Republic* (New York: Vintage Books, 1996).

21. For a deeper sense of the importance of upstate New York's settlement after the Revolution to the development of early-nineteenth-century American culture see, in addition to Taylor's *William Cooper's Town*, Evan Cornog, *The Birth of Empire: DeWitt Clinton and the American Experience, 1769–1828* (New York: Oxford University Press, 1998); Paul E. Johnson, *A Shopkeeper's Millennium: Society and Revivals in Rochester, New York, 1815–1837* (New York: Hill and Wang, 1978); Thomas Summerhill, *Harvest of Dissent: Agrarianism in Nineteenth-Century New York* (Urbana: University of Chicago Press, 2005); and Thomas S. Wermuth, *Rip Van Winkle's Neighbors: The Transformation of Rural Society in the Hudson River Valley, 1720–1850* (Albany: SUNY Press , 2001).

22. Taylor, 317.

23. Wayne Franklin calls *A Guide* a "song of possession throughout," pointing to the ways in which Cooper's bluster guides his treatment of his subject. See Wayne Franklin, *The New World of James Fenimore Cooper* (Chicago: University of Chicago Press, 1982), 122.

24. It was the loss of this rootedness that, for James Fenimore Cooper, signaled the surefire declension of American settlements, which he charts in *Home as Found*.

25. In fact William Cooper's failure to re-create the success of Cooperstown may be the proof of his vision of community construction, for he never resided at the scene of his other speculations.

26. The novel sold 3,500 copies, an astounding number at the time, on its first morning of publication. While the popularity of *The Pioneers* has long been ascribed to Cooper's success with *The Spy*, Signe O. Wegener has recently redirected attention to the fact that the title page of the original edition "stressed that this was a new work by the author of *Precaution*." Whether this marketing decision was made by Cooper or his publisher remains unknown, but as Wegener suggests, in terms of creating an audience for *The Pioneers*, "domesticity was a better marketing ploy than revolution." As Wegener advances in her reading of *The Pioneers*, considering the novel as a commentary on domestic concerns is not as far-fetched as some residual readings of the novel have maintained. See Wegener, 45.

27. See chapter 6, "Leatherstocking and the Problem of Social Order," in Henry Nash Smith, *Virgin Land: The American West as Symbol and Myth* (Cambridge, Mass.: Harvard University Press, 1950).

28. Smith, 62.

29. Susan Scheckel, *The Insistence of the Indian: Race and Nineteenth-Century American Culture* (Princeton: Princeton University Press, 1998), 15.

30. Scheckel, 25.

31. Kelly, 13.

32. James Fenimore Cooper, *The Pioneers; or, The Sources of the Susquehanna: A Descriptive Tale*, ed. James Franklin Beard (Albany: SUNY Press, 1980), 8. Hereafter, all page references are to this volume and are cited parenthetically within the chapter.

33. Cooper reaffirms this point in the final Leather-stocking novel, *The Deer-*

slayer (1841). At the end of that novel the squatting Hutter family is left dis-possessed, and the two armies that have struggled for control of the area both prepare to depart. In Cooper's version of New York's settlement history, nei-ther the Iroquois nor the British create ties that bind them to the area. Natty's resistance to personal entanglements stems from a sense of self that dictates that he not mix his "gifts." None of the figures presented in *The Deerslayer* could, for Cooper, found a community on the lakefront that would ensure a lasting, stable society. Cooper presents *The Deerslayer* as a final version of the presettlement history of the Cooperstown region. In moving all human players from the stage, the narrative clears the ground for Judge Temple's arrival and his foundation of the first viable, and coterminously first post-Revolutionary, settlement in the region.

34. See Clifford Geertz, *After the Fact: Two Countries, Four Decades, One Anthropologist* (Cambridge, Mass.: Harvard University Press, 1995).
35. Geertz, 168.
36. Kelly, 18.
37. Richard Godden, "Pioneer Properties, or 'What's in a Hut?'" in *James Fenimore Cooper: New Critical Essays*, ed. Robert Clark (New York: Vision Press, 19850), 121.
38. Godden, 123.
39. Indeed, by the narrative time of *Home as Found* no Native American population exists at all within the boundaries of Cooperstown. Quite literally, Chingachgook is the last of Cooper's Mohicans.
40. *Home as Found*, 129.
41. James Fenimore Cooper, *Wyandotté; or, The Hutted Knoll: A Tale* (Albany: State University of New York Press, 1982), 12. All further references to this text are to this volume, and page numbers will be noted parenthetically in the chapter.
42. Willoughby's farm lay near Butternut Creek on the western border of modern Otsego County. See Francis Whiting Halsey, *The Old New York Frontier* (New York: Charles Scribner's Sons, 1901). Halsey identifies the location of *Wyandotté* based not only on the specifies of Cooper's navigational directions but also on the topographical features of both the region and the novel.
43. By negotiating with the British Crown and with several Native American parties claiming the area, Willoughby also avoids any difficulties that would arise from land claims harking back to a period prior to his settlement of the area.
44. Donald A. Ringe, *The Pictorial Mode: Space & Time in the Art of Bryant, Irving & Cooper* (Lexington: University of Kentucky Press, 1971), 193. See also McWilliams, 90–100.
45. McWilliams, 96.
46. Newman, 48.
47. Franklin, 166.
48. The oddity of Willoughby's design is that he never hangs, throughout a ten-year period, the two massive wooden gates that were built to guard the one opening he provided in the walls surrounding his house. The failure to hang these gates allows his house to be invaded in the final gesticulations of the novel and effectively causes Willoughby's undoing.

49. It is worth noting that the only violence that ever threatens the house is from the internal resentment that Willoughby's refusal to sell any land on his patent causes. No external threat ever menaces the Knoll.

50. As his son informs him early in the novel, Captain Willoughby has, by the death of an English relative, actually inherited an aristocratic title, which he refuses to adopt. A title "without the estate" is meaningless to Willoughby, and since his patent in New York does not deliver him a title he refutes the notion that he should import a landless aristocratic label from England (52). This does not mean that he does not seek to erect a manor house in America, but simply reveals his conception that titles are tied to particular landscapes and are not portable property.

51. Jeffrey Walker, "Fenimore Cooper's *Wyandotté* and the Cyclic Course of Empire," in *James Fenimore Cooper: His Country and His Art*, ed. George A. Test (Cooperstown: The James Fenimore Cooper Society), 6:99.

52. This sentiment again echoes Cooper's argument in *The Deerslayer*, wherein Thomas Hutter's attempts to build a floating castle (very similar in its design to Willoughby's Hutted Knoll) on the surface of Lake Otsego proves to be an ungenerative foundation. At the end of that novel, nature engulfs Hutter's failed attempt at ordering the area, and Cooper finishes the Leather-stocking saga by redirecting his readers to its earliest volume, where the prehistory of the lake is reordered. By fixing the region's pre-Revolutionary history, he asserts that the first meaningful attempt at settlement was that of Judge Temple. The poor foundations laid by Hutter and those like him are, for Cooper, better left mute, buried under the waves of the lake.

53. As such, Willoughby's aesthetic reflects that of *The Deerslayer*'s Thomas Hutter, which for Cooper is an unstable foundation that he wipes from the scene. Both of these "houses" appear more like a fortress than a domestic house, and like the Effinghams, who decry the ill-suited Greek Revival houses lining the Hudson, Cooper works, in his novels, to eliminate all improper buildings from the American scene in order to teach his readers which houses they should admire and copy when they undertake their own building projects.

54. Susan Cooper's distaste for the importation of European cultural forms registers in her critique of the unfortunate practice of naming American settlements after European cities. See Susan Fenimore Cooper, *Rural Hours*, ed. Rochelle Johnson and Daniel Patterson (Athens: University of Georgia Press, 1998), 298–309. Hereafter references to page numbers in this volume are cited parenthetically in the chapter. References to "A Dissolving View" are to *The Home Book of the Picturesque: Or American Scenery, Art, and Literature* (1852; reprint, Gainesville: Scholar's Facsimiles & Reprints, 1967), 79–94; hereafter page numbers are cited parenthetically in the chapter.

55. For a more detailed portrait of Susan Cooper's use of natural histories in her writing see my longer version of this argument, "'The Borderers of Civilization': Susan Cooper's View of American Development," in *Susan Fenimore Cooper: New Essays on Rural Hours and Other Works*, ed. Rochelle Johnson and Daniel Patterson (Athens: University of Georgia Press, 2001).

56. Richard L. Bushman, *The Refinement of America: Persons, Houses, Cities* (New York: Vintage, 1993), xiv.

57. Consistently in *Rural Hours,* Cooper suggests that Americans manufacture interior decorations based on the superior variety of colors and shades found in the nature around them, rather than continue to follow foreign trends.

58. Downing also published volumes titled *The Fruits and Fruit Trees of America* (1845), *Cottage Residences* (1842), and *The Architecture of Country Houses* (1850). For in-depth treatments of Downing's influence see Judith K. Major, *To Live in the New World: A. J. Downing and American Landscape Gardening* (Cambridge, Mass.: MIT Press, 1997); David Schuyler, *Apostle of Taste: Andrew Jackson Downing, 1815–1852* (Baltimore: The Johns Hopkins University Press, 1996); and Adam Sweeting, *Reading Houses and Building Books: Andrew Jackson Downing and the Architecture of Popular Antebellum Literature, 1835–1855* (Hanover: University Press of New England, 1996).

59. As quoted by Major, 2.

60. Downing, *The Architecture of Country Houses,* 26.

61. Andrew Jackson Downing, *Landscape Gardening and Rural Architecture* (1852; reprint, New York: Dover, 1991), 54. This volume is a reprint of the seventh edition of *A Treatise on the Theory and Practice of Landscape Gardening* (1852).

62. Downing, *Landscape,* 82.

63. Downing, *Landscape,* 19.

64. See Downing, *Landscape,* 7.

65. A tool familiar to those searching for the picturesque, the Claude glass (named for the French landscape artist Claude Lorraine) was a convex mirror used to concentrate the features of a landscape. Here Cooper suggests that the cliff and trees create a natural frame for her vision.

66. Employing a tactic familiar to Hudson River School painters, Cooper locates her narrator within wild nature, but casts her field of vision into a settled landscape. See Angela Miller's reading of Cole's painting *The Oxbow* (1836), in *The Empire of the Eye: Landscape Representation and American Cultural Politics, 1825–1875* (Ithaca, N.Y.: Cornell University Press, 1993), 39–48.

67. Cooper in particular singles out the architecture of Babylon, Greece, and Rome for its fortitude in surviving numerous attacks at the hands of "savages" and "barbarians."

68. The best account of Agassiz's importance is Edward Lurie's *Louis Agassiz: A Life in Science* (Baltimore: The Johns Hopkins University Press, 1988); see especially chapters 4 and 5.

69. Lurie, 82.

70. Lurie, 52, 50.

71. Louis Agassiz, *Lake Superior: Its Physical Character, Vegetation, and Animals, Compared with Those of Other and Similar Regions* (1850; reprint, New York: Arno Press, 1970), 144.

72. Washington Irving, *A Tour of the Prairies* (1832; reprint, Norman: University of Oklahoma Press, 1956), 50. Cooper would also have been familiar with her father's treatment of this myth in his novel *The Oak Openings; or, The Bee-Hunter* (1848).

5. "In the Midst of an Uncertain Future": Remodeling the Legacies of American Domesticity (pages 162–202)

1. Edgar Allan Poe, "The Light-House," in *Poetry and Tales* (New York: Library of America, 1984), 928. All references to Poe's fiction are from this volume unless otherwise noted, and page numbers will be cited parenthetically in the chapter. The manuscript of the unpublished and untitled sketch was first published by Thomas Ollive Mabbot in 1942. See Mabbot, "The Light-House," *Notes and Queries* 182.17 (1942), 226–27.

2. Maurice S. Lee, "Absolute Poe: His System of Transcendental Racism," *American Literature* 75:4 (2003), 774.

3. Louis A. Renza, "Never More in Poe's Tell-Tale American Tale," *Edgar Allan Poe Review* 4.2 (2003), 33.

4. Renza, 33.

5. Vernon Parrington, *Main Currents in American Thought: An Interpretation of American Literature from the Beginning to 1920* (New York: Harcourt, Brace, and World, 1927), 2:58.

6. Both F. O. Matthiessen and David S. Reynolds connect Poe to the center of American literary production, even if they maintain, in Reynolds' words, Poe's "distance from reality." While Poe figures much more centrally in Reynolds' work than in Matthiessen's, Matthiessen does continually refer to Poe in his study of "major" authors. Reynolds' treatment of Poe traces the ways in which Poe drew on actual events and pseudoscientific trends in crafting his fiction. Yet Reynolds almost reductively concludes that Poe's aim in doing so was to gain "victory over the popular Subversive imagination," or to redraw in essence the boundaries of popular forms of U.S. literary production. More than understanding Poe's fiction as part of a dialog concerning literary production, I would argue that his texts (like Irving's before him) are aimed at critiquing cultural practices, specifically in terms of figurations of the domestic. Poe's work is far from ungrounded, even if it contains sensationalistic episodes. Like Brockden Brown and Irving, Poe uses the spectacular to explore the effects of location on personality. His tales relentlessly interrogate the connections between architectural location and identity formation. Reading the connections between architecture and identity allowed Poe to root in a tangible center his examination of the cultural codes of the United States. See F. O. Matthiessen, *American Renaissance: Art and Expression in the Age of Emerson and Whitman* (New York: Oxford University Press, 1941), and David S. Reynolds, *Beneath the American Renaissance* (Cambridge, Mass.: Harvard University Press, 1988). For a persuasive account of Matthiessen's "inclusion" of Poe, see Gillian Brown, *Domestic Individualism* (Berkeley: University of California Press, 1990), 204.

7. Terence Whalen, "Edgar Allan Poe and the Horrid Laws of Political Economy," *American Quarterly* 44.3 (1992), 383.

8. See for instance the essays collected in *The American Face of Edgar Allan Poe*, ed. Shawn Rosenheim and Stephen Rachman (Baltimore: The Johns Hopkins University Press, 1995); *Romancing the Shadow*, ed. J. Gerald Kennedy and

Liliane Weissberg (New York: Oxford University Press, 2001); and *A Historical Guide to Edgar Allan Poe* (New York: Oxford University Press, 2001). Additional work in this vein includes Joan Dayan, *Fables of Mind: An Inquiry into Poe's Fiction* (New York: Oxford University Press, 1987); Jonathan Elmer, *Reading at the Social Limit: Affect, Mass Culture, and Edgar Allan Poe* (Stanford: Stanford University Press, 1995); and Terence Whalen, *Edgar Allan Poe and the Masses: The Political Economy of Literature in Antebellum America* (Princeton: Princeton University Press, 1999).

9. Whalen, *Edgar Allan Poe and the Masses*, 27.

10. Whalen, *Edgar Allan Poe and the Masses*, 29.

11. In recent years critics have labored to undo the historic dismissal of Poe as a writer of timeless tales of terror, and for a deeper sense of the range of scholarship that seeks to locate Poe within a historical context, see (in addition to the work of Elmer, Dayan, Lee, and Whalen) Katrina E. Bachinger, "Peacock's Melincourt and the Politics of Poe's 'The Sphinx,'" *Nineteenth-Century Literature* 42.2 (1987), 217–25; Theron Britt, "The Common Property of the Mob: Democracy and Identity in Poe's 'William Wilson,'" *Mississippi Quarterly* 48.2 (1995), 197–210; Monica Elbert, "'The Man of the Crowd' and the Man outside the Crowd: Poe's Narrator and the Democratic Reader," *Modern Language Studies* 21.4 (1991), 16–30; J. Gerald Kennedy, "'A Mania for Composition': Poe's Annus Mirabilis and the Violence of Nation-building," *American Literary History* 17.1 (2005), 1–35; and Meredith L. McGill, *American Literature and the Culture of Reprinting, 1830–1860* (Philadelphia: University of Pennsylvania Press, 2003).

12. For a deeper trajectory of the history of literary interpretations of the domestic see Nina Baym, *Novels, Readers, and Reviewers* (Ithaca, N.Y.: Cornell University Press, 1984); Gillian Brown, *Domestic Individualism;* Ann Douglas, *The Feminization of American Culture* (New York: Knopf, 1977); Lora Romero, *Home Fronts: Domesticity and Its Critics in the Antebellum United States* (Durham: Duke University Press, 1997); and Jane Tompkins, *Sensational Designs* (New York: Oxford University Press, 1985).

13. The best works on the cultural impact of Jacksonian politics remain John William Ward, *Andrew Jackson: Symbol for an Age* (New York: Oxford University Press, 1953), and Charles Sellers, *The Market Revolution: Jacksonian America, 1815–1846* (New York: Oxford University Press, 1994). See also Marvin Meyers, *The Jacksonian Persuasion: Politics and Belief* (Stanford: Stanford University Press, 1957); Louis Masur, *1831: Year of Eclipse* (New York: Hill & Wang, 2001); Sean Wilentz, *Andrew Jackson* (New York: Henry Holt, 2006); and Ted Widmer, *Martin Van Buren* (New York: Henry Holt, 2005).

14. Gillian Brown, 3.

15. See Charles Sellers, *The Market Revolution*.

16. Recently, J. Gerald Kennedy has argued that "Poe's first significant foray into the terrain of national myth and iconography came in 1839," when Poe composed "The Man That Was Used Up," one of the last tales he wrote as he was assembling *Tales of the Grotesque and Arabesque* ("'A Mania for Composition,'" 8). While Kennedy makes compelling arguments in *The American Turn of*

Edgar Allan Poe (Baltimore: Edgar Allan Poe Society, 2002) about the settings of Poe's tales, I believe that we have to probe beyond the surface settings of tales to accurately chart Poe's representations of American cultural mores. Without question, Poe's preface to *Tales of the Grotesque and Arabesque* encourages a consideration of even his unworldly tales as registers of domestic structures of thought and feeling, as I have argued elsewhere, in "'A Certain Unity of Design': Edgar Allan Poe's *Tales of the Grotesque and Arabesque* and the Terrors of Jacksonian Democracy," *Edgar Allan Poe Review* (Philadelphia: St. Joseph's University Press) 6.2 (Fall 2005), 4–21.

17. Kenneth Silverman's biography of Poe is an essential resource for any accounting of Poe's constant mobility; see Kenneth Silverman, *Edgar A. Poe: Mournful and Never-Ending Remembrance* (New York: Harper Perennial, 1991).

18. Romero, 19.

19. McGill, 161.

20. McGill, 162.

21. Whalen, *Edgar Allan Poe and the Masses*, 247.

22. Silverman, 221.

23. Silverman, 219.

24. The relationship between private domesticity and public personality was a theme that dominated Poe's writing during his time in New York, and was indeed the motivating principle behind his magazine column titled *The Literati of New York City*. A collection of personal sketches about famous New Yorkers, published in *Godey's Lady's Book* throughout 1846, the series seeks to define the real character of people by offering portraits of them in their intimate domestic spaces.

25. Joel R. Kehler, "New Light on the Genesis and Progress of Poe's Landscape Fiction," *American Literature* 47.2 (1975), 178.

26. Catherine Rainwater, "Poe's Landscape Tales & The 'Picturesque' Tradition," *Southern Literary Journal* 16:2 (1984), 39. For a very similar argument about "Landor's Cottage" see also Beth L. Lueck, *American Writers and the Picturesque Tour: The Search for National Identity, 1790–1860* (New York: Garland, 1997).

27. Wilentz, *Andrew Jackson*, 11.

28. Eric Sundquist's suggestive book *Home as Found: Authority and Genealogy in Nineteenth-Century American Literature* does not analyze "The Fall of the House of Usher," though his arguments about how Cooper turns to incest as a solution to the crisis of authority in late 1830s America is similar to the argument that I am making about Poe's tale.

29. For more information on New York's emergence as the nation's economic center see Sellers, *The Market Revolution*, and Sean Wilentz, *Chants Democratic: New York City and the Rise of the American Working Class, 1788–1850* (New York: Oxford University Press, 1984).

30. Alexis de Tocqueville, *Democracy in America*, trans. Harvey C. Mansfield and Delba Winthrop (Chicago: University of Chicago Press, 2000), 511.

31. Tocqueville, 394 and 117.

32. Tocqueville, 512.

33. Nathaniel Hawthorne, *Twice-Told Tales*, ed. Fredson Bowers, L. Neal Smith, John Manning, and J. Donald Crowley, in *The Centenary Edition of the Works of Nathaniel Hawthorne*, vol. 9 (Columbus: Ohio State University Press, 1974), 192. All references to Hawthorne's short fiction are from this volume (unless otherwise noted), and page numbers will be cited parenthetically in the chapter.

34. Frederick Crews, *The Sins of the Fathers: Hawthorne's Psychological Themes* (New York: Oxford University Press, 1966), 158.

35. Nancy Bunge, *Nathaniel Hawthorne: A Study of the Short Fiction* (New York: Twayne, 1993), 64.

36. In his influential study of the American novel, Richard Chase argues that, in Hawthorne's romances, "the field of action is conceived not so much as a place as a state of mind—the borderland of the human mind where the actual and the imaginary intermingle" (19). For Chase, Hawthorne does not care about the settings of his texts, because his interest resides in trying to interpret his characters' mental states, and Chase's reading has promulgated the idea (born from Henry James' biography of Hawthorne) that the lack of a sophisticated cultural nexus during the antebellum period caused Hawthorne to turn away from social concerns and focus instead on psychological ones. See Richard Chase, *The American Novel and Its Tradition* (Baltimore: The Johns Hopkins University Press, 1957).

37. Michael J. Colacurcio, *The Province of Piety: Moral History in Hawthorne's Early Tales* (Cambridge, Mass.: Harvard University Press, 1984), 484.

38. Colacurcio, 484.

39. McGill, 225.

40. Colacurcio argues that "though it has been possible to fold 'Wakefield,' 'Fancy's Show Box,' and 'Dr. Heidegger's Experiment' into a pseudo-historical recipe for 'the Hawthornesque,' no one (I think) should want to whip up a counterformula out of ingredients mixed equally from 'Sir William Pepperell,' 'Little Annie's Ramble,' 'A Rill from the Town Pump,' 'The Toll-Gatherer's Day,' 'Mrs. Bullfrog,' and 'The Lily's Quest.'" Colacurcio, 485.

41. McGill, 225.

42. Milette Shamir, *Inexpressible Privacy: The Interior Life of Antebellum American Literature* (Philadelphia: University of Pennsylvania Press, 2006), 168.

43. Shamir, 168.

44. Teresa A. Goddu, *Gothic America: Narrative, History, and Nation* (New York: Columbia University Press, 1997), 115.

45. Joel Pfister, "Hawthorne as Cultural Theorist," in *The Cambridge Companion to Nathaniel Hawthorne* (New York: Cambridge University Press, 2004), 36.

46. Kristie Hamilton, "Hawthorne, Modernity, and the Literary Sketch," in *The Cambridge Companion to Nathaniel Hawthorne* (New York: Cambridge University Press, 2004), 111.

47. Hawthorne as quoted by Edwin Haviland Miller, *Salem Is My Dwelling Place: A Life of Nathaniel Hawthorne* (Iowa City: University of Iowa Press, 1991), 86.

48. Among the construction projects that Hawthorne undertook at Wayside was, as Edwin Miller describes, the erection of a "tower that elevated him above

the roof level and commanded a panoramic view of the environs." Like his perch in the steeple and the garret of his grandparents' house, the tower allowed Hawthorne to look down on the houses surrounding him as he undertook his own work. See Edwin Haviland Miller, 86.

49. See Terence Martin, "Hawthorne's Public Decade and the Values of Home," *American Literature* 46.2 (1974).

50. For an in-depth analysis of the cultural circulation of the Willey family's story see Eric Purchase, *Out of Nowhere: Disaster and Tourism in the White Mountains* (Baltimore: The Johns Hopkins University Press, 1999).

51. Purchase, 13.

52. John F. Sears, "'The Ambitious Guest' and the Willey Disaster," *American Literature* 54.3 (1982), 359. Hawthorne returns to considering the import of ruins in the tale "Old Ticonderoga." For Hawthorne, Ticonderoga signifies that the pre-Revolutionary history of the United States comprised a series of violent conquests. Yet, his tale suggests, this famous scene now has an ordered and familiar history; its British and French occupations are traceable, as is its American pedigree. These are not ruins in the middle of a wilderness but splintered walls, whose context is understood and thus rendered harmless amid a domesticated landscape marked with cultivated farms. The ruins of Ticonderoga are not a cause for a remembrance of America's warlike past but a register of how houses are sites of stability for the nation. The physical evidence of colonial history exists as broken relics amid a settled and ordered terrain. America's national history is figured as a countervailing tradition to the disorder of distant foreign powers struggling for colonial toeholds; one family has owned the land since the Revolution, and one house has stood upon the field where foreign troops contended for survival and dominance.

53. Purchase, 1.

54. In his reading of the tale, John F. Sears argues that Hawthorne uses the restless, ambitious stranger who visits the family to stress how content and secure the unnamed family remains in its home. Such a reading seems to overstress the family members' happiness; in many ways they seem as restless as their guest.

55. Nathaniel Hawthorne, *Mosses from an Old Manse*, ed. Fredson Bowers, L. Neal Smith, John Manning, and J. Donald Crowley, in *The Centenary Edition of the Works of Nathaniel Hawthorne*, vol. 10 (Columbus: Ohio State University Press, 1974), 138–39. All references to "Fire-Worship" and "The Old Manse" are from this volume, and page numbers will be cited parenthetically in the chapter.

56. Pfister, 38.

57. Larry J. Reynolds, "Hawthorne's Labors in Concord," in *The Cambridge Companion to Nathaniel Hawthorne* (New York: Cambridge University Press, 2004), 12.

58. Leland S. Person Jr., "Hawthorne's Bliss of Paternity: Sophia's Absence from 'The Old Manse,'" *Studies in the Novel* 23.1 (1991), 58. Person argues that Hawthorne erases the presence of his wife from the sketch, even as he labors

to disassociate the house from the productions of other writers while they were tenets of the building. As such, Person offers a provocative reading of the ways in which Hawthorne moves to "modify" the house to suit his own creative needs at this juncture in his career.

59. Robert Milder, "Hawthorne's Winter Dreams," *Nineteenth-Century Literature*, 54.2 (1999), 170.

60. Nathaniel Hawthorne, *The Scarlet Letter*; ed. William Charvat, in *The Centenary Edition of the Works of Nathaniel Hawthorne*, vol. 1 (Columbus: University of Ohio Press, 1962), 8. All further references to *The Scarlet Letter* are from this volume, and hereafter page numbers will be cited parenthetically.

61. Michael Davitt Bell, *The Development of American Romance* (Chicago: University of Chicago Press, 1980), 179.

62. Dan McCall, *Citizens of Somewhere Else: Nathaniel Hawthorne and Henry James* (Ithaca, N.Y.: Cornell University Press, 1999), 38.

63. Gloria C. Erlich, *Family Themes and Hawthorne's Fiction: The Tenacious Web* (New Brunswick: Rutgers University Press, 1984), 30.

64. Bryce Traister, "The Bureaucratic Origins of *The Scarlet Letter*," *Studies in American Fiction* 29.1 (2001), 80.

65. Shamir, 174.

66. Donald E. Pease, "Hawthorne in the Custom-House: The Metapolitics, Postpolitics, and Politics of *The Scarlet Letter*," *boundary 2* 32.1 (2005), 64.

67. In *American Renaissance*, F. O. Matthiessen most prominently deals with Hawthorne's dismissal from the Custom-House by noting in the appended chronology that in 1849 "Hawthorne lost his position in the Customhouse."

68. Jonathan Arac, "The Politics of *The Scarlet Letter*," in *Ideology and Classic American Literature* (New York: Cambridge University Press, 1986), 251.

69. Robert K. Martin, "Hester Prynne, C'est Moi: Nathaniel Hawthorne and the Anxieties of Gender," in *Engendering Men: The Question of Male Feminist Criticism*, ed. Joseph A. Boone and Michael Cadden (New York: Routledge, 1990), 124.

70. Michael T. Gilmore, *American Romanticism and the Marketplace* (Chicago: University of Chicago Press, 1985), 72.

71. Sandra Tomc, "'The Sanctity of the Priesthood': Hawthorne's 'Custom-House,'" *ESQ* 39.2 and 3 (1993), 163.

72. T. Walter Herbert, *Dearest Beloved: The Hawthornes and the Making of the Middle Class Family* (Berkeley: University of California Press, 1993), 163.

73. Brook Thomas, "Love and Politics, Sympathy and Justice in *The Scarlet Letter*," in *The Cambridge Companion to Nathaniel Hawthorne* (New York: Cambridge University Press, 2004), 163.

74. David Leverenz, *Manhood and the American Renaissance* (Ithaca, N.Y.: Cornell University Press, 1989), 262.

75. Michael J. Colacurcio, "Footsteps of Ann Hutchinson: The Context of *The Scarlet Letter*," *ELH* 39.3 (1972), 459.

76. Gilmore, 76. See also Michael Ragussis, "Family Discourse and Fiction in *The Scarlet Letter*," *ELH* 49.4 (1982), 863–88; Louis K. Barnett, "Speech and Society in *The Scarlet Letter*," *ESQ* 29.1 (1983), 16–24; and chapter 6 of

Michael P. Kramer, *Imagining Language in America: From the Revolution to the Civil War* (Princeton: Princeton University Press, 1992).

77. Nina Baym, *The Scarlet Letter: A Reading* (Boston: Twayne, 1986), 44.

78. Baym, 44.

79. Sacvan Bercovitch, *The Office of The Scarlet Letter* (Baltimore: The Johns Hopkins University Press, 1991), 30–31.

80. Romero, 99.

81. Herbert, 188.

82. Brook Thomas, "Citizen Hester: *The Scarlet Letter* as Civic Myth," *American Literary History* 13.2 (2001), 203.

83. Herman Melville, "Hawthorne and His Mosses," in *The Piazza Tales and Other Prose Pieces, 1839–1860*, vol. 9 of *The Writings of Herman Melville*, ed. Harrison Hayford et al. (Evanston and Chicago: Northwestern University Press, 1987), 239. All further quotations from Melville's prose are from this volume unless otherwise noted, and page numbers will be cited parenthetically in the chapter.

84. Matthiessen, 187.

85. Newton Arvin, *Herman Melville* (New York: Viking, 1957), 136.

86. Andrew Delbanco, *Melville: His World and Work* (New York: Knopf, 2005),127.

87. Richard H. Brodhead, *The School of Hawthorne* (New York: Oxford University Press, 1986), 20.

88. Robert K. Martin and Leland S. Person, "Missing Letters: Hawthorne, Melville and Scholarly Desire," *ESQ* 46.1 and 2 (2000), 100. See also the other essays in this special issue of *ESQ* (edited by Martin and Person) dedicated to exploring the relationship between the two. For examples of how Melville's biographers have recently attended to the erotic undertones of the review see Edwin Haviland Miller, *Melville* (New York: Braziller, 1975), 32, and Hershel Parker, *Herman Melville: A Biography*, vol. 1, *1819–1851* (Baltimore: The Johns Hopkins University Press,1996), 760.

89. Clark Davis, *Hawthorne's Shyness: Ethics, Politics, and the Question of Engagement* (Baltimore: The Johns Hopkins University Press, 2005). Davis proceeds later in his text to suggestively assert that "the intimacy that Melville proposes curiously echoes the parasitic bond of the doctor and the minister," and while Davis steers away from unpacking the homoerotic dimensions of the allusion (or of the Melville/Hawthorne relationship), the comparison of the two relationships is an interesting, if unexamined, argument.

90. Gillian Brown, 146.

91. Ellen Weinauer, "Plagiarism and the Proprietary Self: Policing the Boundaries of authorship in Herman Melville's 'Hawthorne and His Mosses,'" *American Literature* 69.4 (1997), 712.

92. See Parker, 1:785.

93. As quoted by Parker, 1:784.

94. Melville, like Hawthorne, envisioned an upper-story, isolated chamber as the ideal vantage point for a writer. See Parker, 1:774–811.

95. Edward Rosenberry, "Melville and His *Mosses*," *ATQ* 7 (1970), 49.

96. John Allison, "Conservative Architecture: Hawthorne in Melville's 'I and My Chimney,'" *South Central Review* 13.1 (1996), 17.

97. See Stuart C. Woodruff, "Melville and His Chimney," *PMLA* 75.3 (1960), 283–92.

98. As quoted by Parker, 1:788.

99. Laurie Robertson-Lorant, *Melville: A Biography* (New York: Clarkson Potter, 1996), 355.

100. Robertson-Lorant, 355.

101. Allen Moore Emery, "The Political Significance of Melville's Chimney," *New England Quarterly* 55.2 (1982), 204.

102. Robert Milder, *Exiled Royalties: Melville and the Life We Imagine* (New York: Oxford University Press, 2006), 142. For another recent version of this critical reading see, Andrew Delbanco, *Melville: His World and Work* (New York: Knopf, 2005), 245–46.

103. Henry H. Glassie, *Pattern in the Material Folk Culture of the Eastern United States* (Philadelphia: University of Pennsylvania Press, 1969), 125.

Index

CPSIA information can be obtained at www.ICGtesting.com
Printed in the USA
BVOW08s0217070216

435830BV00001B/1/P